RESEARCH IN
LAW AND
ECONOMICS

Volume 9 • 1986

Call for Papers:

The editor welcomes the submission of papers.
Editorial correspondence pertaining to manuscripts should be sent to:

Professor Richard O. Zerbe, Jr., *Series Editor*
Graduate School of Public Affairs
DP-30
University of Washington
Seattle, Washington 98195
(206)543-4920

Three copies should be sent. Manuscripts must be put into the Journal's style before final acceptance.

RESEARCH IN LAW AND ECONOMICS

Editor: RICHARD O. ZERBE, JR.
Graduate School of Public Affairs
University of Washington

VOLUME 9 • 1986

 JAI PRESS INC.

Greenwich, Connecticut   *London, England*

BOARD OF REFEREES

CONTENTS

LIST OF PARTICIPANTS

Carson E. Agnew	Engineering-Economic Systems Stanford University
Paul H. Brietzke	School of Law Valparaiso University
Peter Bronsteen	Analysis Group, Inc. Brooklyn, New York
Malcolm B. Coate	Bureau of Economics Federal Trade Commission Washington, D.C.
Mark Frankena	Bureau of Economics Federal Trade Commission Washington, D.C.
Richard G. Gould	Telecommunication Systems Washington, D.C.
Kenneth V. Greene	State University of New York at Binghamton
George D. Moulton	State University of New York at Binghamton
Paul A. Pautler	Bureau of Economics Federal Trade Commission Washington, D.C.
Patricia Reagan	Department of Economics Ohio State University
William F. Shughart II	Center for the Study of Public Choice George Mason University

Pablo T. Spiller   Senior Research Fellow
                                  Hoover Institution
                                  Stanford, California

Robert D. Tollison   Center for the Study of Public Choice
                                  George Mason University

RESALE PRICE MAINTENANCE:
A RE-EXAMINATION OF THE
OUTLETS HYPOTHESIS

Patricia B. Reagan

ABSTRACT

The outlets hypothesis suggests that through minimum resale prices a manufacturer acting unilaterally can increase its profits by controlling the density of the distributors that stock its product. This theory has been overlooked in recent debates about RPM in part because of the lack of a formal model detailing the conditions under which the theory holds. It is shown that the outlets hypothesis is valid only in the short run when new distributors cannot enter the market. The validity of the outlets hypothesis also requires that marginal distribution costs are dissimilar across retailers and that the marginal disutility of travel increases with the distance the consumer must travel to obtain the product. In this case there are conditions under which the manufacturer profits from setting a minimum resale price. RPM establishes the manufacturer's preferred density of retail outlets.

Research in Law and Economics, volume 9, pages 1–12.
Copyright © 1986 by JAI Press Inc.
ISBN: 0-89232-657-3

I. INTRODUCTION

The process whereby goods and services are produced and distributed arises from the activities of manufacturers, wholesalers, jobbers, and retailers who are, for the most part, independent decision-making entities. The diverse activities in this process are rarely coordinated by a single, vertically integrated organization. Instead, the production-distribution process is characterized by multiple market transactions that often involve restrictions on distribution. One such vertical restraint is resale price maintenance. Under resale price maintenance the manufacturer sets a minimum, or occasionally maximum, resale price at which its distributors can resell the product.

There is little debate that a group of manufacturers or distributors can increase its profits by colluding to restrict output and raise price through resale price maintenance; see, for example, Telser (1960) and Overstreet and Fisher (1985). However, debate continues over why a single manufacturer, acting alone, can benefit from setting a minimum resale price. Principles of economics seem to suggest that once a manufacturer sets a wholesale price its profits are greatest if its distributors resell the product at the lowest possible price. However, there is a long history of attempts by manufacturers to establish minimum resale prices.

One explanation of minimum resale prices, articulated by Telser (1960) and formalized by Matthewson and Winter (1983a), suggests that RPM protects dealers' property rights in dealer-provided, product-specific presale services. RPM restricts retail price competition and, so the story goes, channels competition into presale services. The increase in presale services shifts out the market demand schedule and thereby raises the manufacturer's profits.

An alternative explanation of minimum resale prices based on quality certification is provided by Marvel and McCafferty (1984). The reputation of the dealers that stock the product is the consumers' only source of information about product quality. If consumers care about where a product is sold but not from whom they purchase, a retailer's reputation for high quality is subject to free riding by low-cost, low-quality competitors. Under a policy of RPM, price cutting is precluded and the free-riding problem is circumvented. RPM keeps dealers' profits margins high and induces high-quality, high-cost retailers to stock the product. If market demand is sufficiently responsive to perceptions of quality, Marvel and McCafferty argue that, even if a manufacturer follows a policy of refusal to deal with certain low-quality retailers, it will profit from minimum resale prices.

There is a consensus that these explanations of minimum resale prices are appropriate in certain instances. For example, the Telser argument performs well in explaining why electrical appliances might be resale price maintained. The Marvel-McCafferty argument performs well in explaining why fashion goods, such as London Fog raincoats and Lenox china, were at one time resale price maintained. However, the majority of products that were at one time sold under RPM are food and drug items sold through grocery stores and pharmacies.

These products include Bon Ami Cleanser, Corning Ware products, Wood Preen wax, Rubbermaid products, Champion spark plugs, Quaker State motor oil, Parker pens, Gillette products, Noxema products, Papermate pens and refills, St. Joseph aspirin for children, Cream of Wheat, Williams Lectric Shave, Coricidin, White Rain Shampoo, Deep Magic Cleanser, Toni Home Permanent, Getsit Corn Remover, Johnson and Johnson Baby Powder, and Unicaps. The marketing of these products involves no dealer-provided, product-specific presale services. Furthermore, these products are not fashion goods for which the dealer's reputation for quality is the consumer's primary source of information about product quality. Therefore, neither the Telser services argument nor the Marvel-McCafferty quality certification argument provides a convincing explanation in the majority of cases observed for why a manufacturer acting alone would benefit from minimum resale prices.

An alternative explanation for minimum resale prices is the outlets hypothesis. This theory has had a long and venerable tradition, for example Yamey (1954), Gould and Preston (1965), and Preston (1965). The outlets hypothesis suggests that through minimum resale prices the manufacturer establishes an optimal density of distributors. The theory is founded on the Hotelling principle that the full cost to consumers is the sum of the listed product price plus transportation costs constituted by the consumer's indirect cost of obtaining the product. Minimum resale prices establish distributors' profit margins and thereby establish the number of dealers that stock the product. If the increased availability sufficiently reduces consumers' transportation costs, the total amount sold increases and the manufacturer increases its profits.

Despite its simplicity and applicability to the majority of products that were at one time resale price maintained, the outlets hypothesis has received relatively little attention in recent debates on RPM. This oversight is explained in part by the lack of a formal model detailing the conditions under which a manufacturer acting alone would want to write a contract specifying a minimum resale price. The lack of a formal model of the outlets hypothesis is itself not surprising since recent spacial models of vertical price restraints, such as Bittlingmayer (1983), Dixit (1983), and Matthewson and Winter (1983b), focus on the need for price ceilings rather than price floors. These authors argue that there are too many rather than too few distributors and that a manufacturer would therefore seek to institute a price ceiling rather than a price floor. Bittlingmayer mentions the possibility of price floors, but the analysis is cursory.

Existing spacial models of RPM assume that entry and exit in the retail market is instantaneous and costless. They are, therefore, models of long-run equilibrium. It is well known from the theory of contestable markets that, given constant marginal costs, costless entry and exit insures that potential competition drives price, in this case retail price, to the zero profit level. Since retailers earn zero profits in any case, the assumption of costless and instantaneous entry and exit implies that retailers would be willing to distribute a manufacturer's product under a zero profit scheme of RPM with a maximum resale price. The maximum resale price allows the manufacturer to choose the density of distributors that it would establish if it were vertically integrated. Without the price ceiling the number of retailers would exceed that which maximizes the manufacturer's profits.

This conclusion of existing spacial models reflects the assumption of costless and instantaneous entry and exit in the retail market. But, if the assumption of costless entry is relaxed, a model emerges in which retailers' market power is not entirely eroded by potential competition. The manufacturer uses RPM to establish the preferred density of distributors. RPM prevents distributors from competing in price which forces some distributors to shut down. The short-run analysis is interesting because the vast majority of observed instances of RPM involve minimum resale prices.

The purpose of this paper is to provide a formal spacial model of minimum resale prices that captures the spirit of the outlets hypothesis. The plan of the paper is as follows. In Section II the model is presented. In Section III the welfare properties of this model are explored. Concluding comments are offered in Section IV.

II. THE MODEL

In this section a stylized model of minimum resale prices is developed that captures the spirit of the outlets hypothesis. The outlets hypothesis presumes that market demand is an increasing function of the number of retail outlets as well as a decreasing function of retail price. As the number of outlets increases, holding constant retail price, transportation costs decline and the full purchase price to consumers which includes transportation costs declines. The manufacturer's profits are therefore a function of the density of distributors. The outlets hypothesis then suggests that manufacturers profit from setting minimum resale prices because they thereby establish an optimal density of retail outlets.

The idea that minimum resale prices economize on transportation costs suggests that RPM can usefully be modeled in a spacial context. Existing spacial models such as Bittlingmayer (1983 a,b), Dixit (1983), and Matthewson and Winter (1983b) consider a monopolist manufacturer selling output to a monopolistically competitive retail sector. However, the assumption that entry and exit in the retail sector is instantaneous and costless insures that potential competition erodes all retail market power and drives the retail price to the zero profit level. Therefore retailers are willing to distribute the manufacturer's product under a maximum resale price that offers them no rents. The manufacturer selects the price ceiling that provides the profit-maximizing density of outlets. These models are appropriately viewed as models of long-run equilibrium between a manufacturer with sustained market power and a retail sector disciplined by potential competition. (From these analyses it can be concluded that there is no substantive role for minimum resale prices in the long run).

If the assumption of costless entry is relaxed, then minimum resale prices can have a nontrivial effect on retail equilibria. Under these conditions the manufacturer may profit from a minimum resale price that prevents price competition from reducing retailer density. Manufacturers use minimum resale prices to purchase distribution, or, alternatively, as a means of preventing excessive competition among retailers in the short run. Profit-maximizing manufacturers do not use minimum resale price to subsidize inefficient retailers with high marginal distribution costs. If one retailer is willing to sell in any market area at a lower delivered price than its rivals, the manufacturer profits from allowing it to do so.

To formalize these notions, consider the following model. The manufacturer produces at constant marginal cost. The market is described by a circle with circumference L. Hence, it is assumed that nonprice competition is unidimensional. In particular, firms compete in only price and location. Although it would be desirable to consider other forms of nonprice competition, focusing on location maintains the spirit of the outlets hypothesis and allows comparison with spacial models of price ceilings, which consider only a single dimension of nonprice competition.

Each firm has a cost function with avoidable fixed costs, F_i, and constant marginal cost equal to the wholesale price, p^w, plus distribution costs, d_i. Each retailer takes its rival's price as fixed. It then selects its own price to maximize profits given the other firm's actions. As in any game theoretic problem, the model is sensitive to the specification of the strategy space; see, for example, Novshek (1980). However, the Price-Nash formulation followed in this paper is the most appropriate to capture the spirit of the outlets hypothesis.

On the demand side of the market, it is assumed that customers are distributed symmetrically around the circle. Each consumer is willing to travel at most one unit distance to procure the good. If two distributors are within one unit from the consumer, the consumer purchases from the distributor charging the lowest delivered price. The assumption that consumers are willing to travel at most one unit approximates the notion that the marginal disutility of travel rises with the distance traveled. The delivered price, denoted P^d, to a customer at location l from a retailer located at l^1 and charging a retail price P^r is given by

$$P^d = P^r + t|l - l^1|,$$

where

$$t = 1 \text{ for } |l - l^1| \leq 1 \text{ and } t = \infty \text{ for } |l - l^1| > 1.$$

This assumption approximates rising marginal costs of transportation, or increasing marginial disutility of travel. The quantity demanded, Q^d, as a function of delivered price is linear as follows: $Q^d = A - BP^d$.

In the short run, it is appropriate to assume that in the retail sector the number and location of distributors are fixed. In this model it is assumed that no entry occurs, because entry costs are high. But fixed costs are avoidable so exit is costless. Under these conditions it is possible that retail price competition will force some competitors to shut down. The manufacturer can establish retailer density only by preventing retail price competition through a minimum resale price. The following example illustrates the role of RPM in creating retail equilibrium. Consider the simplest case of three consumers, two retailers, and a manufacturer with constant marginal costs of production, c. Suppose the two retailers are located with a distance of two units on one side and four on the other. Suppose that one retailer, denoted h, has high costs and the other, denoted l, has low costs, so that $d_h > d_l$ and $F_h > F_l$. The three consumers are located symmetrically. This configuration of retailers and consumers is depicted in the figure below.

In the short run, distributors possess some monopsony power vis à vis the manufacturer because distributors are differentiated by location and are not disciplined by the threat of entry. Retailers are not passive agents for the manufacturer. They react to any wholesale price by choosing a retail price to maximize profits, provided they cover avoidable fixed costs. The manufacturer's choice of wholesale price in turn depends on its knowledge of dealers' responses. In particular the optimal wholesale price depends on the number of dealers that carry the product and the retail price(s) that will be set. Since the manufacturer is selling to distributors with monopsony power, there are limitations on the variety of

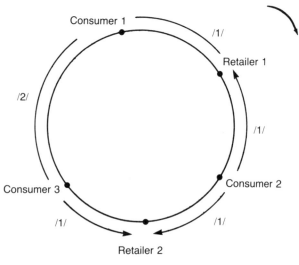

Figure 1

pricing policies that it can impose. To reflect this limitation, two pricing strategies are considered: unfettered resale prices and minimum resale prices.

One alternative open to the manufacturer is to sell only to the low cost distributor, in which case there would be no role for minimum resale prices. The low cost distributor would sell only to the two adjacent customers, as $t = \infty$ for distances greater than one unit. In this case, for any wholesale price, the low cost retailer would select a retail price to maximize profits as follows:

$$\max_{P^r} 2(A - B(P^r + 1))(P^r - P^w - d_l),$$

assuming that at this retail price the low cost distributor covers its avoidable fixed costs. This implies that

$$P^r = \frac{A + B(P^w - 1 + d_l)}{2B}.$$

The manufacturer then chooses a wholesale price to maximize its profits, subject to the retailer's retail price response. Its optimization problem is

$$\max_{P^w} \quad 2(A - B(P^r + 1))(P^w - c)$$
$$\text{s.t. } P^r = \frac{A + B(P^w + 1 - d_l)}{2B}$$

Table 1 enumerates the prices, quantities and profits of the single retailer case.

Alternatively, the manufacturer could choose to distribute its product through both distributors. There are configuration of the parameters of the model under which the manufacturer earns higher profits if it distributes through both outlets, but a minimum resale price is required to obtain distribution through both outlets. Each distributor sells to 3/2 consumers, since they split the sales from the consumer located halfway between them.

Table 1

$$p^w = \frac{A - B(1 + d_l - c)}{2B}$$

$$p^r = \frac{3A - B(3 - d_l - c)}{4B}$$

$$Q = \frac{A - B(1 + d_l + c)}{4}$$

$$\pi_l^r = \frac{(A - B(1 + d_l + c))^2}{16B} - F_l$$

$$\pi^m = \frac{(A - B(1 + d_l + c))^2}{4B},$$

The minimum resale price is determined by the solution to the high cost distributor's optimization problem:

$$\max_{P^r} \frac{3}{2} (A - B(P^r + 1)(P^r - P^w - d_h)$$
$$\text{s.t. } \frac{3}{2} (A - B(P^r + 1)(P^r - P^w - d_h) - F_h \geq 0.$$

Consider the case in which the high cost firm earns zero profits, so that at its optimal choice of retail price it just covers its avoidable fixed costs. It follows that

$$P^r = \frac{A + B (P^w - 1 + d_h)}{2B}.$$

The manufacturer then selects a wholesale price to maximize profits subject to the retail price imposed by the high cost distributor. Its problem is the following:

$$\max_{P^w} \quad 3(A - B(P^r + 1)(P^w - c)$$
$$\text{s.t. } P^r = \frac{A + B (P^w - 1 + d_h)}{2B}.$$

Table 2 enumerates the prices, quantities and profits under such a policy of minimum resale prices. One set of parameters for which RPM is necessary to insure that the product is carried by both outlets is $A = 10$, $B = 1$, $c = 1$, $d_h = 3$, $d_l = 2$, $F_h = 75/32$, $F_l = 0$.

Resale price maintenance is necessary to insure that both outlets operate. Without RPM the low cost distributor would charge a price below the resale

Table 2

$$p^w = \frac{A - B(1 + d_h - c)}{2B}$$

$$p^r = \frac{3A - B(3 - d_h + c)}{4B}$$

$$Q_i = \frac{3}{2} \frac{[A - B(1 + d_h + c)]}{4}, \; i = h, l$$

$$\pi_h^r = \frac{3}{32B} [A - B(1 + d_h + c)]^2 - F_h$$

$$\pi_l^r = \frac{3}{32B} [A - B(1 - 3d_h + 4d_l + c)]^2 - F_l$$

$$\pi^m = \frac{3}{8B} [A - B(1 + d_h + c)]^2$$

Table 3

$$P^w = \frac{A - B(1 + d_h - c)}{2B}$$

$$P^r = \frac{3A - B(3 + d_h - 2d_l - c)}{4B}$$

$$Q = \frac{A - B(1 - d_h + 2d_l + c)}{2}$$

$$\pi_l^r = \frac{1}{8B} [A - B(1 - d_h + 2d_l + c)]^2 - F_l$$

$$\pi^m = \frac{1}{4B} [A - B(1 + d_h + c)][A - B(1 - d_h + 2d_l + c)]$$

price floor. The high cost distributor has two alternatives. It could match the price cut and retain its customer base or it could maintain a high price but suffer a loss in its customer base. In either case the low cost distributor cannot cover its avoidable fixed costs and will shut down. Recall that in the RPM equilibrium the low cost distributor was just breaking even given its customer base. Either an erosion in price or an erosion in its customer base will lead to negative profits if it remains open. Table 3 enumerates the prices, quantities and profits if the low cost distributor circumvents the minimum resale price.

A comparison of Tables 1-3 indicates that under certain parameters of the model the manufacterer's profits are highest if it can enforce a minimum resale price so as to be able to distribute through both outlets. The price floor is a binding constraint in that at the RPM wholesale price the low cost distributor would profit from cutting its retail price below the resale price specified by the manufacturer. If the manufacturer cannot enforce minimum resale prices it will select a different wholesale price and sell only through the low cost outlet.

This example captures the essence of the "outlets" explanation of minimum resale prices. A manufacturer prefers to distribute its output with a particular density of distributors. But that density is eroded by retail price competition. The manufacturer maintains its preferred retailer density by setting a minimum resale price. The following section analyzes the welfare implication of outlets driven RPM.

III. WELFARE EFFECTS OF RPM

The welfare implications of outlets motivated RPM can be assessed by comparing the RPM equilibrium with an equilibrium in which RPM is prohibited. In the simple example presented in the previous section the manufacturer would sell through a single distributor. Under such a policy the manufacturer would recalculate its wholesale price and the resulting market equilibrium would have the characteristics displayed in Table 1.

A comparison of the RPM equilibrium described in Table 2 and the single distributor equilibrium described in Table 1 makes it clear who gains and who loses under RPM. The manufacturer increases its profits under RPM. Consumers in the aggregate also gain because sales are greater under RPM. The third possible gainer from RPM is the distributor that does not survive without RPM. The only potential loser from a restriction against RPM is the distributor that would survive without price maintenance. It is possible for a variety of configurations of the parameters of the model that the surviving retailer earns more profits under the no-RPM equilibrium. Producer surplus as measured by the sum of manufacturer and retailer profits is increased by RPM if retailer costs are not too low. Therefore, RPM could, in some cases, represent a Pareto improvement.

Using a Kaldor-Hicks criterion for welfare improvement, consumer surplus is increased by RPM and producer surplus, measured as the sum of manufacturer and retailer profits, is also increased by RPM if retailer fixed costs are not too large. The source of the welfare improvement is the increase in output brought about by RPM. This argument suggests a new criterion, based on quantity, for determining the legality of RPM. RPM should be legal when it increases the quantity sold. An attempt by manufacturer to increase or maintain retailer density unambiguously results in an increase in output. By the output criterion outlets motivated RPM should be presumptively legal.

The quantity criterion requires readily available information on sales. It complements a price–based criterion proposed by Fisher, McGowan, and Greenwood (1983). They suggest that actions which lead to lower prices should be presumptively legal. But such a criterion is inappropriate for RPM cases where the relevant price, the delivered price, is unobservable.

The quantity approach to assessing the legality of RPM is consistent with a standard proposed by Leffler (1985) in a comment on Marvel and McCafferty (1985). Leffler suggests that RPM should be judged to be illegal only if it can be shown that there is an injury to a competitor. The rule proposed by Leffler would lead to significant changes in the legal treatment of minimum resale prices. In particular, RPM motivated by a manufacturer's desire to increase the density of its outlets would generally be presumptively legal because the restraint is designed in principle to protect retailers rather than to harm them.

In addition, the numerical example developed in this paper illustrates an important caveat to Leffler's proposed rule, viz., that the wholesale price under RPM cannot be used as a bench mark to determine the possibility of an injury to a competitor. In assessing whether such an injury has occurred, the RPM equilibrium must be compared with the complete equilibrium absent RPM. The fact that the wholesale price is altered by RPM must be considered.

IV. CONCLUSIONS

The outlets hypothesis suggests that through minimum resale prices a manufacturer acting unilaterally can increase its profits by increasing the density of the distributors that stock its products. This theory has been overlooked in recent debates about RPM in part because of the lack of a formal model detailing the conditions under which the theory holds. It is shown that the outlets hypothesis is valid when the number and locations of retailers are fixed. These retailers possess market power vis-à-vis the manufacturer and can command rents. If the manufacturer cannot compensate its retailers with a two-part tariff, it may be forced to compensate retailers by allowing them to mark up the wholesale price above marginal distribution costs. In this case there are conditions under which the manufacturer can increase its profits with a minimum resale price by keeping retailer density high and preventing retail price competition which forces some distributors to shut down. RPM motivated by desire to keep retailer density high protects rather than harms individual retailers. Under Leffler's proposed rule that a vertical restraint should be presumptively legal if it does no injury to competitors, RPM under the outlets hypothesis should in general be presumptively legal. Similarly, under an output rule under which a vertical restraint is presumptively legal if it increases output, the outlets motivation would be presumptively legal.

ACKNOWLEDGMENTS

I would like to thank Tom Overstreet, Howard Marvel, Bill Sjostrom, Dick Startz, and Richard Zerbe for helpful discussions.

REFERENCES

Bittlingmayer, George. (October 1982) "Decreasing Average Cost and Competition: A New Look at the Addyston Pipe Case," *Journal of Law and Economics,* Vol. 25, No. 2, pp. 201–230.

_____ . (1983a) "Price Fixing and the Addyston Pipe Case," *Research in Law and Economics,* Vol. 5, pp. 57–130.

_____ . (December 1983b) "A Model of Vertical Restriction and Equilibrium in Retailing," *Journal of Business,* Vol. 56, No. 4, pp. 477–498.

Dixit, Avinash. (March 1983) "Vertical Integration in a Monopolistically Competitive Industry," *International Journal of Industrial Organization,* Vol. 1, No. 1, pp. 63–78.

Fisher, Franklin M., John J. McGowan, and Joen E. Greenwood. (1983) *Folded, Spindled, and Mutilated: Economic Analysis and U.S. v. IBM,* Cambridge, Mass. MIT Press.

Gould, J. R., and L. E. Preston. (August 1965) "Resale Price Maintenance and Retail Outlets," *Economica,* Vol. 32, No. 127, pp. 302–312.

Leffler, Keith. (May 1985) "Toward a Reasonable Rule of Reason: Comments," *Journal of Law and Economics,* Vol. 28, No. 2, pp. 381–386.

Marvel, Howard P., and Stephen McCafferty. (Autumn 1984) "Resale Price Maintenance and Quality Certification," *Rand Journal of Economics,* Vol. 15, No. 3, pp. 346–359.

_____ . (May 1985) "The Welfare Effects of Resale Price Maintenance," *Journal of Law and Economics,* Vol. 28, No. 1, pp. 363–380.

Matthewson, G. F., and R. A. Winter. (July 1983a) "The Incentives of Resale Price Maintenance under Imperfect Information," *Economic Inquiry,* Vol. 21, No. 3, pp. 337–348.

_____ . (December 1983b) "Vertical Integration by Contractual Restraints in Spacial Markets," *Journal of Business,* Vol. 56, No. 4, pp. 497–526.

Novshek, William. (April 1980) "Equilibrium in Simple Spacial (or Differentiated Product) Models," *Journal of Economic Theory,* Vol. 22, No. 2, pp. 313–326.

Overstreet, Thomas, Jr., and Alan A. Fisher. (Spring 1985) "Resale Price Maintenance and Distributional Efficiency: Some Lessons from the Past," *Contemporary Policy Issues,* Vol. 3, No. 3, Part 1, pp. 43–58.

Preston, Lee E. (Summer 1965) "Restrictive Distribution Arrangements: Economic Analysis and Public Policy Standards," *Law and Contemporary Problems,* Vol. 30, No. 3, pp. 506–529.

Telser, Lester G. (October 1960) "Why Manufacturers Should Want Fair Trade," *Journal of Law and Economics,* Vol. 3, No. 3, pp. 86–105.

MARKET SHARE AND MARKET POWER IN THE DOMESTIC LEMON INDUSTRY

Peter Bronsteen

ABSTRACT

Antitrust economists have become increasingly fascinated with legal proceedings that raise fundamental issues in the field of law and economics. One such proceeding began in May of 1977 when the Federal Trade Commission issued a complaint alleging that the Sunkist Growers, Inc. had monopolized the domestic market for fresh lemons. A key issue in that proceeding was the extent to which Sunkist's large market share provided reliable evidence of the firm's monopoly power. This article examines the structure and federal regulation of the domestic lemon industry to determine what if any relationship exists between Sunkist's market share and market power in that industry. Analysis of variables that should fluctuate when market power is exercised reveals that there is no significant relationship between

Research in Law and Economics, volume 9, pages 13–28.
ISBN: 0-89232-657-3

Sunkist's position in the industry and the exercise of market power. Instead, evidence of market power is found to be attributable in large part to a federal marketing order that was imposed in 1941 and is administered by the Department of Agriculture. This suggests that at least in the domestic lemon industry, federal regulation attenuates whatever relationship might otherwise exist between market share and market power.

I. INTRODUCTION

It is not at all surprising that this nation's antitrust laws make it illegal to monopolize or to attempt to monopolize an industry. After all, economic theory predicts that a monopolist will exploit consumers by restricting output and raising price above the competitive level.[1] What is surprising, however, is the difficulty that economists and other analysts have in identifying a firm that has monopolized its industry and is restricting output. As a result of this difficulty, market share is frequently used as an indicator of market power. However, in spite of the fact that market share may be important in identifying a firm with monopoly power, there is little if any agreement among economists as to the precise relationship between market share and market power.[2]

This article will explore the relationship between market share and market power by examining a single case study. The case study involves a regulated agricultural industry that is dominated by a single large firm. The industry is the domestic lemon industry; the industry's largest firm is the Sunkist Growers; and the regulation governing the industry is one of the many so-called federal marketing orders.

Concern over competition in the lemon industry was first formally expressed in 1977 when the Federal Trade Commission issued a complaint alleging that the Sunkist Growers had monopolized the domestic sale of fresh lemons.[3] Although the case was settled in 1981, no conclusion was reached about the exercise of monopoly power by the industry's largest and allegedly dominant firm.[4] The analysis presented in this article addresses the possibility that monopoly power has been exercised in the domestic lemon industry. This article examines evidence of output restriction and determines the extent to which this evidence is attributable to the industry's largest firm. The article concludes that evidence of output restriction is not attributable either directly or indirectly to the Sunkist Growers but instead is attributable, in large part, to the federal regulation that was imposed in 1941 and is currently administered by the U.S. Department of Agriculture. This result suggests that, at least in the domestic lemon industry, federal regulation attenuates whatever relationship may otherwise exist between market share and market power.

The next three sections provide background information on the industry, the Sunkist Growers, and the federal marketing order for lemons. The fifth section presents a statistical analysis of output restriction in the domestic lemon industry, and the final section summarizes the implications of this analysis for the relationship between market share and market power.

II. THE DOMESTIC LEMON INDUSTRY

California and Arizona together produce approximately 97 percent of the lemons grown in the United States. The remainder of the domestic crop is cultivated in Florida, but due to that state's relatively inferior growing conditions, most of Florida's lemons are processed rather than sold for fresh consumption. Imports account for a small share of domestic consumption and come primarily from the Mediterranean countries.[5]

The growing districts in California and Arizona produce lemons virtually the entire year. When lemons reach an appropriate size, they are picked and trucked to a local packing house where the fruit is washed, sized, and graded. The lowest quality lemons are hauled to a processing plant where the fruit is converted into a wide variety of juice and peel products, including both lemon oil and lemon juice. Higher quality lemons are stored in the packing house to mature for future sale as fresh fruit.

Historically, it has been most profitable for growers to sell their lemons in domestic fresh fruit markets. This is considered to be the primary market. In recent years, roughly one-quarter of the domestic lemon harvest has been sold in the primary market, one-quarter has been exported as fresh fruit, and one-half has been devoted to lemon products.

III. THE INDUSTRY'S LARGEST FIRM

The largest firm in the domestic lemon industry is the Sunkist Growers, Inc. Sunkist is a nonstock, nonprofit cooperative marketing association that was first organized in 1893. The cooperative now has approximately 6,500 members in California and Arizona who work jointly to improve the handling and sale of their citrus fruit.

To ensure that members' fruit is handled, packed, and graded in a consistent fashion, Sunkist has established rigid operating guidelines for all packing houses that are affiliated with the cooperative (Sunkist Growers, 1975). Affiliated packing houses are monitored very carefully by Sunkist's field department. At least twice and up to four times daily, each affiliated packing house will be scrutinized by an inspector who may, if necessary, suspend packing operations to rectify violations of the cooperative's packing and grading standards.

The cooperative's grading standards, which are more stringent than those established by the Department of Agriculture (U.S. Dept. of Agriculture, 1964), require affiliated packers to separate fresh lemons into three categories or grades. These grades are: premium, extra choice, and choice. The cooperative's premium grade fruit receives the "Sunkist" stamp. Extra choice grade fruit may receive the "Excel" label, and choice fruit may receive either the "SGI" or "SK" brand. Fruit that does not qualify for Sunkist's choice grade is sent to processing plants rather than being sold for fresh consumption.

All of the fruit grown by members of the cooperative is sold through the cooperative. Revenue from the sale of fruit, minus the cost of the cooperative's operations, is returned to member growers. Membership in the cooperative is strictly voluntary and may be terminated by the grower at the end of any growing season. In order to attract and maintain members, the cooperative must provide useful services and an attractive rate of return to its grower members.

IV. THE FEDERAL MARKETING ORDER

Since 1941, an agency of the federal government has regulated the domestic sale of lemons grown in California and Arizona. Under the authority granted by the Agricultural Marketing Agreement Act of 1937, the Department of Agriculture oversees what is known as a marketing order for the domestic lemon industry. The declared purpose of this and similar marketing orders is to "establish and maintain parity prices" and "to avoid unreasonable fluctuations in supplies and prices."[6]

The marketing order is administered by the Lemon Administrative Committee which operates under the ultimate jurisdiction and supervision of the Department of Agriculture. The Lemon committee is composed of 13 members. Twelve of the members are elected by the industry, and these 12 in turn elect a nonindustry member to be their chairman. At the present time, the Committee consists of eight growers, four packers or handlers, and one nonindustry chairman.

The Lemon committee administers essentially two restrictions: a size restriction and a quantity restriction. Both restrictions apply to all packing houses that handle fruit produced in the growing districts of California and Arizona.

The size restriction states that lemons must exceed a given size in order to be marketed domestically as fresh fruit. The size limit is set annually but may be changed over the course of the season if deemed necessary by the Lemon Committee.

The quantity restriction is somewhat more complicated. It is designed to regulate the flow of fresh lemons to domestic markets. The Lemon Committee meets each week to determine the maximum quantity of fresh lemons that may be shipped to domestic markets during the following week from the growing districts in California and Arizona. This total is then allocated across packing houses based approximately on the quantity of fruit on hand in each packing house. In any particular week, lemons that the marketing order prevents from being sold domestically as fresh fruit may be exported, sold to a citrus processing plant, or held for possible future sale.

The expressed purpose of the lemon order is to raise and support the domestic price of fresh lemons.[7] The order does this simply by restricting the supply of western fruit in a market where no alternative sources of supply exist. The order does not restrict entry of new growers nor does the order restrict the production of lemons by existing growers. Prior to enactment of the legislation authorizing the establishment of marketing orders, the Supreme Court invalidated production controls as an unconstitutional exercise of federal power to regulate interstate agriculture.[8] Based on this ruling, language in the Agricultural Marketing Agreement Act of 1937 clearly states that the Act is "not . . . intended for the control of production of Agricultural Commodities."[9] The Act simply authorizes the Department of Agriculture to establish marketing orders that restrict sales but do not directly restrict production.

V. IDENTIFYING MONOPOLY POWER

The preceding sections of this paper describe a regulated industry where one firm accounts for an exceedingly large share of the industry's total sales. The position of that firm was challenged in 1977 when the Federal Trade Commission alleged that Sunkist had monopolized the domestic sale of fresh lemons. The foundation for this allegation seems clear. The cooperative accounts for a large share of its market,[10] it operates as a central sales agency; members are prohibited from selling their fruit independently; and the cooperative exports or processes fruit that it diverts from the primary market. Based on these facts, it is plausible to suspect that the cooperative organization has the power to maintain the domestic price of fresh lemons by diverting fruit to export and lemon product markets.

Analysis suggests, however, that successful output restriction requires more than the structural conditions just described. The structure and position of the cooperative may not be sufficient to insulate Sunkist from the forces of a competitive marketplace. Any attempt by the cooperative to restrict output would set in motion a competitive response by the cooperative's own growers, other growers, and new entrants. Member growers, who are free to leave the cooperative at the end of any fiscal year, would do so to join other growers and possibly new entrants to sell a larger share of their harvest in the primary market where the cooperative was attempting to maintain high prices.

As a result, if output is being restricted in the domestic lemon industry, perhaps an alternative explanation exists. One possible explanation is that the federal marketing order, not the Sunkist cooperative, is the source of output restriction. The marketing order may effectively cartelize the industry in a way that makes it unnecessary for a single firm to attempt unilaterally to restrict output. This alternative explanation, the regulation hypothesis, suggests that the marketing order is enforced to restrict all firms' output whereas the prior explanation, the monopoly hypothesis, implies that the Sunkist cooperative restricts its own output.[11]

In this section of the paper, empirical analysis is used to determine the extent to which Sunkist and the marketing order are responsible for output restriction in the domestic lemon industry. Two types of statistical analyses are performed. The first analysis relies on correlation coefficients to determine whether the monopoly hypothesis or the regulation hypothesis is more consistent with observed data. The second analysis, which relies on a more sophisticated regression analysis, identifies the degree to which monopolizing behavior can be attributed to Sunkist and the marketing order.[12]

A. Correlation Coefficients

The model developed below will determine whether observed data are more consistent with the single-firm output restriction suggested by the monopoly hypothesis or the industrywide restriction suggested by the regulation hypothesis. Due to the nature of the lemon industry, statistics that reflect output restriction may be relatively easy to identify. In contrast to output restriction in a manufacturing industry, output restriction in the lemon industry does not involve a restriction on production. Sunkist's membership contract does not entitle the cooperative to restrict a member's production, and the Lemon Committee does not have the authorization to restrict production.[13] Instead, to the extent that output restriction does occur, it will entail a restriction on sales or a diversion of sales rather than a restriction on production. If Sunkist restricts output directly, that firm will shift sales from the primary market to the secondary markets. Alternatively, if the marketing order enforces output restriction, all firms will shift sales from the primary market to the secondary markets. In either case, output restriction will reduce the ratio of domestic fresh lemon sales to total lemon sales. This ratio will be referred to as the primary sales rate.

In order to determine which alternative hypothesis is most nearly correct, this model examines three statistics that are based on the primary sales rate. These statistics will be called: (1) the primary sales rate correlation, (2) the primary sales rate difference, and (3) the market share correlation. The first statistic is the correlation between the primary sales rate for Sunkist and the primary sales rate for the rest of the industry. The second statistic is the difference between the average primary sales rate for Sunkist and the average primary sales rate for the rest of the industry. The third statistic is the correlation between Sunkist's market share and the difference between the primary sales rate for Sunkist and the primary sales rate for the rest of the industry.

The alternative hypotheses generate differing predictions for the signs (positive or negative) of these three statistics. By comparing the actual values of these statistics against the values predicted by the competing hypotheses, analysis will identify the hypothesis that is most nearly consistent with observed data.[14]

The monopoly hypothesis predicts that if Sunkist restricts output directly, all three statistics should be negative. This is shown in Table 1. As Sunkist diverts sales from the primary market, the cooperative's primary sales rate will decline, the domestic price of fresh lemons will rise, and the rest of the industry will have the incentive to increase its primary sales rate. This should produce a negative correlation between the primary sales rate for Sunkist and for the rest of the industry. As displayed in Table 1, the primary sales rate correlation should be negative.[15]

The monopoly hypothesis also predicts that the second statistic in Table 1 will be negative. Output restriction by Sunkist gives other firms the incentive to increase their primary sales rate. Assuming other factors are constant, the primary sales rate for Sunkist should fall below the primary sales rate for the rest of the industry.

The third statistic in Table 1 tests the structural belief that market power is derived from market share. If this belief is true, Sunkist's market share should be negatively correlated with output restriction as indicated by the difference between Sunkist's primary sales rate and the primary sales rate for the rest of the industry. As shown in Table 1, the market share correlation should be negative.

In contrast to the monopoly hypothesis, the regulation hypothesis predicts different values for the three statistics in Table 1. If output restriction is attributable to a marketing order which is applied uniformly throughout the industry, then the domestic fresh sales rates for Sunkist and for the rest of the industry should move together. As noted on Table 1, this implies that the primary sales rate correlation should be positive.

With respect to the second statistic, if the lemon order effectively restricts output across the industry, there is no eason to expect, as the monopoly hypothesis predicts, that Sunkist's primary sales rate would fall below the domestic fresh sales rate for the rest of the industry. Instead, the regulation hypothesis is consistent with the second statistic in Table 1 being either zero or positive. If Sunkist achieves roughly the same primary sales rate as the ret of the industry then the second statistic in Table 1 will be zero. Another possibility, suggested elsewhere

Table1.   Implications of the Competing Hypotheses

	Statistic	Monopoly Hypothesis	Regulation Hypothesis	Estimated Value
(1)	Primary sales rate correlation	negative	positive	.834*
(2)	Primary sales rate difference	negative	positive or zero	3.9*
(3)	Market share correlation	negative	zero	.25 **

*Significant at the .01 level.
**Not significantly different from zero at the .20 level.

(Bronsteen, 1981), is that Sunkist is well organized to sell as much fresh fruit as the lemon order permits, and consequently the cooperative's primary sales rate may actually exceed the primary sales rate for the rest of the industry. Thus, the second statistic in Table 1 may be positive.

With respect to the third statistic in Table 1, the regulation hypothesis does not imply any relationship between market share and output restriction. As such, the market share correlation is predicted to be zero.

To test the implications of the competing hypotheses, the three statistics in Table 1 were computed from a data set containing annual observations from 1956 through 1972.[16] The first statistic reveals a positive correlation between the primary sales for Sunkist and for the rest of the industry. The correlation coefficient is .834, which is significant at the .01 level. Such a strong positive correlation is inconsistent with the hypothesis that Sunkist alone diverts fruit from the primary market and suggests that any diversion occurs on an industrywide level.

The second statistic reveals that the primary sales rate for Sunkist is not lower than the primary sales rate for the rest of the industry. In fact, during the 23-year period spanned by the data set, Sunkist on average marketed a higher percentage of its lemon harvest in the primary market than did the rest of the industry. On average, Sunkist sold 39.7 percent of its lemons domestically as fresh fruit while the remainder of the industry sold 35.8 percent of its harvest in the same market. This difference of 3.9 points is significant at the .01 level. This result also casts doubt on the possibility that Sunkist alone is restricting output. As discussed above, if Sunkist were restricting sales to the primary market the rest of the industry would have the incentive to increase output and Sunkist's primary sales rate would probably fall below the primary sales rate for the rest of the industry.

The third statistic reveals no significant correlation between Sunkist's market share and the difference between the primary sales rate for Sunkist and for the rest of the industry. The correlation coefficient was estimated to be .25 but this value is not statistically different from zero.[17] This result is consistent with the regulation hypothesis but runs contrary to the claim that market share is a measure of directly exercised market power.

Each of the results presented in Table 1 provides support for the belief that output restriction in the domestic lemon industry is attributable to the federal regulation that operates in this industry. As noted, however, these results do not indicate whether the operation of the marketing order is in some way influenced by the market power of the industry's largest firm.

B. Regression Analysis

Regression analysis provides further insight into output restriction in the domestic lemon industry. The following analysis explains the variation in two statistics that are likely to fluctuate when market power is exercised. The two statistics are the industry's primary sales rate, and what will be referred to as fresh output per bearing acre, or more simply, output per acre.

The first variable, the primary sales rate, is defined to be the percentage of the lemon harvest that is marketed domestically as fresh fruit. If output restriction occurs, other factors remaining constant, the value of this variable should decline as fruit is diverted from the primary market to the secondary markets.[18]

The second statistic, fresh output per bearing acre, is defined to be the quantity of lemons sold domestically as fresh fruit, divided by the total number of bearing acres. This statistic should also provide evidence of output restriction. If fruit is being withheld or diverted from the primary market, fresh domestic sales per bearing acre should decline.[19]

An ordinary least squares regression model was used to explain the fluctuation in the two variables just described. Each regression equation contains the same explanatory variables. The explanatory variables are:

D = A dummy variable representing the period in which the marketing order was in effect;

SOM = Sunkist's share of the market; and

H = The size of the lemon harvest.

The first two explanatory variables are included to determine the extent to which output restriction is attributable to the marketing order and the Sunkist Growers, respectively. The last variable is also expected to have explanatory power, as will be discussed below. It is therefore included to avoid contaminating the regression estimates.[20]

In certain cases, the independent variables were split into pre- and post-1941 variables. This will reveal any changes in the explanatory power of the segmented variables that may have occurred in 1941 when the marketing order was imposed. Variables that represent only the preorder period are designated with the suffix 1, and variables that represent only the postimposition or the effective period of the order are designated with the suffix 2.

The estimates produced by this regression analysis are presented in Table 2. The first equation explains the variation in what was described earlier as the primary sales rate. Recall that this is the percentage of the industry's harvest that is sold domestically as fresh fruit. As revealed by the r-squared statistic, this equation explains 98.3 percent of the variation in the dependent variable. Simply summarized, the pattern of estimates in this equation shows that evidence of output restriction is correlated with the operation of the federal order and is uncorrelated with the Sunkist harvest share.

The coefficient for the preimposition dummy variable, $D1$, exceeds the coefficient for the postimposition dummy variable. This indicates that when other factors are held constant, the operation of the federal marketing order is associated with a smaller percentage of the entire harvest being marketed domes-

Table 2. Explaining Output Restriction

Independent Variables	Dependent Variables		
	Primary Sales Rate	Output per Bearing Acre	Output per Bearing Acre
D1	127.9**	216.1**	159.6*
	(33.7)	(81.1)	(64.7)
D2	68.1*	129.6**	197.3**
	(20.1)	(48.4)	(40.0)
SOM1	−.292	−.655	.634
	(.390)	(.938)	(.738)
SOM2	.391	.488	.0328
	(.216)	(.520)	(.417)
H	−.00310**	−.00213**	
	(.000331)	(.000796)	
H1			.00442**
			(.00132)
H2			−.00402**
			(.000711)
R-Squared	.9833	.9810	.9885

Note: Standard errors reported in parentheses.
  *Significant at the .05 level.
  **Significant at the .01 level.

tically as fresh fruit. Both coefficients are significantly different from zero, and the first coefficient is statistically greater than the second coefficient at the .1 level of confidence. Although the estimates are statistically very precise, the level of significance at which the first coefficient may be said to exceed the second dictates caution in relying on conclusions supported by this piece of evidence alone.

The parameter estimates associated with Sunkist's market share, SOM1 and SOM2, are not significantly different from zero. This indicates that Sunkist's market share provides no explanation for output restriction. This result casts doubt on the validity of the monopoly hypothesis as well as a multiple hypothesis that Sunkist and the marketing order both restrict output and a mixed hypothesis that Sunkist exercises its market power by controlling the marketing order. If the latter hypothesis were valid, to the extent that market share generates market power, Sunkist's market share in the post-1941 period would be negatively correlated with the dependent variable.

The negative value of the first market share coefficient, SOM1, is consistent with the possibility that prior to imposition of the marketing order Sunkist did attempt to divert some fruit from the primary market. However, the imprecision of this estimate suggests concluding that the true coefficient is zero.

The relatively small standard deviation that is associated with the estimate of the second market share coefficient, SOM2, permits making a slightly more confident interpretation of this coefficient. The positive value suggests that, following imposition of the federal order, Sunkist did not restrict output but instead, relative to the industry, marketed a higher percentage of its harvest in the primary market.[21] Again, however, the imprecision of this estimate prevents concluding that its true value is different from zero.

The estimated coefficient for the harvest variable, H, is negative and significantly different from zero at the .01 level. The estimated coefficient is consistent with both the monopoly hypothesis and the regulation hypothesis. If either Sunkist or the Lemon Committee were attempting to maintain the domestic price of lemons, there would be a negative correlation between the size of the harvest and the percentage of the harvest that was sold in the primary market. In order to maintain domestic fresh lemon prices, a larger percentage of the crop would have to be diverted during a boom year than during a lean year. The estimated coefficient for the harvest variable is also consistent with a competitive industry where demand in the primary market is less elastic than demand in the outlet markets.

The second regression equation explains the variation in output per bearing acre, which was defined earlier to be the industry's domestic fresh lemon sales, divided by total bearing acreage. This regression explains 98.1 percentage of the variation in the dependent variable and supports the conclusions drawn from the first equation. Again, evidence of output restriction is not related to the market share of the largest firm but instead is attributable to the federal marketing order.

The estimated coefficient for the first dummy variable exceeds the coefficient of the second dummy, and each estimate is extremely precise. However, in this equation the difference between these values is not significant at the 0.1 level.

The market share of the dominant firm exhibits no explanatory power. Again, as in the first equation, statistical evidence is insufficient to conclude that the true values of the market share coefficients are different from zero. This, of course, is inconsistent with the structural belief that market share implies market power.

The coefficient associated with the size of the harvest is negative and statistically significant. This produces the unusual implication that larger harvests are associated with less fruit per acre being sold domestically as fresh fruit. This result is inconsistent with either a competitive market or a monopolized market, but may be consistent with a regulated market. In either a competitive market or a market characterized by a single seller, a larger harvest will, ceteris paribus, lead to more fruit per acre being sold in the primary market. Only in a regulated market would it be possible for larger harvests to be consistently associated with smaller quantities supplied in the primary market. A possible explanation is that during a boom year the Lemon Committee might further restrict sales in the primary market in order to compensate for what will be unusually low prices in the outlet markets.[22]

Although there is little evidence to support or refute this hypothesized response, further evidence indicates that the negative coefficient for the total har-

vest variable is determined by behavior when the marketing order was in existence. This can be demonstrated by re-estimating the second equation after
separating the harvest variable into two variables. One harvest variable, TQ1,
will contain observations for the preorder period, and the other variable, TQ2,
will contain values for the postimposition period. As shown in the last column of
Table 2, the resulting estimates show a positive coefficient for the preorder harvest variable, and a negative coefficient for the postimposition harvest variable.
Both estimates are statistically significant at the .01 level. These estimates indicate that the negative coefficient on the harvest variable in the second equation is
attributable to the impact of the marketing order. The negative coefficient simply
indicates that output restriction under the marketing order is more severe in boom
years than in lean ones.

The estimates produced by re-estimating the second regression reinforce the
conclusions reached earlier. As was demonstrated in the first two equations, the
third equation also indicates that output restriction is unrelated to market share.
The coefficients for Sunkist's market share are not statistically different from
zero, which leads to the conclusion that there is no relationship between
Sunkist's market share and output restriction in the lemon industry.

The third equation also indicates that the marketing order functions to restrict
output. The impact of the order can be estimated by holding Sunkist's market
share constant and using the estimated coefficients to predict the level of fresh
domestic sales per acre in both the preorder period and in the postimposition period.[23] Equation (3) can be split into two equations as listed below.

$$QPBA1 = A1 + C1(TQ) \tag{1}$$
$$QPBA2 = A2 + C2(TQ) \tag{2}$$

The first equation approximates the output per acre prior to imposition of the
marketing order, QPBA1, and the second equation approximates the output per
acre following imposition of the marketing order, QPBA2. The difference between the predicted values of these equations demonstrates the effect that the
marketing order is predicted to have upon the quantity of fresh lemons supplied
to the domestic market. These equations predict that when there is an average
lemon harvest of 13 million boxes, the Lemon Committee will divert nearly 72
boxes of lemons per acre from the primary market.[24] Based on this result, it is
easy to understand the impact of the marketing order when you realize that for
the past 10 years, the average annual output per acre was 345 boxes of lemons.
In light of this, the conclusion can not be avoided that the federal marketing order has a dramatic influence on the domestic market for fresh lemons.

The pattern of results supports the conclusion that evidence of output restriction is solely attributable to the imposition and operation of the federal marketing
order. The estimated equations explain virtually all of the variation in the dependent variable. None of this variation is attibutable to the market share of the

Sunkist cooperative, and a large portion is attributable to the imposition of the federal marketing order.

VI. CONCLUSION

This analysis indicates that in the domestic lemon industry there is no clear relationship between market share and market power. Evidence demonstrates that in spite of exhibiting what might be considered a dominant market share, the Sunkist Growers has not monopolized its industry. Output restriction in the primary market is not related to the market share of the Sunkist cooperative but instead is closely related to the operation of the federal marketing order that was imposed in 1941. The marketing order was intended to regulate the domestic supply of fresh lemons and it appears to be doing just that. This analysis suggests that it is unnecessary for any firm unilaterally to exert market power in a market where output is effectively restricted by the federal government.

Although there appears to be no close relationship between market share and market power in the domestic lemon industry, this does not rule out the possibility that there is indeed some general relationship between market share and market power in other industries. However, if in fact there is some general relationship between market share and market power, this article demonstrates that mitigating factors, such as the regulations that operate in the domestic lemon industry, may attenuate this relationship. As such, it is worth reiterating an often heard but less often believed caution that a large market share is necessary but not a sufficient condition for the exercise of market power.

ACKNOWLEDGMENTS

Peter Bronsteen, formerly an antitrust economist for the law firm of Skadden, Arps, Slate, Meagher & Flom, is currently a litigation consultant with Analysis Group, Inc., in New York. The author gratefully acknowledges the comments and assistance of Eugene M. Singer, Robert J. Larner, and the author's thesis committee which included Benjamin Klein, Harold Demsetz, and Wesley J. Liebeler.

NOTES

1. Richard Posner (1975) notes that a monopolist may also waste scarce resources by devoting its expected monopoly profits to a privately productive but socially useless effort to obtain or protect its monopoly position.

2. See, for example, Goldschmid et al. (1974), ch. 4.

3. Federal Trade Commission (May 31, 1977) Complaint. See also Federal Trade Commission (Feb. 7, 1978; Feb. 17, 1978; March 23, 1979; April 17, 1979; Feb. 25, 1980; May 5, 1981).

4. The settlement agreement, which was signed in August of 1980 and issued in May of 1981, focused on concerns over bad conduct. The agreement required Sunkist to divest but continue supplying fruit to one of its lemon-processing facilities. See Federal Trade Commission (May 5, 1981) Order.

5. Although imports were relatively significant in the early 1900s, a series of protective tariffs and improvements in domestic cultivation have vitiated the competitive effect of imports on the domestic market. Since 1940 the import share of domestic consumption has remained well below 5 percent.

6. *Agricultural Marketing Agreement Act of 1937.*

7. U.S. Dept. of Agriculture, Consumer and Marketing Service (1971).

8. *United States v. Butler et al., receivers of Hoosac Mills Corp.* (1936).

9. *Agricultural Marketing Agreement Act of 1937.*

10. The trial brief of the Federal Trade Commission (1980) indicates that from 1959 to 1977 Sunkist's share of the domestic market ranged from a low of 70.0 percent to a high of 85.9 percent.

11. It may be plausible to consider a mixed hypothesis that Sunkist uses the marketing order as the vehicle for the firm's market power. In such a case, the single-firm exercise of market power would be transformed into an industrywide output restriction. Although it is not clear how market power would be converted into regulatory control, this possibility will be considered more closely later in the article when analyzing regression estimates.

12. Data for these tests was provided by the U.S. Department of Agriculture (various years), the California Crop and Livestock Reporting Service (various years), and the Sunkist Growers (various years). The final aggregated data set contained annual observations for the period from 1924 to 1978.

13. *Agricultural Marketing Agreement Act of 1937.*

14. This procedure, however, does not consider either the mixed hypothesis that Sunkist uses the marketing order as the vehicle for output restriction, or the multiple hypothesis that both Sunkist and the marketing order restrict output. The mixed and multiple hypotheses will be addressed later in the article.

15. If demand in the primary market is more elastic than demand in the outlet markets, then to the extent that fluctuations or a trend in harvest size do not correspond to shifts in the demand for lemons, the true value of the primary sales rate correlation may be positive even if the monopoly hypothesis is correct. This combination of occurrences seems unlikely, however, and the results presented in the next section of the paper, where harvest size is explicitly considered, indicate that harvest size is not solely if at all responsible for the sign of the primary sales rate correlation computed in this section.

16. Firm specific observations for the years preceding 1956 were not available.

17. The correlation remains statistically insignificant even at the point where there is a 20 percent chance of falsely concluding that it is significant.

18. The primary sales rate was computed for the years 1924 through 1978. Its value ranges from 19.3 percent to 91.4 percent and exhibits an average value of 58.2 percent.

19. Fresh output per acre was also computed for the years 1924 through 1978. Its value ranges from 86.8 boxes per acre to 176.9 boxes per acre and exhibits an average value of 136.8 boxes per acre. A box of lemons weighs approximately 76 pounds.

20. Leamer and Leonard (1983) explain that excluding a relevant variable is equivalent to including that variable and constraining its coefficient to equal zero. To the extent that the excluded variable has explanatory power and is correlated with the included variables, the parameter estimates for the included variables will be predictably biased.

21. This result is consistent with the second statistic presented in Table 1. That statistic revealed Sunkist's domestic fresh sales rate to exceed the domestic fresh sales rate for the rest of the industry. The coefficient from Table 2 indicates that a 10 point increase in Sunkist's market share would produce a 4.0 point increase in the percentage of the harvest that is marketed domestically as fresh fruit.

22. The effectiveness of this strategy depends on the elasticity of demand in both the primary and secondary markets.

23. In the first two equations, the mean impact of the marketing order was identified by comparing the values of the two dummy variable coefficients. This procedure cannot be applied to the third equation because the impact of the marketing order is in part reflected in the preorder and postimposition harvest coefficients.

24. In calculating this figure, note that the dependent variable is measured in units of 1,000 boxes per acre.

REFERENCES

Agricultural Marketing Agreement Act of 1937, 7 U.S.C. §§ 601 et seq., 671 to 673 (1976) (enacted June 3, 1937).

Bronsteen, Peter. (1981) "Allegations of Monopoly and Anticompetitive Practices in the Domestic Lemon Industry," Ph.D. dissertation, University of California, Los Angeles.

California Crop and Livestock Reporting Service. (Annual) *California Fruit and Nut Acreage,* Sacramento.

_____ . (Annual) *California Fruit and Nut Statistics,* Sacramento.

_____ . (November, 1955) *California Fruit and Nut Crops: 1919–1953,* Sacramento.

_____ . (1962) *California Fruit and Nut Crops: 1949–1961,* Sacramento.

Federal Trade Commission, Docket No 9100. (May 31, 1977) Complaint.

_____ . Docket No. 9100. (February 17, 1978) Complaint Counsel's Principal Subpoena Instructions and Definitions.

_____ . Docket No. 9100. (March 23, 1979) Sunkist Grower's, Inc.'s Statement of its Defense.

_____ . Docket No. 9100. (April 17, 1979) Response to Sunkist's Statement of its Defense.

_____ . Docket No. 9100. (February 25, 1980) Trial Brief of Complaint Counsel.

_____ . Docket No. 9100. (May 5, 1981) Order.

Goldschmid, Harvey J., H. Michael Mann, and J. Fred Weston, eds. (1974) *Industrial Concentration: The New Learning,* Boston, Little Brown.

Leamer, Edward, E., and Herman B. Leonard. (May 1983) "Reporting the Fragility of Regression Estimates," *Review of Economics and Statistics,* Vol. 65, No. 2, pp. 306–317.

Posner, Richard A. (August 1975) "The Social Costs of Monopoly and Regulation," *Journal of Political Economy,* Vol. 83, No. 4, p. 807–827.

Sunkist Growers, Inc. (Annual: 1913–1951) *Annual Report of the General Manager of the California Fruit Growers Exchange,* Sherman Oaks.

_____ . (Annual: 1952–1980) *Annual Report of the Sunkist Growers, Inc.,* Sherman Oaks.

_____ . (Revised June 1, 1975) "Rules and Regulations Governing Fruit Packed for Marketing by Sunkist Growers, Inc. Under Its Trademarks Sunkist, SGI. Excel, SK and Red Ball and Under Association Non-Advertised Brands," Sherman Oaks.

_____ . (Annual) "Statistical Information on the Citrus Fruit Industry," Sherman Oaks.

_____ . (Annual) "Citrus Fruit Industry Statistical Bulletin," Sherman Oaks.

U.S. v. Butler et al., Receivers of Hoosac Mills Corp. 297 U.S. 1 (1936).

U.S. Dept. of Agriculture. (1937) *Agricultural Statistics,* Washington, D.C.

_____ , Agriculture Marketing Service. (1975) *Marketing Agreements and Orders for Fruits and Vegetables,* Washington, D.C.

_____ , Agriculture Marketing Service. (1964) *United States Standards for Grades of Lemons,* Washington, D.C.

_____ , Agriculture Marketing Service, Fruit and Vegetable Division. (Annual) *Fresh Fruit and Vegetable Prices,* Washington, D.C.

_____ , Bureau fo Agricultural Economics, Crop Reporting Board. (January 1949) *Fruit and Nuts; Bearing Acreage: 1919–1946,* Washington, D.C.

_____ , Consumer and Marketing Service. (1971) *Reprint from the Federal Register, 36 F.R. 9061, Sec. 910, May 19, 1971,* Washington, D.C.

_____ , Economics, Statistics, and Cooperatives Service. (Monthly) *Fruit Situation,* Washington, D.C.

_____ , Economics, Statistics, and Cooperatives Service, Crop Rotating Board. (Monthly) *Agricultural Prices,* Washington, D.C.

_____ , Foreign Agricultural Service. (March 1976) *Foreign Agricultural Circular; World Citrus Fruit Production and Trade Statistics,* Washington, D.C.

_____ , Statistical Reporting Service, Crop Reporting Board. (Monthly) *Agricultural Prices,* Washington, D.C.

_____ , Statistical Reporting Service, Crop Reporting Board. (Annual) *Citrus Fruit: Production, Use and Value,* Washington, D.C.

AN ANALYSIS
OF THREE APPROACHES
TO MARKET DEFINITION

Malcolm B. Coate

ABSTRACT

This paper compares the gap in the chain of substitutes, the Boyer optimal cartel and the Department of Justice (DOJ) 5 percent test market definition methodologies. All of the approaches suffer from some theoretical flaws so a spatial simulation model is defined to compare the ability of each definition to identify noncompetitive pricing. The DOJ 5 percent test appears to generate the best results with all the correlations between the Herfindahl index for the DOJ market and the price premium statistically significant and most correlations greater than .50. Of course, the spatial structure of the simulation limits our ability to draw a general conclusion on the best market definition concept.

Research in Law and Economics, volume 9, pages 29–43.
Copyright © 1986 by JAI Press Inc.
All rights of reproduction in any form reserved.
ISBN: 0-89232-657-3

I. INTRODUCTION

Classical economic theory tended to ignore the question of market definition, because the assumption of homogeneous products minimized the need for a detailed market definition analysis.[1] Products were in the same market if they were physically similar and in separate markets if they were physically different. Firms were assumed to recognize that direct competitors limited their ability to set price while businesses in other markets did not. Marshall (1920, p.324) noted the importance of market definition for products that differ in geographic location, and concluded that a market was an area where "prices of the same goods tend to equality" with due allowance for transportation costs. The relaxation of the homogeneity assumption by Chamberlin (1948) and Robinson (1934) created a need for a system to classify heterogeneous products into product markets.[2] In the first attempt to satisfy that need, Robinson (p. 17) introduced the notion of a "gap in the chain of substitutes" as the boundary of a product market. The cross elasticities of demand and supply evolved as tools to proxy the degree of substitutability between various products. Since the data necessary to measure the cross elasticities are difficult to quickly obtain, a checklist of characteristics has been defined to proxy the demand and supply cross elasticities. For example, the Federal Trade Commission (1982) notes the factors which indicate nonsubstitutability include the persistance of sizable price disparities, the presence of sufficiently distinctive characteristics which render a product suitable for a specialized use, the preference of particular purchasers for one product, and the judgment of purchasers or sellers that the products do not compete. However, it is well recognized that these factors must be closely scrutinized, because no single factor can definitively identify a market. Moreover, there is always the problem of the qualitative and potentially self-serving nature of the evidence.

Recently, two innovative approaches to market definition have been advanced to supplement and perhaps replace the existing methodology. They are the optimal cartel approach of Boyer, and the 5 percent test of the Department of Justice (DOJ). Boyer (1979, p. 92) defines a market from the point of view of a single firm as "the smallest group of sellers such that, were all members of the group to collude, bringing additional members into the collusive group would give the firm only minimal short term advantage." Thus, a market is really the ideal cartel for the product of a particular firm. The DOJ (1984, p. 5) defines a market as a group of products "such that a hypothetical firm that was the only present and future seller of those products (i.e., a monopolist) could profitably impose a small but significant and nontransitory increase in price."[3] The DOJ (p. 7) test uses the prevailing price charged by the firm for the relevant product as a base, and usually considers a price increase of 5 percent for one year to be sufficient for identifying a market.[4]

Once a market is defined, it can be used to structure an analysis of the ability of firms to implement and maintain a price increase. In particular, the DOJ merger guidelines (1984) base their analysis on the Herfindahl statistic calculated for the relevant market. This simple market-share based calculation generates an initial evaluation of the state of competition in a market.[5] However, the Herfindahl index is affected by the choice of the relevant market. Thus, the value of the index as a proxy for the state of competition may depend on the approach used to define the market.

Given the three methodologies to delineate a market, it is useful to study the definitions to identify the strengths and weaknesses of each approach. In the first section, we highlight the fundamental theoretical difficulties and then discuss the various application problems with each approach. Next we utilize a spatial simulation model to investigate the ability of each definition to identify a market in which concentration is linked to noncompetitive performance under different assumptions for collusion. We conclude by summarizing our results and suggesting an approach to use the three market definition methodologies in antitrust analysis.

II. EVALUATION OF THE MARKET DEFINITION CONCEPTS

The optimal market definition procedure would define a market that (1) includes all the firms that influence competitive decisions in a market, (2) contains only firms that influence competitive decisions in a market, (3) generates the same relevant market for any state of competition,[6] (4) offers a simple system to operationalize, and (5) results in an unambiguous market when implemented in practice. We evaluate the characteristics of the gap in the chain of substitutes, Boyer and DOJ approaches to market definition, and draw comparisons when relevant. We conclude this section by highlighting the problems with the various approaches to market definition.

A. Gap in the Chain of Substitutes Market

The gap in the chain of substitutes (GCS) approach depends on the idea that some products are closer substitutes than others. Market boundaries are placed to separate products into clusters, with competition more intense within the cluster than without. The nature of the definition allows firms with minimal competitive significance to be incorporated in the market if a gap does not exist in the prior chain of substitutes. Moreover, there is no theoretical reason why a gap should actually appear in a chain of substitutes. In fact, if product groups vary by either geographic or product characteristics and competition is more intense between close products than it is for distant products, the price for products in a particular group can be raised until the cross substitution among the groups becomes significant. The collusive price increase could mask the gaps in the chain of substitutes that could define a product market. Thus, it is conceptually possible for the definition to fail to identify a relevant market.

The GCS market uses price information, product characteristics, and qualitative opinions to define a relevant market. However, in many industries, reliable price data will not be available, because firms offer discounts that reduce the transaction price paid by customers.[7] Also, the information on product characteristics and the qualitative opinions of industry participants may not create a clear indication of the boundaries of a relevant market. Thus, in practice, the GCS analysis will face operational difficulties.

The GCS methodology can be ambiguous, because the evidence regarding each factor is open to interpretation and must be weighed against the evidence regarding the other factors. In some industries, the characteristics necessary to define a gap in the chain of substitutes can be interpreted to support either narrow or broad markets. Even if all the characteristics are interpreted in an unambiguous manner, the absence of a formula or procedure for weighing the factors means that a case can be made for either accepting or rejecting a relevant market if any of the characteristics differs in implication.

Recently, Horowitz (1981) created a regression model that uses historical price data to statistically test potential market definitions. The Horowitz model assumes that the price difference between two products will tend to a long-run value if two products are in the same product or geographic market. However, the Horowitz test uses a simple autoregressive process to characterize this adjustment. If the actual adjustment process is more complex, this misspecification could give biased estimates of the dynamic behavior. Howell (1984) notes a general statistical test would be preferable, with the historical adjustments in the price data determining the appropriate Box-Jenkins autoregressive moving average model (ARMA).[8] Moreover, Howell observes that the Horowitz methodology can fail when the prices involved are causally unrelated but serially correlated. Howell suggests fitting separate ARMA models to the price data and calculating residual series. If the cross correlations between the residual series are significant, there is evidence for assuming the series are jointly determined and proceeding with the market definition analysis. If the series are unrelated, there is little reason to assume that they are generated in the same market. The improved version of the Horowitz analysis offers some hope for determining the appropriate GCS market. However, even with these improvements in technique, Howell (p. 1170) notes it is still possible to spuriously infer membership in a common market if an exogenous causal factor influenced the price differences over time. Although these limitations do not destroy the usefulness of the GCS market definition, they do suggest that a search for a better definition should be undertaken.

B. Boyer Market

The Boyer definition of a market as an ideal collusive group appears to define the broadest possible market. By its very nature, the Boyer market would include all close substitutes and many more distant substitutes. One could argue that the definition includes too many substitutes, because products that are not considered substitutes by consumers for small price changes would be included in the market as long as consumers would switch for large price changes.

The Boyer analysis requires a definition of an optimal cartel for the product of a particular firm. In a recent article, Boyer (1984) proposed the ratio of a particular firm's monopoly earnings generated by a given hypothetical cartel to the assets held by the hypothetical cartel members as the profitability measure to be maximized. If adding a marginal firm to the cartel increases this ratio, the firm should be included in the market; otherwise, the firm is excluded. The Boyer approach is difficult to operationalize, because identifying the members of a hypothetical cartel is complex and use of the return on assets ratio can distort the results.

Werden (1985) observes that the use of return on assets as the profitability variable to be maximized can exclude capital intensive firms from the cartel, while including labor intensive firms in the cartel. Also, the use of a particular firm as the base for the cartel may create an optimal cartel that was not viable, because some of the potential cartel members could significantly increase their profits by inviting other close competitors to join the cartel. These problems might be eliminated by basing the definition of the optimal cartel on a return on sales measure for a group of collusive firms. Since it is necessary for the collusive firms to restrict sales to earn supracompetitive profits, the distribution of monopoly profits on the basis of sales seems reasonable.

Klein (1985) notes that the Boyer standard "ignores the time frame of the analysis and consequently the concept of acceptable levels of welfare losses associated with market definition." Theoretically, the size of any cartel could be increased by hypothesizing a longer cartel life, because more outside firms would enter the market for any fixed cartel price in the long run. This problem would be solved by considering the discounted present value of the monopoly profit.

In addition to the problems with defining an optimal cartel, it may be difficult to project all the hypothetical responses of potential cartel members necessary to define a market. However, the structure of the optimal cartel concept should make this market definition process more quantitative than the GCS methodology.

C. DOJ Market

The DOJ definition of a market, as a group of products for which a potential monopolist could profitably raise price 5 percent, represents a relatively narrow definition of a market. The DOJ market boundary excludes close substitutes if the potential increase in the production of the substitute would not render a 5 percent price increase unprofitable. For example, if a close substitute held a 10 percent share of the market and the core product held a 90 percent share, the cross elasticity would have to be huge before the increase in the sales of the close substitute would render a price increase for the core product unprofitable. Moreover, the 5 percent test could exclude fringe competitors from the market for exactly the same reason, even if the fringe produced an identical product. Assuming the fringe firms could not increase output drastically, the dominant core firms would be able to raise price. This suggests that the DOJ 5 percent test implicitly assumes that small fringe firms have no competitive significance. In other words, the DOJ test assumes that small firms have perfectly inelastic supply schedules such that they cannot increase output in response to a collusive price increase. A concentration statistic defined for a DOJ market will exclude the fringe firms and generate a biased measure of the ability of the dominant firms to raise price if the fringe firms actually have some positive supply response to an increase in price. Thus, the DOJ definition seems to ignore the procompetitive effect of small firms. The DOJ test would also exclude any firm currently operating at capacity, assuming expansion takes more than one year.[9] Although this result seems reasonable if one has shown demand will not decline in the next year to free up some capacity, the exclusion of firms operating at capacity only transfers their competitive impact to the analysis of entry, because existing competitors may be able to build new plants if prices tend to increase. To be fair to the DOJ definition, we should note that it allows for a broader market definition if the firms in such a market could raise price significantly more than 5 percent.[10] It is not clear when the DOJ would decide to use a broader market.

A second problem with the 5 percent test involves the ability to define different markets for competitive and noncompetitive markets. Assume that a group of substitute products exists such that producers of a product can raise the price of the product 6 percent without losing significant sales, but a 10 percent increase would result in a significant loss of sales. If the core market is competitive, the DOJ would find the core is the appropriate market, because the firms could raise price by 5 percent. However, if the core firms had already colluded to raise price 5 percent, so that an additional five percent increase was unprofitable, the DOJ would find a broader market is required. Thus, the DOJ's market definition process could have the perverse effect of blocking a merger in a competitive market and allowing a merger in a similarly concentrated but not as competitive market.[11]

The implementation of the DOJ approach requires the definition of a base price for the 5 percent increase. Werden (1983, pp. 534–542) discusses the advantages and limitations of four possible prices: (1) the price charged by the firm, (2) the value added, (3) the cumulative price, and (4) the final consumer price. He concludes that there is no one correct way to measure price and suggests the choice be made on a case-by-case basis. In the latest version of the guidelines, the DOJ (1984, p. 7) specifies that the price charged by the firm is usually the appropriate base price. Once the appropriate price is defined, the analyst need only identify the relevant responses to a 5 percent price increase from historical data or interview responses.

Although the need to choose a base price and then consider a 5 percent increase introduces some ambiguity into the market definition process, the DOJ test should leave the market definition process less susceptible to gerrymandering than the GCS method. Moreover, the DOJ 5 percent approach appears to be defined better than the Boyer method.

D. Summary

In conclusion, none of the three market definition criteria satisfy the five conditions set forth at the beginning of this section. The DOJ methodology appears to exclude some competitors from a market just because of their small size. On the other hand, the Boyer approach can include firms in the market that do not usually influence the competitive decisions made in a market. Both the GCS and DOJ analyses can generate different market definitions for competitive and noncompetitive situations. Also, the GCS and Boyer methodologies fail to offer a system that can be easily operationalized. Finally, the GCS approach allows the analyst to manipulate the market definition process through the choice of weights for the various factors. Thus, it is not possible to chose one definition as superior in all situations. Since theoretical analysis fails to define an optimal approach to market definition, we turn to simulation to compare how the three market definitions perform.

III. A SIMULATION ANALYSIS OF THE MARKET DEFINITION CONCEPTS

A. The Model

The three approaches to market definition can be analyzed with a spatial simulation model. The simulation framework can represent the behavior in a market to allow an examination of the ability of each market definition process (in combination with a concentration index) to predict supracompetitive pricing. The market definition methodology that most closely proxies the elevation of price would seem to be the best approach for defining markets in industries that fit the assumptions of the simulation model.

We represent product or geographic differences among the various products by their location on a grid, with one product located at the center of the grid and the other products randomly distributed in the surrounding area. In a geographic market, the other products would be located in cities or industrial complexes and in a product market the other products would be positioned to represent popular combinations of attributes for differentiated products. This methodology envisions that spatial product demand is localized (or at least peaks) at particular locations in the product space.

A base firm is assumed to be the only seller of the center product and thereby represents the subject of the market analysis.[12] For example, the aquiring firm in a merger would be considered the base firm in an antitrust analysis and the firm constructing a business plan would be used as the base firm in a strategic analysis. The other firms are assumed to sell the competitive products located at areas of high product demand. Each firm has a spatial advantage with respect to sales to the customer group clustered at its location. However, this advantage is limited by the ability of competitors to sell at a competitive disadvantage proportional to their distance from the customer's location. Of particular interest is the assumption that competitors will be able to limit the ability of the base firm to set price for the customers located at the origin.

Rules can be defined to allow the three market definitions to identify groups of firms in particular markets. The gap in the chain of substitutes approach requires a complex algorithm to delineate a spatial market while the Boyer and DOJ approaches are much easier to implement. In particular, the gap in the chain of substitutes is defined by first averaging the distance between the groups of firms in potential markets and then calculating the change in the average as each additional firm is included in the group. The largest jump in the average from increasing the number of firms in the potential market defines a gap in the chain of substitutes.[13] The Boyer test is easily implemented as the area that includes all the firms close enough to the base firm such that their competitive behavior would prevent the base firm from selling at the monopoly price. Finally, the DOJ market would include all firms that could prevent the base firm from raising its price by 5 percent.

We define the price of the base firm as a function of the distance between the base firm and its competitors.[14] The closest firm to the origin would limit the ability of the base firm to raise price if all the firms behaved as competitors. This implies that the distance from the closest firm to the origin defines the amount by which the competitive limit price can exceed marginal cost. However, if the closest firm colluded with the base firm, the limit price would rise until competition from a more distant rival made further price increases unprofitable. If all the firms colluded, the price of the base firm would rise to the monopoly level.[15]

Our simulation model assumes that the probability of any competitor participating in a cartel depends inversely on both the average distance between the potential cartel members and the total number of potential relationships between the collusive firms.[16] Thus, as the cartel increases in size, the probability that an additional firm will also collude declines. If the cartel achieves the size necessary to price at the monopoly level, no additional firms are allowed to participate in the collusion.

Three different simulation structures for collusions are considered in the analysis. The initial collusion structure weights the average distance and potential relationship data to generate relatively low probabilities of collusion so the market would tend to be highly competitive. In fact, the price can equal the competitive limit price in some of the individual trials of the simulation. The second structure allows for moderate probabilities of collusion so the closest firms to the origin can participate in the cartel. The final collusive system incorporates high probabilities of collusion in the model. Thus, the price can approach and even equal the monopoly price. The exact probabilities of collusion in any of the simulations depends on the other assumptions of the model.

In any of the simulations, the base firm's price would be determined by the distance between the base firm and the closest firm found not to collude (i.e., to compete) in the simulation. The supracompetitive surcharge above the competitive limit price can then be compared to the resulting Herfindahl index for the firms alleged to be in a market and the usefulness of various market definitions for predicting noncompetitive performance can be noted.[17] The results of the simulations should be independent of the particular assumptions of the model. Thus, we investigate the robustness of the results by first analyzing a base case and then determining how changing the various assumptions affects the results.

The base case assumptions are given in Table 1. In all the simulations, we locate the firms on a 2500 square unit grid with a distance of one unit being associated with a 1 percent price premium. We initially place 10 firms on the grid and hypothesize a 20 percent monopoly surcharge. Also, we measure the unit distance between two firms with the Euclidean norm (i.e., the geometric distance between two points on the grid). These assumptions allow us to define a Boyer market as a circle 20 units from the base firm. The DOJ market is defined as a circle 5 units beyond the closest firm to the origin, because the base firm would charge a price determined by this firm's location in a competitive equilibrium. The GCS market would be defined based on the location of the particular firms in any simulation.

Table 1 also lists three adjustments in the model. First, the number of competitors is increased from 10 to 20. This increases the density of firms on the grid so the number of firms in the various markets will tend to increase. Second, the monopoly price is increased from 20 percent to 25 percent. This increase allows the simulation to consider a market with different demand and supply elasticities generating another monopoly price. The higher monopoly surcharge increases

Table 1.   Assumptions of the Simulation Model

	Base	Adjustment
Number of firms	10	20
Monopoly surcharge	20%	25%
Distance index†	Euclidean norm	Maximum segment

†The Euclidean norm is the distance between two points on the grid. (For example, (0,0) and (4,3) would have an Euclidean norm of $((4-0)^2 + (3-0)^2)^{1/2}$ or $(16+9)^{1/2}$ or 5.) The maximum segment is the largest element in absolute value from the vector difference between two points. (For example, (4,3) and (10,8) would have a difference of (6,5) which generates a maximum segment of 6.)

the number of competitors in the Boyer market. Finally, the competition index is changed to reflect the larger of the horizontal and vertical distances between the grid positions of the firms, because differences in product space may be best proxied by distances measured on the axes. This would require Boyer and DOJ markets to be defined as squares. Thus, a total of four simulations are considered in this study.

B. The Results

For each simulation, a total of 200 iterations were performed and the results are summarized in Tables 2-4. The mean and standard deviation of the expected number of firms in a particular market are given in Table 2. The number of firms in the average DOJ market may not be responsive to the total number of firms, because an increase in the number of potential competitors has two effects on the DOJ market. First, the increase in competitors tends to force the competitive price downward, thus shrinking the size of the DOJ market area. On the other hand, the additional firms may fall inside the DOJ market area and increase the number of competitors. On balance, the table shows a significant increase in the average number of competitors.

The number of competitors in a Boyer market increases if either the total number of firms or the monopoly price is increased. Also, the number of Boyer competitors grows if the distance index is adjusted. Finally, the number of firms in the GCS market remains relatively constant. However, the GCS market has the largest standard deviation of the three markets. The table also notes that the Boyer market is the largest and the DOJ market the smallest in most scenarios. This result is not surprising given the definitions of the three markets.

Table 3 presents the correlation statistics for the number of firms classified into the three markets during the simulation. The DOJ and GCS markets seem to be the most closely related with significant correlations ranging from .20 to .36.

Table 2. Average Number of Firms in Market for Various Simulations

Simulation	DOJ	Boyer	GCS	N†
Base case	3.12	5.54	4.91	67.0%
	(1.09)	(1.48)	(1.92)	
Additional firms	3.77	10.48	5.13	77.5%
	(1.48)	(2.25)	(2.72)	
Higher monopoly price	3.23	8.13	4.89	84.5%
	(1.23)	(1.30)	(1.83)	
New Distance Index	3.38	6.78	4.70	77.5%
	(1.20)	(1.49)	(1.71)	

Note: Standard deviations in parentheses.

†The percentage of the simulations where the number of firms in the Boyer market was greater than or equal to the number of firms in the GCS market which was greater than or equal to the number of firms in the DOJ market.

Table 3. Correlations between Number of Firms in
Particular Markets

Simulation	Correlations for		
	DOJ Boyer	*DOJ/GCS*	*Boyer/GCS*
Base case	.36*	.36*	.17*
Additional firms	.15*	.21*	.11
Higher monopoly price	.12	.20*	.10
New distance index	.17*	.33*	.12

*Significantly different from zero at the 5 percent level.

The number of firms in the DOJ and Boyer markets is correlated in the base scenario but the strength of the relationship is reduced when the structure of the simulation model is adjusted. Because the DOJ market is based on the competitive price and the Boyer market is tied to the collusive price, we should expect the two definitions to be related in some industries and not in others. The Boyer and the GCS approaches are only significantly related in one of four simulations.

The fundamental results of the analysis are presented in Table 4. The statistics represent the correlation between the Herfindahl index for a market[18] and the collusive price premium over the competitive limit price.[19] This proxies the ability of a market definition concept to identify noncompetitive pricing with a structural market power index. The DOJ market outperformed the Boyer and GCS approaches in all the simulations. Thus, it seems that the DOJ approach represents the best market definition methodology if the spatial competition model is valid, the competitive limit price is the appropriate base price and the price is not elevated to the monopoly level.[20] These three caveats require a little explanation. First, the spatial competition approach leads to a significant correlation between the competitive limit price and the number of firms in a Boyer market.[21] Since the competitive price is deducted from the collusive price to determine the monopolistic premium in the spatial model, much of the correlation between the number of firms in a Boyer market and the price is washed out. For a homogeneous product with a single competitive price, the Boyer methodology could outperform the DOJ approach in markets prone to collusion. The spatial competition structure also leads directly to the empirical definition of the GCS market. If a different simulation model was used, different GCS results could be generated. Second, the base firm might not elevate its price to the competitive limit price. Thus, the simulated collusive price increase would be greater and it is not clear if the DOJ definition would continue to dominate. However, we see no reason why the base firm would not behave strategically and raise its price to the competitive limit price. Finally, the failure of the spatial model to reach a monopoly price also biases the results in favor of the DOJ market.[22] This problem may not be serious, because the supracompetitive premium in one scenario averaged 85 percent of the monopoly price and the DOJ market still significantly outperformed the Boyer market.

Table 4. Correlation of the Herfindahl with
the Monopolistic Premium

Degree of Noncompetitive Performance†	DOJ	Boyer	GCS
Base case			
Low (23%)	.46*	.14	.12
Moderate (39%)	.61*	.17*	.31*
High (65%)	.56*	.11	.21*
Additional firms			
Low (15%)	.47*	.06	.01
Moderate (25%)	.64*	.11	.13
High (51%)	.51*	.06	.10
Higher monopoly profit			
Low (25%)	.53*	.15*	.13
Moderate (41%)	.54*	.07	.17*
High (86%)	.46*	.14*	.23*
New distance measure			
Low (20%)	.53*	.04	.23*
Moderate (33%)	.72*	.20*	.27*
High (61%)	.55*	.17*	.21*

*Significantly different from zero at the 5 percent level.
†The percentage of the full monopoly premium in the scenario is
given in parentheses.

In conclusion, the results in Table 4 offer some support for the DOJ approach to market definition, especially where spatial competition is important (i.e., geographic markets and differentiated products). However, it may be possible to define a simulation structure where the Boyer or GCS outperforms the DOJ test. Thus, it would be inappropriate to draw a final conclusion on the best approach to market definition from this evidence.

IV. CONCLUSION

The three approaches to market definition all face shortcomings that limit their general usefulness. These problems will affect their applicability to antitrust analysis. The standard GCS methodology can be subjectively interpreted to define either broad or narrow market definitions. Thus, extreme care must be used when applying the definition to ensure the market shares are reasonable proxies for the competitive position of the firms in the industry. The Boyer approach will incorporate too many substitutes in the market, if some substitutes are only relevant when the price approaches the monopolistic level. This implies that market shares based on the Boyer definition can understate the ease of collusion. Of course, if one were interested in the likelihood that the price could be raised to the monopoly level, the Boyer approach would be useful. The DOJ analysis can eliminate apparent substitutes if the sales of these substitutes are either small relative to the basic market or very price inelastic. Moreover, the DOJ rule can define a narrow market if the core products are currently priced competitively, and a broad market if the core products are priced supracompetitively. The narrow market can lead to the conclusion that a merger in a competitive market should be blocked while the broad market can support the conclusion that a merger in a noncompetitive market should not be blocked. These results seem inappropriate, because a merger should cause more concern in a market that is performing poorly.[23] Thus, the various market definition approaches all have some theoretical flaws that limit their use in antitrust analysis.

Our analysis of the spatial simulation model found the DOJ approach outperformed the GCS and Boyer methodologies. However, the structure of the simulation seemed to allow for the problems with the GCS (high standard deviation suggesting particular markets were either too narrow or too broad) and Boyer (monopoly concept allowed too many firms in the market) markets but not the DOJ. No firms were excluded from the DOJ market because they were too small and the current price was fixed at the competitive limit price. This may suggest that the DOJ market definition process can be superior if it is carefully applied to spatial competition situations.

Even though the DOJ approach appears superior in certain situations, all the market definition methodologies can give some unambiguous insight for merger analysis. A Boyer market that appears to be concentrated certainly creates some cause for concern, because the concentration data underestimates the competitive problem. Alternatively, a DOJ market that is unconcentrated is unlikely to suffer from collusion. The remaining cases are harder to analyze. If the Boyer market is used, the share analysis should be supplemented with a study of the elasticity of the distant substitutes to determine if the prices of the core products can be easily increased. If the DOJ approach is used, the market universe should be increased to include fringe firms and other small close substitutes to guarantee the procompetitive force of these products is incorporated in the merger analysis. Finally, the GCS methodology could be used in combination with either the Boyer or the DOJ approaches to verify the market definition.

ACKNOWLEDGMENTS

The analyses and conclusions set forth in this paper are those of the author and do not necessarily reflect the views of other members of the Bureau of Economics, other Commission staff or the Commission. I would like to thank John Howell, Christopher Klein, James Hurdle, Randall Marks, Steven Newborn, and two anonymous referees for valuable comments on previous drafts of this paper.

NOTES

1.   A product type is homogeneous if all consumers consider the varieties to be perfect substitutes. Economists did not consider the issue of whether one homogeneous product (e.g., steel) is in the same market as another homogeneous product (e.g., aluminum).

2.   Chamberlin and Robinson introduced the concept of product differentiation to allow for differences between related products. This concept implied that consumers had a choice among relatively close but not perfect substitutes.

3.   The DOJ (1982) introduced this methodology in the 1982 version of the guidelines.

4.   The DOJ (1984, p. 7) notes it may use a price increase either larger or smaller than five percent in certain cases.

5.   Of course, the DOJ (1984) recognizes that detailed analysis is necessary to confirm the initial indication of the Herfindahl index.

6.   Although one could argue that the current state of competition is irrelevant for market definition purposes (because one is only interested in the ability to raise price), this argument ignores the potential for a noncompetitive market to return to a competitive state.

7.   Although standard discounts offered to all customers can be factored into the analysis, special discounts offered to meet competition or obtain new accounts will not be easy to capture in the price data.

8.   The simple autoregressive process relates the current value of the price difference to the price difference lagged one period. More complex autoregressive moving average models link the current value of the price difference to lagged values of the price difference and to lagged values of the stochastic innovations (error terms). See Howell (1984) for a more detailed explanation of autoregressive moving average models.

9.   This would also exclude foreign firms operating under an import quota which is expected to last for more than one year. However, these foreign firms would have to be considered entrants if the quotas could expire.

10.   In an article on market definitions and the Guidelines, Werden (1983, pp. 532–33) notes a market defined with the 5 percent test should be expanded if (1) uncertainty exists as to the boundaries or (2) a small expansion to a "natural boundary" would allow for a significantly greater price increase.

11.   A similar analysis would conclude that a firm with a differentiated product would be placed in a broader market than a firm with a commodity product, because the differentiated product's price would tend to be raised to reflect unilateral market power.

12.   The model could be generalized to allow more than one firm to sell the center product without significantly changing the market definition process.

13.   The definition does not allow for a GCS market of either one or two, because the probability of finding firms close to the base firm is small. This restriction minimizes the likelihood of the simulation procedure generating artificially small markets.

14.   A naive firm could charge a competitive price equal to its constant marginal cost. However, a strategic firm would recognize that it could raise price to some degree without losing sales, because its competitors must sell at a spatial cost disadvantage.

15.   The collusion could be based on either an explicit agreement or a tacit recognition of mutual dependence.

16.   The average distance between cartel members is defined by calculating the distance on the grid between all of the individual cartel members and averaging the results. For example, one would average the distance between the base firm and the second firm, the base firm and the third firm and the second and third firm to calculate an average distance value for a three firm cartel. The number of relationships is computed by applying the factorial function to the number of firms (excluding the base firm) in the cartel. For example, only one relationship exists in a two firm cartel, while three relationships exist in a three firm cartel and six relationships in a four firm cartel.

17. This analysis is based on the assumed relationship between concentration and profitability. If these variables are not related, our approach cannot be used to evaluate the market definition concepts.

18. The Herfindahl was calculated by assuming each firm in the market has an equal share. The four firms concentration ratio gave similar but somewhat lower correlations for the DOJ approach.

19. Since the competitive limit price represents the price the base firm can charge without losing sales, it was defined by the distance of the closest competitor to the origin.

20. Also, one would have to assume that either no small fringe firms exist or the DOJ definition was adjusted to include fringe producers.

21. The correlation between the Herfindahl index for the Boyer market and the limit price in the base model was .27. This correlation is guaranteed to be high, because it is unlikely that any firm will be close enough to the origin to prevent the base firm from pricing substantially above marginal cost if the Boyer market contains only a few firms.

22. The Boyer market might be able to predict performance better than the DOJ market for prices close to the monopoly level, because the Boyer approach is based on the monopoly price.

23. This conclusion would be wrong if collusion was inevitable once a critical concentration ratio was reached, so the anticompetitive effect would be larger in a competitive market.

REFERENCES

Boyer, K. (1979) "Industry Boundaries," pp. 88–106 in T. Calvani and J. Siegfried, eds. *Economic Analysis and Antitrust Law,* Boston, Little, Brown.

————— . (January 1984) "Is There a Principle for Defining Industries?" *Southern Economic Journal,* Vol. 50, pp. 761–770.

Chamberlin, E. (1948) *The Theory of Monopolistic Competition,* Cambridge, Harvard University Press.

Horowitz, I. (July 1981) "Market Definition in Antitrust Analysis: A Regression Based Approach," *Southern Economic Journal,* Vol. 48, pp. 1–16.

Howell, J. (1984) "A Comment on Horowitz's Market Definition in Antitrust Analysis: A Regression Based Approach," *The Journal of Reprints for Antitrust Law and Economics,* Vol. 15, pp. 1161–1172.

Klein, C. (October 1985) "A Principle for Defining Industries: Comment," *Southern Economic Journal,* Vol. 52, pp. 537–541.

Marshall, A. (1920) *Principles of Economics, Book V,* London, Macmillan.

Robinson, J. (1934) *The Economics of Imperfect Competition,* London, Macmillan.

U.S. Federal Trade Commission. (1982) "Statement of the Federal Trade Commission Concerning Horizontal Mergers," Washington, D.C.

U.S. Department of Justice. (1982) "U.S. Department of Justice Merger Guidelines," Washington, D.C.

————— . (1984) "U.S. Department of Justice Merger Guidelines," Washington, D.C.

Werden, G. (June 1983) "Market Delineation and the Justice Department's Merger Guidelines," *Duke Law Journal,* pp. 514–557.

————— . (October 1985) "Is There a Principle for Defining Industries?: Comment," *Southern Economic Journal,* Vol. 52, pp. 532–536.

TREBLE DAMAGES AND OPTIMAL SUING TIME

Pablo T. Spiller

ABSTRACT

This paper examines the implications of the buyers' compensation doctrine for antitrust deterrence. The main theme of the paper is that the doctrine generates strategic incentives for purchasers from potential antitrust defendants. Particularly, it is an important determinant in their decision of when to file suit against an upstream firm allegedly committing an antitrust offense: direct buyers have an incentive to delay suing, while increasing the purchases of the good and thus the expected value of their antitrust litigation. This paper also develops a Nash equilibrium model to analyze the interactions between buyers' and suppliers' strategies. Buyers and suppliers have unbiased expectations about the different probabilities and suing time. The equilibrium determines: (1) the probability of suppliers actually being engaged in illegal activities, (2) the plaintiff's success probability, and (3) the optimal suing time.

Research in Law and Economics, volume 9, pages 45–56.
Copyright © 1986 by JAI Press Inc.
ISBN: 0-89232-657-3

I. INTRODUCTION

This paper examines the implications of the buyers' compensation doctrine for antitrust deterrence.[1] This doctrine holds that direct buyers should be compensated by the monopoly overcharge, trebled.[2]

The theme of this article is that the doctrine generates strategic incentives for purchasers from potential antitrust defendants.[3] The trebling provision is an important determinant in a buyer's decision of *when* to file suit against an upstream firm alledgedly committing an antitrust offense. Since buyers are compensated by the amount they buy times a multiplier larger than one, the larger the amount of purchases the larger their expected returns from suing the upstream firm. Thus direct buyers have an incentive to delay suing, while increasing the purchases of the good and thus the expected value of their antitrust litigation.[4]

In a simple model it is shown that if firms have unlimited liability, then the optimal decision is to postpone filing suit until the gains from postponing (i.e., increasing the total damages trebled) equal the losses from waiting (i.e., a smaller success probability, and a reduction in the present value of the total compensation). In this case the damage multiplier affects, in the margin, the optimal suing time. In particular, if the buyer would (not) find it profitable to file suit when there is only injunctive relief, then an increase in the damage multiplier would increase (decrease) the optimal suing time. If, however, courts award interest on damages, and court costs and success probabilities are time independent, then, the optimal decision is to postpone filing suit indefinitely (even in the presence of discounting). In this case the damage multiplier determines when to sue, but does not, in the margin, determine whether a buyer will sue or not. Since defendants have limited liability,[5] the incentives to file suit may be affected by bankruptcy constraints. If these are binding, the direct buyer will postpone filing suit until the actual damages, plus court costs, will equal the assets of the offenders.[6] In this case the damage multiplier determines both when the buyer will sue, as well as whether to sue or not.[7]

A Nash equilibrium model is developed to analyze the buyer and supplier strategies. The buyer's strategy is to decide whether and when to sue. The suppliers' strategy is whether or not to form a cartel. The equilibrium is a rational expectations one. Both the buyer and the supplier are assumed to assess each other's decision rules, and thus will have unbiased expectations about the different probabilities and suing time. The equilibrium determines: (1) the probability of suppliers actually being engaged in illegal activities, (2) the plaintiff's success probability, and (3) the optimal suing time.

II. THE MODEL

The problem is the following: The industry is composed of a single buyer and one or many suppliers.[8] The buyer buys either K units per period if the price does not exceed P, or if price exceeds P, does not buy at all. Suppliers' capacity is also assumed to be K.[9] At time zero the buyer thinks that there is a probability (π_c) that for L periods the upstream suppliers have been charging a monopoly price of $P > c$ where c is the marginal cost of the suppliers.[10] The buyer has to decide when to file suit. It could file suit immediately and recover damages with probability π_w based on the amount it purchased during the L periods. With probability $1 - \pi_w$ it may lose the case. If the buyer postpones its decision for some time, it will continue buying at a rate of K units per period until it files suit. Postponing the filing of a suit has two implications. On the one hand, damages are accumulated by increased purchases. On the other hand, if courts do not grant interest on accumulated damages, postponing the filing of the suit reduces the present value of "old" damages. Similarly, the probability of a plaintiff's success may decay with time, thus reducing the incentives to delay suing.

After filing suit, if the defendants lose and stay in business, the price falls to the competitive price (c). If the upstream firms go bankrupt, then the assets are transferred to the buyer who then produces the good at a cost equal to the competitive price.

Court costs (D) are assumed to be fixed and equal for both sides. The cartel (if it exists) is assumed to charge a price that extracts the whole surplus from the buyer, that is, it charges the 'perfect monopolistic' price. These two assumptions are chosen so as to simplify the model. Their implications are discussed in the notes.

To develop the basic intuition, I will analyze first the case where courts grant interest on damages, and where the plaintiff's success probability is time independent.

A. The Buyer's Problem

Case A1: Unlimited Liability, Interests Awarded

The benefit to the buyer from filing suit at time t is given by,

$$
\begin{aligned}
B_t = & \pi_w \int_t^\infty (P-c)K e^{\{-rs\}}ds \\
& + e^{\{-rt\}}[\pi_w K(P-c)M \int_{-L}^t e^{\{rs\}}ds - D].
\end{aligned}
\tag{1}
$$

The benefits from filing suit at time t are composed of three components: First, if the suit is successful, the price will fall from P to marginal cost, c, from time t on. Second, in that case the buyer also receives a compensation equal to the accumulated damages from the time the cartel started to overcharge times a multiplier of M. Each period's damages equals the per unit overcharge times the quantity purchased. These damages are then compounded by an interest rate of r.[11]

The first order condition is given by

$$
\partial B / \partial t = e^{\{-rt\}}[(P-c)K\pi_w(M e^{\{-rL\}} - 1) + Dr] = 0
\tag{2}
$$

Observe that the term in brackets is independent of t, it is either positive or negative. If positive, then the optimal decision is to postpone indefinitely the filing of the suit. If it is negative, it is worthwhile to file suit immediately.[12]

The condition, then, to indefinitely postpone filing suit is given by

$$M \geq \{1 - rD/[(P-c)K\pi_w]\}/e^{\{-rL\}}. \tag{3}$$

Thus, if $L - 0$, that is, the buyer identifies an antitrust offense the moment it is committed, a multiplier equal to 1 will provide buyers with incentives to postpone indefinitely the filing of suits. Observe that postponing until infinity is an optimal strategy because the present value of court costs goes to zero as $t \to \infty$, while by granting interests on damages, the present value of the award remains positive. The value of this strategy is given by taking the limit of Eq. (1) when t tends to infinity:

$$\lim_{t \to \infty} B_t = \pi_w (P-c)KM/r. \tag{4}$$

Since the benefits from such a strategy are positive always (if π_w is positive), as long as Eq. (3) holds, buyers will postpone filing suits to the limit. Moreover, changes in M (for $M > 1$) do not change the incentives to file suits.[13]

There are, however, reasons for buyers to file suits in finite time. First, the success probability (π_w) may decay with time because of memory or witness losses, as well as the statute of limitation. Second, courts do not usually award interest on damages. Thus, as long as there is a positive discount rate, filing suits at infinity may not be an optimal strategy. Finally, firms have limited liability, thus restricting the amount of damages that can actually be collected.

Case A.2: Unlimited Liability, No Interest Awarded, Time Dependent Success Probability

The benefit from filing a suit at time t is now given by

$$B_t = \pi_w \int_t^\infty (P-c)Ke^{\{-rs\}}ds + e^{\{-rt\}}[\pi_w K(P-c)M(T+L) - D], \tag{5}$$

with the first order condition being

$$\partial B/\partial t = e^{\{-rt\}}K(P-c)\{\pi_w'/r + (\pi_w' - r\pi_w)M(t+L) + \pi_w(M-1) \\ + rD/K(P-c)\} = 0 \tag{6}$$

Thus the optimal time to sue is

$$t^* + L = \{[\pi_w'/r + \pi_w(M-1)]K(P-c) + rD\}/\{MK(P-c)(\pi_w r - \pi_w')\}. \tag{7}$$

Thus, if $L = 0$, even with $\pi_w' = 0$, Eq. (7) provides a finite solution for $t > 0$, as long as $M > 1$. Observe that $M = 0$ (that is, if the plaintiff gets only injunctive relief), then, if $rD < \pi_w(P - c)K$, suits will be filed immediately (i.e., at $t = 0$). If, however, $rD > \pi_w(P - c)K$ then the benefits from filing suits are negative and no suit will be filed.

In general, the optimal time to file a suit depends on the parameters of the model. It can be seen that

$$dt^*/dM = e^{\{-rt\}}\{K(P-c)\pi_w[\epsilon_{\pi_{w,t}} - r]/r + rD\}/\Delta, \qquad (8)$$

where

$$\Delta = \partial^2 B_t/\partial t^2 < 0, \text{ and } \epsilon_{\pi_{w,t}} = \pi'_w/\pi_w.$$

Therefore,

$$\text{sign } dt^*/dM = \text{sign } \{K(P-c)\pi_w(r-\epsilon_{\pi_{w,t}})/r - r D\}.$$

If $\pi'_w = 0$, t* increases with M if $K(P - c)\pi_w > rD$, which is the condition for a plaintiff to file a suit when M = 0. Thus, whether a bigger multiplier delays filing suit further, depends on whether the expected annual injunctive relief exceeds the annualized court costs. Observe also that as long as M > 0, the plaintiff will always file suit at some t > 0, since for $\pi'_w = 0$,

$$B(t^*) = e^{\{-rt^*\}}\pi_w(P-c)KM/r > 0.$$

Finally, it can also be seen that the optimal suing time falls with K, (P − c), r and π_w, but increases with D.[14]

B. The Sellers' Problem

The previous section discusses the optimal strategy for a plaintiff given his expectations of the sellers actually being a cartel. In this section I analyze whether forming a cartel is an optimal strategy for the sellers, given the buyer's optimal suing strategy.

Case B.1: Unlimited Liability, Interests Awarded

In this case the gains to forming a cartel are given by:[15]

$$
\begin{aligned}
G_t &= \int_0^{L+t} K(P-c)e^{-rs}ds - \pi_{wc}e^{\{-r(t+L)\}}[D + \int_0^{L+t} K(P-c)Me^{rs}ds] \\
&\quad + (1-\pi_{wc})\int_{L+t}^{\infty} K(P-c)e^{\{-rs\}}ds \\
&= K(P-c)/r - \pi_{wc}\{K(P-c)M[1 - e^{\{-r(t+L)\}}] \\
&\quad + De^{\{-r(t+L)\}} - e^{\{-r(t+L)\}}\}/r. \qquad (9)
\end{aligned}
$$

The gains from collusion equal the abnormal profits obtained until detection (from time 0 to L + t),[16] minus the expected costs if found guilty (equal to the actualized value of the overcharge times the multiplier plus court costs), plus the expected gain if found innocent (the discounted value of future abnormal profits from continuing pricing at the monopoly price).[17]

It can be seen that

$$\lim_{t \to \infty} G_t = K(P-c)[1 - \pi_{wc}M]/r. \qquad (10)$$

Thus, a cartel will not form if $M \geq q\ 1/\pi_{wc}$. If all cartels had the same probability of conviction (i.e., the same π_{wc}), then cartels could be eliminated by setting a multiplier larger than $1/\pi_{wc}$. Observe, however, that such a case may not be an equilibrium. If $M \geq 1/\pi_{wc}$, then the probability of a price increase being collusive is zero. That is, a well-informed buyer will assess $\pi_c = 0$. But then, it will never pay to sue and cartels would then form. Thus, to be able to get a 'rational expectations' solution in terms of the probability of price increases being collusive, we need to have, across cartels, different probabilities of being convicted. Let π_{wci} be the probability that a cartel i be convicted. π_{wci} is known by the cartel but not by the buyer.[18] Let π_{wci} be distributed uniformly in $(0, \pi_{max})$, with mean equal t $\pi_{max}/2$. Then, let the government determine a given M, thus those cartels with $\pi_{wci} \geq 1/M$ will not form. The proportion of cartels formed is[19]

$$\pi_c(M) = 1/(M\pi_{max}). \tag{11}$$

Thus, a rational consumer will assess the probability of a price increase to be collusive (π_c) to be equal to $\pi_c(M)$. Thus, there is a sufficiently large M for which all cartels are deterred from forming.[20]

As discussed above, if the success probability falls with time or interests are not awarded, the optimal t is finite. These cases are discussed below.

Case B.2: Unlimited Liability, No Interests Awarded

The gains from forming the cartel are now given by

$$G_t = \int_0^{L+t} K(P-c)e^{\{-rs\}}ds + (1-\pi_{wc})\int_{L+t}^{\infty} K(P-c)e^{\{-rs\}}ds$$
$$- \pi_{wc}e^{\{-r(t+L)\}}(P-c)KM(L+t) - e^{\{-r(t+L)\}}D. \tag{12}$$

Substituting Eq. (7) (the optimal buyer's suing time) in Eq. (12), and assuming for simplicity that $\pi_w' = 0$, we obtain:

$$G_t = e^{\{-rL(L+t)\}}\{K(P-c)(1-\pi_{wc}M) - D(1+\pi_{wc}/\pi_w)\}/r. \tag{13}$$

Observe that a sufficient condition for $G_t < 0$ is that $M > 1/\pi_{wc}$. For a cartel to be formed, however, it is necessary that

$$0 < \pi_{wc} < [K(P-c) - D]/[MK(P-c) + D/\pi_w] = \hat{\pi}_{wc}. \tag{14}$$

The inequalities in Eq. (14) provide the Nash equilibrium probability of the sellers actually being a cartel, which is given by

$$\pi_c = [1/(\pi_{max} - \pi_{min})] (\hat{\pi}_{wc} - \pi_{min}). \tag{15}$$

Observe that π_c falls with M. Moreover, there is a $\hat{M}$, given by Eq. (16), for which $\pi_c = 0$,

$$\hat{M} = 1/\pi_{min} - D(1+\pi_{min}/\pi_w)/[\pi_{min}K(P-c)]. \tag{16}$$

To summarize, if firms have unlimited liability, and if $M \geq 1$, buyers will postpone filing suit to the limit, and only $\pi_c(M)$ cartels will be formed.[21] The cartels that are going to be formed are those with relatively low probability of being convicted if detected. The average probability of being convicted if detected is $\hat{\pi}_{wc}/2$ (see Eq. [14]). Thus, unless $M \geqq \hat{M}$ (see Eq. [16]) this doctrine does not necessarily eliminate cartels, but it deters their creation. The doctrine, however, creates incentives to delay prosecution.[22]

The next section examines the implications of this doctrine for the limited liability case.

III. LIMITED LIABILITY

In this section we assume that the total damages implied by the optimal suing times discussed in Section II exceed the assets of the defendants. Thus, the buyer will choose its timing so as to maximize its expected benefits subject to the constraint that the total damages cannot exceed the value of the upstream firms minus court costs. For simplicity we will assume that interests on damages are awarded and that
$\pi'_w = 0$. Then limited liability implies that

$$\int_0^{L+t} M(P-c)Ke^{(rs)}ds \leqq K - D. \tag{17}$$

From Eq. (17) we get that the optimal timing cannot exceed t* such that

$$e^{\{r(t^* + L)\}} = 1 + (K-D)r/[M(P-c)K]. \tag{18}$$

Since, as seen above, the unconstrained first order condition is positive for $M > 1$, then the optimal t will be t*.
Substituting Eq. (18) into Eq. (1) we obtain:

$$\begin{aligned} B_{t^*} = \{\pi_w[(P-c)K(1+Me^{(-rL)} + Dr(1-e^{(-rL)}) \\ + Kre^{(-rL)}] - Dr\}e^{(-rt^*)}/r. \end{aligned} \tag{19}$$

Thus, a buyer will file suit at t* if

$$\begin{aligned} \pi_w \geqq Dr/\{K[(P-c)(1+Me^{(-rL)} + re^{(-rL)}] \\ + Dr(1-e^{(-rL)})\}. \end{aligned} \tag{20}$$

Consequently, an increase in the multiplier increases, at the margin, the number of suits, since buyers with even lower π_{ws} will find it worthwhile to file suit.[23]

Let us now examine the benefits to the supplier from collusion, given that Eq. (20) determines who actually files suit at t*. The gains from collusion are:

$$\begin{aligned} G_t &= \int_0^{L+t} K(P-c)e^{(-rs)}ds - \pi_{wc}e^{\{-r(t+L)\}}K \\ &+ (1-\pi_{wc}) \int_{L+t}^\infty (P-c)Ke^{(-rs)}ds \\ &= [(P-c)e^{\{r(L+t)\}} - \pi_{wc}(P-c+r)]Ke^{\{-r(L+t)\}}/r. \end{aligned} \tag{21}$$

Substitute Eq. (17) and Eq. (21) we obtain:

$$\begin{aligned} G_{t^*} &= [(P-c)KM(1-\pi_{wc}) + (K-D)r \\ &- r\pi_{wc}KM]e^{\{-r(L+t^*)\}}/(Mr). \end{aligned} \tag{22}$$

From Eq. (22) only cartels whose π_{wci} is such that G_{t*} is positive will have an incentive to form. That is, cartels will begin to operate if

$$\pi_{wci} \leqq [(P-c)KM + (K-D)r]/(KM(P-c+r)). \qquad (23)$$

Thus, for a given M, there is a maximum π_{wci} such that cartels will form. That M, in turn, will determine (a) the proportion of cartels that are going to be formed, and thus the probability that a price increase is collusive ($P_c(M)$), and (b) the probability, as expected by the buyer, of it winning the suit if one is brought.[24] But even if M is very large, the maximum π_{wci} is not going to fall below $(P-c)/(P-c+r)$. The rationale for this result is that given limited liability, there is a limit to what can be lost at the courts.[25] Thus, increasing M may not further reduce antitrust violations. A very large M, however, brings $t*$ to zero, since damages will tend to exceed K, consequently reducing the incentives to delay prosecution. Finally, for a given M, if the probability of being acquitted is relatively large, the collusion gains from the periods following the suit are, in an expected sense, large. However, the larger the discount rate, the lower the maximum π_{wci}.

To summarize, when firms have limited liability, buyers' compensation has the potential to deter cartels from forming. Since buyers will postpone suing until the total damages equal the assets of the cartel (minus court costs), the larger the multiplier, the sooner buyers will bring suit. For very large M, the proportion of cartels that are going to be formed is given by $[(P-c)/(P-c+r)]/\pi_{max}$.

IV. FINAL COMMENTS

In this paper I analyze through a model of cartel formation and litigation some of the problems that a policy of compensating buyers may generate. The model solves for the endogenous number of cartels being formed, the probability of conviction, the number of cases filed, and their timing. While the results are extreme because of the simplicity of the model, the implications are robust to its specification. The main results are the following:

First, buyers have incentives to postpone the filing of suits. This incentive is extreme if court costs and the probability of winning a suit are constant, interest on damages are awarded, and the suppliers have limited liability. In this case the buyer will simply accumulate damages, the return from postponing the filing of a suit being always positive. While this strategy may seem to deter cartels from forming, that is not the case if the probability of being acquitted is sufficiently large. However, in this case a sufficiently large multiplier may deter the formation of cartels.

Second, if suppliers have limited liability, buyers will bring suit whenever the damages (plus court costs) equal the net worth of the suppliers.[26] In this case, trebling damages may not be very effective in deterring cartels. As long as the probability of losing the case is not too high, the suppliers will find it optimal to become a cartel, even if they know for sure that they will be brought to court.

Third, when the probability of winning a case decays with time, the damage multiplier affects the optimal timing of the suit. In particular, if the plaintiff would (not) file a suit if $M = 0$, then the optimal timing and M are positively (negatively) correlated.

ACKNOWLEDGMENTS

I would like to thank Kenneth Elzinga, Mitch Polinsky, Mike Riordan, and an anonymous referee for helpful comments.

NOTES

1. For simplicity of the discussion I will concentrate the analysis on price fixing. The analysis can easily be extended to other types of antitrust violations, as well as to punitive damages in tort cases (e.g., Polinsky and Shavell, 1984).

2. This doctrine is based on assessing the monopolistic damages as its overcharge. Thus, injured parties' compensation, which after the *Illinois-Brick* decision implies direct buyers only, would be based on trebling the amount they purchased times the per-unit overcharge. The classic reference for calculating the monpolistic damages is the electrical equipment cases; see Bane (1973). The deterrence effects of the doctrine were analyzed by Landes (1983), and see also his footnote 1 for further references. A critical view of it can be found in Breit and Elzinga (1974).

3. The strategic incentives that this compensation policy generates has been recognized in the literature before. See, for example, Breit and Elzinga (1974), Elzinga and Breit (1976), Easterbrook (1981), and Butler (1983).

4. This incentive to increase the amount of damages was perceived by the courts. See *SCM Corp. vs. Xerox Corp.* 463 F. Supp. 983,990 (1978) for a case where the jury sustained that SCM should have mitigated damages by filing suit earlier. See also Breit and Elzinga (1985) for other references.

5. Limited liability means that the defendant is liable for not more than its net wealth. Thus, damages cannot exceed that amount.

6. See also notes 8, 21, and 23 below.

7. Many of the inefficiencies associated with enforcement by buyers could be eliminated by other types of private enforcement. On this, see Becker and Stigler (1974) and Friedman (1984). See, however, Landes and Posner (1975).

8. The assumption of a single buyer is important for two purposes. First, it simplifies the analysis. Second, it clearly shows the incentives the buyers' compensation doctrine generates. In footnotes, however, the results will be qualified for the case when there are multiple buyers.

9. The assumption that the buyer buys only K units is only a simplifying one. Assuming a 'normal' demand curve would provide similar results at the cost of complicating the algebra. It should, however, be emphasized that in the case being analyzed here there are no "inefficiencies" due to monopolization. This, however, is an assumption of the model. Similar results would be obtained if monopolization generated social inefficiencies. Observe, however, that if the supplier can increase its production above K, then we will observe both a delay in suing as well as an increase in he quantity bought per period. This increase should be accounted for when measuring the social costs of the cartel. Thus, to simplify the analysis, a capital constraint is assumed. Thus, the cartel, if formed,

agrees on building K units of capacity and on a given price, to be specified below. Once the cartel is formed there is no incentive to cheat since firms cannot exceed their capacity constraints.

10. It is assumed here that the buyer has unbiased expectations of the costs of producing the good by the suppliers.

11. We are assuming away the problem of a binding statute of limitation. Moreover, we assume here that if the courts agree with the plaintiff, they will also assign damages starting from period $-L$.

12. Observe that if D was a function of, say, the amount of damages or of time, then Eq. (2) would have an interior solution. Similarly, courts could actually treat M as endogenous, depending on the asked damages. Courts actually may be reluctant to let firms go bankrupt, and thus may try to reduce the actual damages, so that when they are multiplied by M, the total will not exceed the cartel's assets. On this, see the next section.

13. It should be observed here that the cartel could affect Eq. (3) by choosing a price below the 'monopolistic' price. That is, for a given value of the exogenous variables, there is a P such that Eq. (3) is reversed. In this case suits will be filed, if at all, at $t = 0$. To deter buyers from filing suits at $t = 0$, the cartel has to choose an overcharge so that $B_0 \leqq 0$. That is, it will have to choose $(P - c)K \leqq rD/\{\pi_w[M(1 - e^{-rL}) + 1]\}$. For simplicity of analysis, it will be assumed that this strategy does not pay off. The conditions for it, however, will depend on M and other exogenous variables.

14. If interests were paid on awards, then $t^* < \infty$ as long as $\pi_w' < 0$. In this case it can be seen that $dt^*/dM \gtrless 0$ as $t^* \gtrless 1/(-\epsilon_{\pi_{w,t}})$.

15. In Eq. (9) π_{wc} is the probability of a 'true' cartel being convicted if brought to court. Thus the relationship between π_w and π_{wc} is:
$\pi_w = \pi_c\pi_{wc} + (1 - \pi_c)\pi_{wcn}$ where π_{wcn} is the probability of convicting an innocent firm given that it was brought to court.

16. It is assumed here that L is common knowledge. That is, the buyer suspects that from time $-L$ the sellers have been charging a collusive price. If sellers have been actually charging a collusive price, then it is assumed that the buyer's assumption about the starting time is correct.

17. It is assumed here that the probability of facing a suit in the future is zero after being acquitted from the current case. That is, once it is proven that the cartel has not actually committed an offense, if it keeps the price at the same level, no other suit can be open on the same grounds.

18. π_{wci} may be a function, for example, of the type of costs the cartel has. If no prosecution will use cost-accounting information to assess whether the price increase was collusive or not, different accounting methods or different cost structures may imply different probabilities of actually being found guilty.

19. In his paper I will assume that the only problem the cartel faces is prosecution. That is, there are no cartel enforcement problems. Thus, if it is worthwhile, cartels will form. Thus the proportion of cartels formed equals the proportion of those cartels which find collusion profitable.

20. If the lowest probability of being convicted, given that the defendant is a cartel, is not zero but, say π_{min}, then, $\pi_c(M) = (1/M - \pi_{min})/(\pi_{max} - \pi_{min})$, thus choosing $M = 1/\pi_{min}$ will be necessary to deter *all* antitrust offenses. Observe, that this generates a rational expectations equilibrium since $M = 1/\pi_{min}$ satisfies Eq. (3), and as long as $\pi_{wn} > 0$, then Eq. (4) is also positive.

21. This result is insensitive to the assumption of a single buyer. Assume there were two buyers. Neither of them would benefit from filing suit earlier. First, since in a symmetric equilibrium each buyer buys K/2 units per period, neither can accumulate larger damages by buying more than the other. Moreover, filing suit earlier only reduces the amount of the damages.

22. We are assuming that courts cannot really distinguish a purchaser who behaves strategically from one that does no. Actually, courts may assign damages depending on the extent of precautionary activities performed by the downstream firm as well as on whether they behaved strategically. However, the main issue in this doctrine, as put forward by Easterbrook (1985), is to make buyers behave strategically. Thus, allowing the courts to detect strategic behavior and to assign damages accordingly may actually go against the main thrust of this doctrine.

23. It should be noted that this result is also insensitive to the assumption of a single buyer, as long as risk neutrality is maintained. Assume, for the moment, that there were two buyers. A game will be developed between the two which will consist of when each will file suit. Since each would be buying K/2 units of the good per period, and since each is aware of the optimal strategy of its competitor, whenever the sum of the accumulated damages equal the suppliers' total assets (minus court costs), both competitors will file suit simultaneously. The optimal timing will remain the same. (Now, however, each one does not wait until its own compensation equals the suppliers' assets, but when total expected damages equal that sum.) Assume one (call it firm A) decides to file suit later. Since firm B filed suit and received its own compensation, what is left is no more than what firm A could have received if it would have filed suit simultaneously with firm B. That is, it will not be able to recover the overcharge for the last period purchases. Thus no firm will postpone the filing. Assume now that firm A decides to file suit earlier. Its damages are smaller than they would have been had it filed suit a time t* (jointly with firm B). Consequently, there are no incentives no file suit before t*. Thus t* is a Nash equilibrium in filing strategies. However, if each buyer is less informed about its own competitors' strategies, and if there is risk aversion on the side of buyers, then the optimal timing may be less than t*.

24. Equations (20) and (23) have to jointly hold so as to have a unique equilibrium with positive probabilities of detection and conviction. A simple look at both equations will show that this is true if M is sufficiently large. For small Ms, however, Eq. (20) may not hold. An equilibrium, then, would be one where $\pi c = 1$ but it does not pay to sue because of $\pi_{wc} < 1$, and thus buyers will not file suits.

25. See Polinsky and Shavell (1984) for a similar result.

26. The fact that we do not necessarily see firms going bankrupt after being sued means that courts may actually take into account the plaintiff's incentives and thus provide compensating damages lower than the 'right' ones. See Breit and Elzinga (1985) for a discussion of the behavior of the courts in the presence of strategic behavior by plaintiffs.

REFERENCES

Bane, C. A. (1973) *The Electrical Equipment Conspiracies: The Treble Damage Actions*, New York, Federal Legal Publications.

Becker, G. S., and G. J. Stigler. (1974) "Law Enforcement, Malfeasance, and Compensation of Enforcers," *Journal of Legal Studies*, Vol. 3, pp. 1–18.

Breit, W., and K. G. Elzinga. (1974) "Antitrust Enforcement and Economic Efficiency: The Uneasy Case for Treble Damages," *Journal of Law and Economics*, Vol. 17, pp. 329–356.

Breit, W., and K. G. Elzinga. (1985) "Private Antitrust Enforcement: The New Learning," *Journal of Law and Economics*, Vol. 28(2), pp. 405–444.

Butler, H. N. (1983) "Restricted Distribution Contracts and the Opportunistic Pursuit of Treble Damages," *Washington Law Review*, Vol. 59, pp. 27–57.

Easterbrook, F. H. (1981) "Predatory Strategies and Counterstrategies," *University of Chicago Law Review*, Vol 48, pp. 263–319.

Easterbrook, F. H. (1985) "Detrebling Antitrust Damages," *Journal of Law and Economics*, Vol. 28(2), pp. 445–468.

Elzinga, K. G., and W. Breit (1976). *The Antitrust Penalties: A Study in Law and Economics*, New Haven, Yale University Press.

Friedman, D. (1984) "Efficient Institutions for the Private Enforcement of Law" *Journal of Legal Studies*, Vol. 13, pp. 379–398.

Landes, W. M., and R. A. Posner. (1975) "The Private Enforcement of Law," *Journal of Legal Studies*, Vol. 4, pp. 1–46.

Landes, W. M. (1983) "Optimal Sanctions for Antitrust Violators," *University of Chicago Law Review,* Vol. 50, pp. 656–678.

Polinsky, A. M., and S. Shavell. (1984), "The Optimal Use of Fines and Imprisonment," *Journal of Public Economics,* Vol. 24, pp. 89–99.

ANOTHER LAW AND ECONOMICS

Paul H. Brietzke

ABSTRACT

The experience of teaching law and economics informs Brietzke's approach to re-
search. He describes exchanges with students of diverse interests, backgrounds,
and abilities in economics. These classroom experiences encouraged him to adopt
a sympathetic but nevertheless rather critical approach to the subject. Casting
about for ways to make abstract theories clear and useful to law students, he chose
to relate economics to their knowledge of legal history, legal philosophy, political
science, and a process-oriented sociology of law. His discussions with students
then demonstrated that these fields can be made to yield cogent and effective criti-
cisms of much law and economics scholarship.
These insights indicate a way to go beyond the carping evident in much of the criti-
cal literature. Law and economics must be brought to bear on the mixed economy
where, like it or not, we all live and work. Theory has failed us here because sensi-
ble policy prescriptions get lost in the middle ground between the false dichotomy
of microeconomics and macroeconomics, and between the congruent dichotomy

Research in Law and Economics, volume 9, pages 57–109.
ISBN: 0-89232-657-3

created by analyses of private and public laws. The perfection of economic or legal theory has become the enemy of policies which are merely good in terms of the "public interest." Theories leading to the identification of such policies have played almost no role in law and economics. Such theories would include those of the second best, of workable competition, of an institutional economics, and of "equity"—lawyers' attempts to ameliorate the extremity of result when canons of either liberty or equality get applied.

I. INTRODUCTION

An explosion in studies of law and economics has outpaced analyses of teaching this subject in law schools. My purpose is to suggest a different, not necessarily a better approach to a subject amenable to a variety of treatments.[1] Like that of John Siegfried (1981, pp. 19–21) at Vanderbilt, my course design grows out of the realization that law students cannot become anything remotely resembling economists while taking one three-hour course. The range of law student competence in economics is so great that the same course must somehow enable the uninitiated to master at least "basic" concepts without boring the economically sophisticated. This is difficult enough, but there follows the often-ignored hazard that a little knowledge can prove a dangerous thing in the hands of new converts to economic analysis.[2] I try to solve these problems by encouraging and "teaching" students to criticize the tools of economic analysis, even as they are reading about them, much as students learn to criticize literary criticism.

How can the uninitiated criticize, when they lack the economics tools to evaluate the economics tools they are beginning to master? Law students *can* begin to develop their own criticisms on the basis of ideas with which they are already familiar, such as those studied in undergraduate courses and developed further in Jurisprudence, Legal History, Legal Process, and Constitutional Law. Students already familiar with economics concepts can profitably spend relatively more time examining their assumptions about economics and comparing the methodologies of law and of economics. Learning is a process of moving outward, from the familiar to the unfamiliar, and students unfamiliar with economics concepts eagerly grasp something "legal" to hang onto while tracking economics analyses which, initially, seem overwhelmingly complex. Fostering a critical approach to law and economics from the very beginning is also essential to an eventual sophistication in the field. Most law and economics scholars are so technically accomplished that their conclusions follow more or less automatically if the reader consciously or unconsciously grants them their initial assumptions. Once embedded in a reader's mind, these assumptions are extremely difficult to dislodge. It is not enough to teach the assumptions and theories favored by the teacher. The field should be presented fully blown, in all of its contradictions. But the teacher's preferences will inevitably come across, and these should thus be made explicit.

When the assumptions of one law and economics scholar conflict with those of another, as they often do, the likely result is the reader's confusion rather than a fruitful integration of ideas. The best way to overcome this confusion and to foster a mastery of law and economics in the process is to encourage student analyses to take account of the ways in which the field evolved. Much was written during the initial stages of a law and economics that sought to explain the whole world and paid insufficient attention to rival inarticulate premises that significantly influence outcomes. These premises came to be analyzed in detail after the frontiers to genuinely new analyses began to close. The result was the emergence of rival "schools" of law and economics, an arguable premature fragmentation of the field rather than a productive synthesis of very real insights. Students are more interested in the academic politics of this fragmentation than I would have expected. They do try to extract the useful teachings of each school and to somehow integrate them—for reasons only partly explained by the need to take a final exam. What is useful varies with student interests and with the anticipated uses for law and economics, and my course structure attempts to foster diverse experiences. I also stress to students that the course is only an introduction to topics meriting a much more extensive exploration while formulating responsible policy arguments for lawsuits, drafting rules and legislation, and playing the often-inescapable lawyer's role as a leader of informed public opinion.

II. COURSE STRUCTURE AND CONTENT

With these perspectives in mind, I attempt to strike a balance between a "directed" learning and a "free" discussion of the issues that arise. A brief lecture outlines a particular concept and explains its most difficult aspects in the shortest possible time. The discussions which follow usually include student criticisms of the inarticulate premises of the lecture; the resulting insights are then applied to hypotheticals[3] based on cases, statutes, and/or public policy notions. I choose hypotheticals which link up with the next topic wherever possible. There are "required" readings, and students choose one or more "optional" readings in line with their own interests for each segment of the course. (See the Appendix to this article.) There are no formal requirements to do so, but students commonly lead the class discussions related to their optional readings and occasionally lecture as well. If there seems to be little class interest in an optional topic, it is treated briefly or omitted, as time permits. What follows is thus a composite portrait of six years' experience with my course.

Like most course designs, mine tries to put two pints' worth of content into a one pint pot. To the extent I succeed, it is because I try to link topics together as often and as tightly as possible to make policy analyses cumulative, and to treat important economics techniques in different contexts and at higher levels of sophistication as the course proceeds. The course consists of five roughly equal segments: an introduction to the main concepts of law and economics, property, contracts, corporations, and politics and administration. This course structure has proved quite successful in encouraging students to build up, brick by brick, a picture of how law operates in the economy.

Students gain a sense of some economic institutions, having thought through several policy issues in comprehensive ways. They ask themselves whether quick insights based on economics can be consolidated in thoroughgoing analyses that display a real feeling for legal tasks and economic life. Cost-benefit analyses are discussed throughout the course; I show how techniques described in Mishan's excellent book[4] can be used to clarify policy problems and solutions. We also consider whether many such analyses, conducted regardless of legal concerns and promptings of the "heart," are feasible and moral: "You can't really trade off an Indian child's education with the future of the whooping crane."[5] My course neglects many areas of law and economics scholarship, chiefly those in which economic motivations are not popularly thought to dominate behavior. This tends to understate the determinism of a scholarship that, like Marxism, often reduces all of behavior to economic dimensions. But it is better to ignore topics than to achieve the superficiality likely to result from attempts to cover all of the subjects treated in, for example, books by Richard Posner (1977) and by Gary Becker (1976). Detailed coverage faces a "diminishing marginal utility," however, particularly in light of the widespread student impression that law exists in neat little packages wrapped up with course syllabi.

Law and Economics can, and in my view should, serve as a "perspectives" course, enabling students to integrate their knowledge across several course boundaries. Jurisprudence responded to this need[6] at many law schools, not always successfully. The continued decline of belief and interest in black letter law, and calls for powerful theories that enable future practitioners to concoct more effective policy arguments, have worked to the advantage of economics. As a counterweight to an arid doctrinalism in law, economics emphasizes the function and purpose of a rule and the need to clarify concepts, so that these can be modeled and then evaluated empirically. As a legal theory, economics would help people figure out what is best done in a world full of opportunities, rather than have people ordered to do things which may prove suboptimal. Unfortunately, economics may offer an incomplete, "Yuppie" theory of law and introduce oversimplifications of its own through a utopian accentuation of certain realities and neglect of others.[7]

My course focuses on the making of economic choices, constrained by a variety of factors, in the allocation, delegation, and aggregation of resources.[8] These resources are scarce in relation to what almost all economists see as unlimited human wants. The law and economics of property analyzes the *allocation* of these resources, answering Harold Lasswell's (1936) "political questions" of who owns what, when where, and, above all, why. Contracts are treated as changing the allocations of resources and as accomplishing the *delegation* of rights to use resources. We approach corporations as combining the functions of resource allocation and delegation—of property and contracts—the whole being greater than the sum of its parts because of the *aggregation* of resources that takes place within corporations. Property, contracts, and corporations are then treated in combination as the legal foundations of private decision making in the economy, and they are compared and contrasted with the law and economics of public decision making. We view the public sector as heavily committed to aggregating, allocating, and delegating the use of resources in ways which partly cooperate and partly conflict with private decisions. Although we study many legislative and judicial interventions in the property, contracts, and corporations course segments, discussions revolve around a scholarship which treats these interventions as unwelcome intrusions into the "private" law of "free" markets. At the end of the course, an examination of government regulation of economic activity applies a corrective which points up the legal significance of a "mixed" economy.[9] The course thus concludes with matters taken up in detail in Antitrust, a course which I teach in the second semester and which about half of the Law and Economics students take.

Studies of the phenomena of economic choice guarantee that Law and Economics will be a policy-oriented course, concerned with devising criteria for evaluating actual and potential choices. Legal rules symbolizing the exercise of economic choice relate to the free alienability of property, freedom of contract, free markets for corporate takeovers, democratic processes of representation, an administrative accountability, etc. These concepts are laden with favorable emotions in law and in economics, and are thus difficult to analyze objectively. I attempt to foster a more balanced analysis through a continuing emphasis on the constraints to choice, particularly the inequalities of power among decision makers that Robert Lee Hale explored long ago.[10] Necessitous decision makers are not free; the exercise of power by others hems the decision maker in and constitutes a counterweight to his freedom of decision. Understanding this counterweight of power is a requisite for realistic policy analyses, as in Robinson's excellent economics monograph, *Freedom and Necessity* (1970).[11]

A. Course Introduction

Most law and economics analyses deploy a small number of interdependent ideas. A sound basis for subsequent analyses can be established by rather briefly examining Posner's four "fundamental concepts,"[12] marginal utility theory,[13] efficiency (or wealth maximization) criteria,[14] and the most difficult concepts in the course, Pareto optimality and potential Pareto superiority.[15] I do not expect full understanding of these concepts at the beginning of the course; these and other concepts are best mastered in context[16] as the need for them arises in evaluating other concepts and in furthering policy analyses. But I stress at the outset that these concepts form the basis for Chicago School analysis, the foundation for an expansive program the likes of which "eluded Bentham, Comte, and Marx": "*all* human behavior can be viewed as involving participants who maximize their utility from a stable set of preferences and accumulate an optimal amount of information and other inputs in a variety of markets" (Becker, 1976, p. 14; emphasis supplied).

Throughout the course, we examine in some detail the ideas of the Chicago School's leading light, Richard Posner. We test his analyses against the friendly but nonetheless effective criticisms of Reder,[17] and against views of more hostile critics. My purpose is not to set Posner up as a straw man, although some of his ideas tempt one to do so, but to stimulate student evaluations of the most comprehensive and internally consistent Chicago School theory of law. Most students agree with at least some of the criticisms: Chicago School assumptions and concepts form a rather murky and tautologous epistemology, they describe rather than explain events, they tempt analysts to be dogmatic, they do not consistently account for the invisible hand of power that lies underneath the Invisible Hand of market processes, or they are used to smuggle value judgments and policy advocacy into an ostensibly positivist economics and law.[18] We find that it is not very difficult to identify and counteract possible biases in Chicago School assumptions, after repeatedly playing a "spot the inarticulate major premises" game similar to the game some law teachers play with students to such good effect. The assumptions used to introduce this technique—a kind of anthropology of law and economics[19]—concern the nature of people, markets, and a perceived economic consensus. The legitimacy and expediency of abstracting a *homo partialis*, the (often sexist) *homo oeconomicus*, are examined to consider whether, as Gunnar Myrdal (1954, p. 137) argues, economic "liberals" set "out to isolate an 'economic' factor in political life" in order to give "a scientific appearance to an individualist, anti-interventionist prejudice."[20] Economists are usually unclear about the place of economic rationality in their schemes, and they frequently seem to argue nothing more than "people willl pursue their interests." This is tautological—there is no way to validate the assumption that is independent of the behavior it predicts—and singularly unenlightening.[21] The neoclassical theories forming the backbone of law and economics were developed late in the nineteenth century, at a time when psychology was in a rather primitive state. We therefore discuss the psychology of economic rationality in class, and consider whether group rationality can ever be a simple summation of individuals' rationality.[22] The class surveys cases and case studies to determine if the congery of assumptions about economic man—such as cool calculation based on near-perfect information, risk aversion,[23] and severely limited altruism[24]—are realistic and relevant to the concepts and policies under study. For example, assuming a severely limited altruism fosters analyses which understate the importance of charitable behavior in the private and public sectors, of fiduciary and good faith obligations, and of corporate social responsibility. Whether this understatement distorts prescriptions for law and policy is an inquiry which continues throughout the course.

By the end of the course about half of the students conclude that a similar understatement proceeds from the conventional law and economics assumption that an essentially private law both does and should mimic the operation of a "market."[25] Explicitly or implicitly, scholars often assume that a relevant market exists in a state of perfect competition or one in which imperfections are minimized. These assumptions have the effect of ruling out a priori the many legal interventions that are predicated upon the nonexistence or failure of markets. Empirical evaluations of the need for and the success of intervention are thus never undertaken. For example, firms in the U.S. auto and steel industries have recently undertaken "efficiency programs" in response to declining consumer demand and more efficient foreign producers. But these programs could have been implemented much earlier and would, indeed, have been essential to corporate survival in a competitive market. Legal interventions in these industries become more plausible to those students who conclude that market imperfections permit, and perhaps perpetuate, a variety of avoidable inefficiencies.

Another bulwark of free market notions, and a justification for limitations on state power, is the consensus model of society developed by Talcott Parsons (1950) et al. This model has so captured the imagination of American social scientists that positivist economists and lawyers alike have adopted it in a more or less unthinking way. Their assumption that law and market activity more or less automatically move toward an equilibrium has the effect of downplaying socioeconomic conflict and change as, for example, isolated instances of "deviance" or calls for a bit of "social engineering" here and there.[26]

B. Property

Each segment of my course begins and ends with brief jurisprudential inquiries for purposes of comparison and contrast with the law and economics analyses in between. These inquiries will be described in greater detail than the course time spent on them warrants, since they may interest other teachers of Law and Economics. The property segment is introduced with Roman law theories, the ideas of Locke (and, briefly, Marxian extrapolations), and the pragmatism of David Hume and Adam Smith that has, with subtle modifications, found great favor among legal and economic positivists. Discussions blend theories of law and of economics while considering the entertaining Anderson and Hill article[27] about the economic history of property rights in the American West.

The property segment focuses on the Coase Theorem[28] because exhaustive critiques[29] of Coase make extended discussion worthwhile and because the theorem best serves to introduce many of the notions which link the segments of my course together: Pareto analyses, externalities ("social" costs, those not borne by the parties to a transaction),[30] the ways in which free riders[31] and holdouts distort or frustrate bargains, the economics of judicial and statutory remedies, and the centrality of transaction costs to many analyses. Some students wind up concluding that externalities and free riders are stereotyped and minimized during the Chicago School's "thrust for endogenization." This is an attempt to account for all effects within the broadest possible theory, even at the expense of a superficial treatment. The incidental, unintended nature of externalities and free riders is assumed by definition. Yet they may be important reasons for exercising property rights in particular ways so as to force others to bear part of your costs. Externalities and free riders effects that cannot be readily measured are often ignored. Ignoring them distorts cost-benefit analyses and begs questions about whether property rights are correctly defined and assigned.[32]

Classroom hypotheticals emphasize the impact of the externalities of pollution, of drug-resistant gonorrhea strains (their effect on public health practices and social behavior—an aberration in terms of my course structure, but an interesting one based on information I gathered in England), and of the Ford Pinto—a topic about which there is much information and interest because of a local prosecution of Ford for reckless homicide. We consider whether, as Posner and many others argue, property rules promote efficiency in the allocation and use of resources. Most students conclude that the answer turns on the ways in which efficiency is defined,[33] and a search for relevant definitions proceeds throughout the course. At this stage, we treat efficiency/wealth maximization as a necessary condition for legal success, postponing discussions of whether it is also a sufficient condition and whether it can be actually measured.

At one level, law students have no need of an elaborate theory to prove that efficiency requires that transaction costs (costs of shopping around and bargaining, monitoring the performance of others, and enforcing bargains gone awry) be minimized. However, a closer examination does demonstrate something far from obvious to students or practitioners: transaction costs all but determine the economic and legal form and function of decisions in both private and public sectors.[34] Having considered a variety of hypotheticals at various points in the course, most students find some of the descriptions and prescriptions offered by transaction cost analyses to be simplistic.[35] Extrapolating from Dahlman's excellent article (Dahlman, 1979, pp. 147–150), we try to improve upon these analyses by treating transaction costs as species of the costs of acquiring, using, and transmitting information that are estimated at 25 percent of GNP. This approach also introduces the currently fashionable economics of imperfect information/rational expectations and provides additional links between course segments. We examine the ebb and flow of information in an economy subject to legal controls, the relationship between possessing certain types of information and possessing a political and economic power, and governments' capacity to acquire and process enough information to engage in sensible regulation.[36] From these perspectives, the "information society" of computers and telecommunications threatens significant new inequalities of power, while procedural due process becomes a fairly efficient means for courts to acquire the information that minimizes the costs of legal error—to the parties and to a society subject to *stare decisis.*

Focusing on Thomas Grey's (1976) excellent article (and see Ginsberg, 1965, pp. 95–101), the property segment of my course concludes with a discussion of relationships between the concepts of property and of justice. Is wealth maximization an "adequate concept of justice," as Posner argues?[37] Is it feasible and moral to maximize the collective pie first and worry about distributing it later, if at all? Should distributions favor the efficient, the worse off, the political supporters of particular programs, or some other group? We survey the ideas of Nozick and of Rawls and conclude that Rawls' neglect of property issues comes close to vitiating his theory.[38] Their ideas are treated as the polar extremes within which an American pragmatism functions, a treatment which makes trespass into Jurisprudence or Constitutional Law unlikely. We examine some of the legal forms available for the pursuit of justice by comparing Milton Friedman's freedom-through-capitalism with Oscar Lange's notions of a market socialism.[39] We also briefly consider the history of the pursuit of justice in America, to evaluate the criticism that many economists approach resource allocation as an ahistorical process which is distinct from resource distribution. For example, Lawrence Friedman (1971, pp. 242, 249–252) asserts that slaves, sharecroppers, Indians, and factory workers received a less than "just" distribution under a system of property designed for middle-class farmers, artisans, businessmen, and professionals. The "nightwatchman" state permitted the unjust acquisition of property through fraud and the exercise of monopoly power.[40] These claims and their policy implications for a corrective justice are evaluated and contrasted with Novick's significant point that no formula of justice can be implemented without continuous state interference with conventionally defined liberties.[41] Many students pragmatically conclude that property rules sometimes "overdetermine" the result; owners' protections go beyond what is necessary to induce desired behavior and thereby inhibit desired behavior by others.

C. Contracts

We deepen our understanding of efficiency in resource allocation by examining the economics of contracts law. Subject to a number of caveats traced in class discussion, contracts serve to shift resources from lower to more highly valued uses. This often occurs without the owners' loss of overall control, reversionary rights, and/or the income from property. Economists usually describe these "use-values" in terms of consumers' or producers' willingness to pay. We consider whether their descriptions neglect important distributional issues and the externalities spawned by contracts. Unlike the externalities of property, the contractual ones receive little academic or judicial attention beyond third-party beneficiary rules and a sporadic and nebulous public policy. Students conclude that production processes are made more predictable by obtaining present contractual commitments to fulfill future needs; contract is treated as a bridge over time, sometimes paved with good intentions but always paved with transaction cost considerations.

The jurisprudence of contracts is introduced as a conjunction of agreement and obligation. The phenomena of agreement are familiar to students from their first year, and discussions thus tend to assess the nature and extent of contractual obligations, a class of duties correlative to rights *in personam*. These choses in action, as they are traditionally classified, are a mixture of property and contract rights. They thus form links between course segments which we explore further at the end of the contracts segment and in relation to corporations. Judicial analyses of contracts are approached historically as reflecting American emphases on the individual rather than the community, and on the feasibility and morality of individuals bargaining out almost all social relations, subject to fewer regulations than are found in property laws. This dominant jurisprudence is then contrasted with Robert Lee Hale's denigration of freedom of contract as the interplay of imposing your will (your power based on rights exercised over things and people) and your capacity to resist the will of others.[42] We discuss briefly the Scots empiricism and pragmatism of Macaulay (1963) and Macneil (1974, 1978) in order to discover whether contracts law really fosters a consensus in particular situations and to test the accuracy of Hurst's (1977, pp. 229–230) assertion that law's role is subordinate to that of business practices in determining market activity. The approach some students adopt initially is to follow Lawrence Friedman (1965, pp. 212–214) in arguing that, in an attempt to keep markets free, the judicial abstractions of contract law consciously ignore many business desiderata. Further analysis shows this attempt to have failed in at least some instances and to mirror an important aim of much law and economics scholarship: the creation of abstractions that are political because they prefer an economic freedom defined in particular ways.[43]

We treat many of the concerns of contracts lawyers in an order that facilitates transaction cost analyses.[44] Risk aversion and transaction costs emerge as prime determinants of the choice among contractual forms and of the costs of market operation. Briefly, contracts tend toward the short-term exchange of predetermined values, if the parties are unable to deal creatively with future uncertainties through flexible yet readily enforceable agreements. Attaining this goal often entails the heavy costs of bargaining out all contingencies in advance. This is so unless, for example, one of the parties (such as an employer) acquires the present right to have commands obeyed in the future, when contingencies become realities. Although it often reduces bargaining costs, this broad delegation of rights to use resources causes other kinds of costs to increase: extensive discretion must be paid for somehow; its exercise is often resisted by the other party, reflecting the desire to remain one's own master; and the costs of monitoring the reluctant

"servant's" performance increase, a problem explored in the corporations segment of the course.[45]

The prescription many economists offer for minimizing the transaction costs
of contracts involves standardized sets of risk allocation terms; when necessary
these sets are contracted around or enforced through flexible, judge-made remedies. Students typically find this prescription wanting in significant respects after
we examine several mistake, frustration, and unconscionability cases and, later,
state incorporation statutes. We therefore move on to consider alternatives which
seem to receive less attention than deserved from economists. The work of Ian
Macneil (1974) and the "invisible handshake" Arthur Okun (1975) finds in implicit contracts suggest significant qualifications to transaction cost analyses.
Transactions are often part of ongoing social (economic only in part) relations
with their own costs and benefits, rather than the isolated bits of business assumed by many economists. We explore ways in which the costs spawned by the
social context of these transactions can be weighed against the benefits of a long-
term business planning under relational contracts, and ways of circumventing the
often inefficient and winner-take-all judicial remedies predicated on the contractual relation coming to an end at each breach. Another type of flexibility which
tends to minimize transaction costs, particularly those costs stemming from unequal access to an imperfect information, can be achieved after the fact by imposing fiduciary and good faith obligations. Evaluations of these techniques for co-
difying what *would have been* the parties' reasonable expectations carry over
from the contracts to the corporations segment of the course along the lines suggested by the merger of good faith and fiduciary obligations in *Hoffman v. Red
Owl*[46] and by Anderson's provocative article.[47]

Student evaluations of transaction cost analyses become, in turn, building
blocks in a critique of the conventional law and economics assertion that contracts are efficient (almost) by definition. Based on somewhat suspect assumptions about economic man, some economists argue that transactions will not take
place unless they augment the wealth/utility of both parties. Society thus benefits
from contracts because they consistently move resources to more highly valued
uses. A judicial or legislative rewriting of the bargain must therefore be
inefficient, once again by definition. We analyze these arguments within a larger
framework, examining the economists' efficiency criteria from different perspectives and at higher levels of sophistication as the course proceeds.

In the contracts portion of the course, we draw out two significant insights
from law and economics. First, the parties will contract around outcomes made
inefficient by judges or statutes, or, if this proves too economically or legally
difficult, refuse to contract at all. These tactics are undoubtedly efficient in at
least some circumstances, but we consider whether they also reflect inequalities
of bargaining power, whether these inequalities are themselves inefficient or otherwise unacceptable in our society, and whether they can be remedied under a
more imaginative contracts regime. Second, we explore the important roles law

plays in streamlining and regularizing the channels through which flow goods, services, and, perhaps most important, information. Our analyses build up a picture of law in the economy by moving from isolated transactions to the markets which sometimes, but far from always, coordinate transactions and lend them continuity. Transactions costs loom large in the costs of operating the markets in which some contracts are formed. We briefly survey the impact of these costs on market conduct, structure, and performance. This forms a basis for subsequent analyses of corporations as attempts to replace markets (to internalize the costs of market operation), and for Antitrust analyses in the second semester. Most students conclude that economists have many interesting things to say about contracts, but that efficient trade-offs between such conflicting policies as predictability and flexibility cannot be generalized for all types of contracts.

The conclusion to the contracts segment of my course extends prior discussions of the relation between property and justice. For example, we examine the economics of Corbin's contention that contract law promotes justice by enforcing the parties' reasonable expectations. Following Dworkin's lead in taking rights seriously, we consider the extent to which economics clarifies the meaning of contract and property rights in law. The general rule of breach-and-pay-damages and the Coase Theorem assumption that the receipt of a bribe for not exercising rights can be equated with court-awarded damages are examined from the vantage points of efficiency and of community moral standards. In the course of analysis, most students conclude that these perspectives on rights contradict each other, at least in part. We also compare the postulate of conventional law and economics that efficiency results from rights defined in a case-by-case fashion with Dworkin's contention that decisions about rights should derive from an overarching conception of the aggregate social good.[48] Some students come to favor the piecemeal approach. Extrapolating from the Coase Theorem, other students reason that transaction costs are so closely bound up with rights definitions that changes in one automatically provoke changes in the other. Almost infinite varieties of efficient solutions and species of distributive justice are thus possible. Defending choices among rights definitions and efficient solutions in a principled manner, something law and economics fails to do, remains essential.

D. Corporations

My jurisprudential introduction to corporations is predominantly historical, a tracing of attempts to attain public purposes through appeals to the interests of the voluntary associations that, many economists argue, are wholly private in nature.[49] Briefly surveyed are the economics of a judicial selectivity in piercing the corporate veil,[50] of courts *choosing* to interpret the Fourteenth Amendment and now the First Amendment ''persons'' so as to include corporations, and of attempting to locate and regulate the ''person'' in multinational corporations operating through tiers of local subsidiaries.

Relatively brief lectures and discussions stress the ingenuity of corporate design in law and in economics.[51] Property and contracts analyses combine in an economics critique of Berle and Mean's notion of the separation of corporate ownership from control.[52] For many economists, this separation is not only efficient but inescapable, given high shareholder costs of information, of monitoring, and of organizing an opposition. (We also discuss whether this argument applies to voters on election day, whether voters perform legitimating functions like those of shareholders while remaining in a more or less powerless isolation because of similar "transaction" costs.) We then consider the conventional economists' argument that derivative suits and laws against fraud protect shareholders' interests adequately. Many students find this argument persuasive only so long as corporate managers are profit maximizers subject to strict market controls and the survivor principle, somewhat dubious assumptions[53] considered later in the corporations segment, elsewhere in the course (see Text at notes 55,72-73 *infra*) and in Antitrust.

Like a public bureaucracy, the corporation is approached as a mixed blessing in economics. It economizes on some transaction costs through a specialization and coordination of functions without exhaustive negotiations in advance, while causing other, chiefly monitoring, costs to increase. Corporations take advantage of the organizing, planning, and control functions of contracts; corporations are really the most extreme forms of Macneil's relational contracts that are potentially perpetual. Discussions focus on the question of whether corporations simply displace markets or also replace them with more efficient "private markets," which encourage information to flow toward those who can make the best use of it.[54] Incorporation tends to increase monitoring costs because the specialization it fosters confers on the knowledgeable an opportunity to cheat investors, consumers, and others at an informational disadvantage. The contribution of each individual to production becomes more difficult to measure and monitor within a complex corporation, and, some economists argue, the incentives to shirk (implement a preference for leisure) increase. Managers and bureaucratic hierarchies have a limited span of control, and a loss of control within corporations (and public bureaucracies, when we link up arguments with those in the next course segment) occurs when this span is exceeded.

We attempt to assess the magnitude of these monitoring costs by considering studies in sociology as well as economics. We evaluate the altruism of corporate social responsibility and the demands for legal intervention spawned by the effects of high monitoring costs. These demands are for fiduciary and good faith obligations, more specific shareholder and consumer protections, corporate criminal responsibility, other forms of regulation, and aggressive enforcement of the antitrust laws. We also examine Alison Anderson's (1978) hypothesis that because too many of these stringent interventions are demanded, costs can exceed benefits. This is because the beneficiaries of a particular regulation (investors, consumers, etc.) do not pay all of the costs; part are borne by taxpayers in general (pp. 788-789).

Perhaps the most interesting of our corporations discussions revolve around the notions that unregulated stock markets would generate information competitively and that such regulations as corporate takeover disclosure requirements paradoxically stem the flow of information and weaken market controls over management.[55] In other words, unregulated stock and corporate control markets (and product and labor markets) are deemed efficient in metering and rewarding productivity, in reducing monitoring costs. These "case studies" are then generalized to evaluate a law and economics proposition carried over the property and contracts segments: self-interested behavior subject to market controls can only be made less efficient by legal interventions, which will fail to achieve their stated aims in any event. This thread is then picked up in the administration segment of the course, when we consider the extent to which regulatory behavior attempts to correct market failures in the public interest, as opposed to attempts to implement the antimarket desires of special interest groups (see text at notes (65–67, 73–74, 90–92).

In the other segments of the course, students tend to pick and choose from among law and economics analyses in accordance with the criteria of evaluation they develop for themselves. However, students have fairly uniformly rejected almost all of the conventional law and economics learning presented in the corporations segment. In its place, they often voice attitudes that the Chicago School might term "populist." The reasons for this are not clear; either I have failed to achieve a balance in the materials chosen (see the "Appendix" for materials presently used), or the students are illustrating Hurst's assertion that large corporations have never managed to legitimate their position in American life (Hurst, 1970; 1977, pp. 49, 273). Student attitudes are perhaps reinforced later by a brief conclusion to the corporations segment about what may be termed the jurisprudence of power. The focus is on Edward Mason's assertion that corporations law registers the inevitable by rather passively mirroring power relations in society (see Mason, 1970, pp. 2-12). We examine different definitions of power and ponder Hale's assertion that every lawful economic power, power based on the exercise of property, contract and corporate rights, and on privileges allocated under administrative laws, is a form of political power.[56] This discussion carries forward into the next segment, in which political power explicitly comes to the fore, and into Antitrust. Does a democratic society entail a democratic economy? If so, what does this mean in terms of, for example, corporate responsiveness and deconcentrated market structures?[57] Students conclude that corporate power gives rise to serious social problems, while acknowledging that law and economics readings raise acute questions of feasibility and fairness concerning attempts to control this power.

E. Politics and Administration

In this course segment I organize discussions around three themes. We return to economists' assumptions about economic man, evaluating the accuracy and adequacy of the assumptions as descriptions of the behavior of politicians, administrators, citizens, and interest groups of varying stripes. The economics-oriented behavior of these actors is then considered in greater detail: Can the "public interest" that many laws purport to advance be discerned in this behavior, in theory and with regard to particular instances of public policy?[58] Here we examine law and economics studies in combination with their close relatives, the pluralist bargaining models so admired by most American political scientists.[59] Finally, we ask whether much of law and economics adopts a double standard, using certain extremely rigorous analyses to criticize the inefficiency of the public sector while neglecting the implications of applying these analyses to private decision making.[60] About half of the students follow me in concluding that this double standard exists to foster such false dichotomies as almost perfectly efficient private markets versus chronically inefficient political and bureaucratic processes, and private production versus political distribution/redistribution as separate and antithetical processes.[61]

The jurisprudential introduction to politics and administration briefly recalls theories familiar to students from Constitutional Law, Administrative Law, and undergraduate courses. We focus on the paradox, described by Rabin among others,[62] of an administrative state growing rapidly within the individualistic society we delineate in the property and contracts course segments. To place this paradox in its historical context[63] and to counter the impression that economic intervention began when the New Deal displaced a nightwatchman state, materials first discussed in the introductory and property segments are recalled briefly. By the end of the course, most students conclude that law and economics captures many, but far from all, of the nuances of Rabin's paradox. Whether or not they reach this conclusion, students identify many economic policy issues which cannot be dealt with adequately within the bounds set by conventional public lawyers: the scope of delegations of authority, the formal aspects of agency procedures, and the scope of judicial review.[64]

We examine the economics of political behavior briefly, primarily as a backdrop to administrative processes. Some students conclude that most contemporary economists' portraits of American politics are not those of a democracy but of a rather crass paternalism. The mainstream economics of politics reduces all of political behavior to the pursuit of individual self-interest, which is certainly one way of resolving Rabin's paradox. Politicians stay in power by keeping the people happy with bread and circuses, rather than by promoting efficiency or any other definition of general welfare. Political wealth redistributions mitigate political opposition through appeals to citizens-as-consumers, whose costs of obtaining "true" political information are high in any event. A political "entrepreneurship" is at work in the organizing of political parties, interest groups, and logrolling opportunities. Many students perceive a double standard at work in most of the law and economics studies[65] we discuss here. The tendency toward monopolization or an oligopolistic interdependence is as overemphasized in analyses of political and public bureaucratic markets as it is neglected with regard to nongovernmental markets. If the Invisible Hand is usefully at work in the latter, why isn't it also helping to advance the general welfare through politics?[66] A few students want to press these analyses further. On their face, contemporary theories of law and economics and political science deny even the theoretical possibility of democracy. There can never be networks of public communication which are fairly free of noise and interference, no analogs of private markets in which information flows more or less free of domination and through which a genuinely communal political will can be formed.[67]

We examine the economics of the relationship between democracy and bureaucracy through surveys of the opportunity costs of administration. These are costs of resource allocation, delegation, and aggregation, directly by governments and through their regulation of private decisions.[68] The conventional law and economics wisdom, typified by Niskanen's provocative article,[69] is that these opportunity costs are excessive and can only be recovered through a deregulation which permits a further privatizing of economic activity. According to Niskanen, governments overspend on inefficient bureaucracies which cater to special interests, produce more than the electorate wants, are overcapitalized, and seek constantly to extend monopoly positions through administrative "rationalizations." Much of this is undoubtedly true and may be changing in response to insights provided by law and economics, but we return to materials examined in the corporations segment to consider whether large private bureaucracies operating through imperfect markets are really so different. This inquiry carries over into Antitrust.

Our comparisons suggest some striking similarities in the behavior of private and public bureaucrats. Members of both groups bid for chunks of resources which cannot be easily valued, seek advancement through organizational growth and by pleasing superiors in similar ways, try to maximize discretion and congeniality in the office, and, according to some economists, shirk when they can get away with it. In other words, heavy transaction costs (mostly costs of monitoring performance) are incurred through the inevitable, and often otherwise efficient, delegations of power to public and private bureaucrats alike. While the law deals with them as "persons" (individuals), public and business bureaucracies both prefer organizational needs to human needs where these conflict. That is, precision, stability, the coercion of would-be free riders, and a formal equality of treatment tend to prevail over an individualized justice, competition, opportunism, and the chance for individual expression.[70] Chains of causation between organizational needs and (individual) wealth maximization frequently seem rather long and tenuous. Many students agree that administrative laws, like state incorporation statutes, register the inevitable as mirrors held up to power relations in society. Neither set of laws offers an efficient monitoring or realistic answers to the question of who monitors the monitor.[71] Many economists argue that private bureaucrats, but not public bureaucrats, are subject to strong market controls which efficiently monitor their performance. This argument is not taken seriously by those students who see it as another instance of a false dichotomy based on an analytical double standard.[72]

The course concludes by considering aspects of politics and administration dealt with in what seems a reductionist fashion or not at all in the mainstream of law and economics and of political science. My argument is that law is no mere consumer good. Governments are much more than a series of voluntary exchanges under the Coase Theorem, more than alternative suppliers of goods and services to households, more than mouthpieces for special interests. With their short-term interests in mind, citizens do not always want to act, act quickly enough, or act in economically rational ways. Canons of a political legitimacy[73] enable governments to pursue effectiveness (in, e.g., defense programs) or income redistributions desirable to some, rather than a narrowly conceived efficiency. Such activities as nation building and repair, the maintenance of order and of social security, and the protection of human rights cannot be dealt with adequately under the ethical relativism of contemporary theories of interest group politics. These theories hold, in Benthamite fashion, or under what lawyers might see as corruptions of Pound's jurisprudence, that the public interest attained through politics and administration can be no greater than a mechanical weighting of its interest group parts. Pursuing such a public interest becomes inefficient almost by definition, in comparison with the weightings assigned by private markets that are assumed to be nearly perfect. The dominant strand of law and economics thus calls for a deregulation because it presently lacks the methodological means of demonstrating how a genuinely public interest can be derived from conflicting special interests. Liberal and social democratic theories, on the other hand, either assume that these means exist or require that they be found.

We thus inquire into whether law and economics, purged of reductionism, analytical double standards, and false dichotomies, can be used innovatively to evaluate rival definitions of the public interest. Students conclude that, at the very least, law and economics plays a significant role in evaluating the attempts by special interests to justify themselves in terms of the public interest. Market failure emerges as the prime, perhaps the only, justification for governmental intervention. But defining markets and deciding when and how they fail and can be fixed turn out to be contentious matters among economists, many of whom take refuge in assumptions rather than analysis.[74] A few students go further, arguing that economists do little more than concoct bogus justifications for special interests, and/or attempt to suppress generalizable public interests by treating most interests as particular. These students adopt Flynn's position: "Where economists abdicate any responsibility (other than counting the results) for the wisdom or morality of the choices made by rational maximizers, economists can claim no right to criticize the lines drawn by the law in performing" these functions.[75] However, George Stigler (1971) commands our consensus when he argues that criticisms of regulations for doing what they were designed to do are misplaced; designs for a new logic of public life are what is needed (pp. 17–18).

III. FROM COURSE TO CRITIQUE

My research interests, like those of many others, often grow out of, and are focused by, class discussions. Three years ago, our Law and Economics discussions generated what I consider to be a significant insight: There is a near-perfect congruence between the antimonies of microeconomics and macroeconomics, on the one hand, and of lawyers' analyses of private and public laws on the other. I will briefly outline the implications of this insight, since they encouraged me to explore it further and to recast my course into its present form.

One reason many undergraduates ratify the view of economics as a "dismal science" is that they get lost when their course perspectives shift from micro to macroeconomics. The same thing happens to many economists, at higher levels of sophistication. Although investigations continue apace, welfare economics and other attempts to bridge the micro/macro gap have proved unsatisfactory from the standpoint of developing realistic policy prescriptions.[76] Similarly, a utilitarian balancing of interests through legal analysis has proved incapable of bridging the private/public law gap, despite the efforts of, for example, Roscoe Pound. We should therefore not be surprised when many law students get lost at the (dis)junctures of private and public law; this confusion is fostered by the ways curricula are organized and courses taught in many law schools.

We may be faintly bemused by the attempts of civil law jurists to grapple with the distinctions between private and public law that they themselves have created. If so, we have failed to recognize that their task is also our own: developing relevant perspectives for Stigler's logic of public life.[77] We have done no better than our continental colleagues through our calculated inattention, a point driven home when we consider the sorry state of legal canons in our mixed economy. What is private and what is public is now blurred beyond recognition, and an examination of the periodic redrawing of the boundaries to match shifts in society's balance of power shows that these lines always have been blurred.[78] The legal mind abhors such indistinct genres, and a few jurists have reacted by attempting analyses based on legal antinomies.[79] Many of our Law and Economics discussions demonstrate that these antinomies have their counterparts in economics, and that, all too often, both sets of antinomies degenerate into false dichotomies. The main reason for this state of affairs is not hard to trace; it is the passion, shared by economists, lawyers, judges, legislators, administrators, businesspeople, and many others, for classifying blurred entities into mutually exclusive categories. This process is spurred on by the tendency toward reductionism that we all share to some extent and by the delusive force of reasoning by analogy. Ridiculous outcomes are reached analogy-by-analogy, with each step seeming self-evident or logically necessary. Public policy suffers when thinkers and doers alike are sucked into the vortex of their own abstractions.[80]

Any genuine attempt to understand the mixed economy by spanning the micro-private law/macro-public law divide would require greatly improved prescriptions for what I have been calling the public interest. These would be based in turn on more accurate descriptions of our "economic constitution":[81] a conception sufficiently broad and novel to arch over the analytical gap. Many law and economics scholars say little about our economic constitution; they would rather replace it with wealth maximization as our legal system's *Grundnorm*. *Pace* Hans Kelsen, this positivist basis for constituting all of our rights and public activities would be legitimated by an austere logic—that of welfare economics. Unfortunately, the "virtual constitution" of welfare economics describes only a partial ordering of economic arrangements; *given* a particular collection of goods, *given* a distinct set of rights, and *given* a particular distribution of rights and goods in society, only some economic arrangements can be ranked as potentially superior to others.[82] Such ranking yields a tautology of the status quo: existing distributions of rights and goods form bases for the wealth maximization that justifies existing distributions. Nevertheless, many economists would have us prefer the substantive values of wealth maximization to other values. This would seemingly be accomplished under techniques of a substantive due process. These techniques are similar to the ones condemned fifty years ago as attempts to implement values rather strongly resembling those of a wealth maximization. Resolving rights conflicts through interpersonal comparisons of utility, what courts regularly do in effect, would be an impermissible strategy for most economists. Questions of distributive justice, of what we want and value as a *society,* and of legal accountability to someone other than yourself, would recede into the background. Yet in many court decisions and certainly in the Framer's minds, answers to these questions are antecedent to a wealth maximization. Elaborate, inefficient safeguards (rights to act as a holdout) were built into the Constitution. In contrast to most economists' assumptions, the Framers assumed (except in the First Amendment) that markets fail, that information and motivations are frequently imperfect, and that the behavior of "factions" is dangerously different from that of individuals.[83]

One set of means to the end of describing economic constitutions was destroyed when artificial distinctions among disciplines were created through the increased specialization in the modern university. Constant attention to the nature of economic constitutions is found in the writings of such academic "outsiders" as Beccaria-Bonesaria, Marx, and John R. Commons, and it is particularly evident in the mainstream of philosophical liberalism in Britain and America. Philosophy, history, economics, political science, and law were all facets of the unified political economy known to Adam Smith, Bentham, and Mill—a political economy by and large devoted to delineating the economic constitution of the time. A reintegration of insights under a modernized political economy is necessary and can be legitimately required of the many specialists who claim the title "liberal" by way of succession. Anything worth saying can be made intelligible to the nonspecialist without recourse to labeling or the arcane language of calculus, statistics, linguistic philosophy, or per se illegality.

The meaninglessness of labels is illustrated by rival descriptions of law and economics as liberal or libertarian, and as advancing the New Right's social agenda. But it is not disputed that the Chicago School has always been openly and strongly antistatist, in analyses extensively informed by Milton Friedman's seminal *Capitalism and Freedom* (1962). Over objections from George Stigler, Chicagoans have pursued their normative preference by constantly injecting it into nominally positivist analyses. When economic analysis thus becomes ideology, it must be treated as such or economists' taste-shaping will inadvertently come to dominate American legal culture. If decisions really are based on economists' political predilections, these decisions are better left to political processes.[84]

A prime example of the Chicago Tendency is Posner's portrait of the "deep unity" of a common law promoting an economic efficiency over time.[85] This description reinvents the wheel, now studded with the language of economics. Cardozo's "social utility" of bodies of law progressing over time[86] is the more useful formulation because it broadly incorporates insights gleaned from additional disciplines and because it (prospectively) rebuts as a false dichotomy Posner's distinction between efficient common law and inefficient statutes.[87] Many students are all too willing to accept this false dichotomy at face value, given the tendency of law school curricula and pedagogies to reinforce the private-public law gap. Posner's overwhelming preference for the microeconomics-private law approach has the effect of placing a heavy[88] burden of proof on advocates of any change in common law rules said to mimic efficient markets over time. A more neutral stance (less conserving of the status quo) seems called for, and we attempt it in class discussions by going behind Posner's late nineteenth-century view of the common law to uncover numerous inefficiencies in Anglo-American antecedents concerning property and contracts.

Descriptions of the economic constitution would involve much going backward, in both legal history and in critiques of interpretations of that history. The historical/institutional perspective that so many conventional economists disdain would usefully inform law and economics scholarship here, enabling it to account for the phenomena of power and the manifest advantages of particular governmental interventions. Prescriptions for the public interest also cry out for analytical leaps forward. Here law and economics showed great promise initially, gaining much ground quickly from political philosophy in general and jurisprudence in particular. One of the singular merits of law and economics is that its extreme skepticism toward conventional philosophical reasoning forced jurisprudence to look to its laurels. Having had the field too long to itself, the argumentation in Anglo-American jurisprudence had become rather loose, stale, inward-looking, and lacking in the surface polish of more concrete methodologies such as those of economics.[89] Posner threw down the gauntlet when he argued plausibly that, until a consensus comes along about attaining the public interest through legal formulae of distribution and redistribution, efficiency is the most politically viable criterion of legal performance.[90]

Underlying this challenge is a powerful ideological claim that disputes the legitimacy of any political attempt to define the public interest. Legitimacy no longer comes from the higher reaches of a philosophy or traditional world views, but from below, from the inherent justice of market exchanges where the vices of power and an antecedent determination of rights are deemed irrelevant. As ideology, this claim amounts to a defense of capitalism, a far-from-idle task since captialism is no longer widely regarded as the natural order of things. Socialism has its ideological rationales, too, but who pauses to rationalize the mixed economy, the system we have to deal with for the foreseeable future?

Responding to these challenges seems a worthwhile task; it would require a cooperation among jurisprudence, law and economics, and other disciplines in the service of public interest prescriptions that are superior to those currently defined in terms of efficiency. One thing the mixed economy teaches us is that realistic prescriptions would have to compromise values such as liberty and equality, which are defined so as to conflict regularly with each other. These realistic prescriptions would thus appear messy to someone accustomed to the austere theoretical elegance of the specialist, and they are in any event politically messy.

Implementing any policy significant enough to be controversial involves a sacrifice of much of the potency of theory to the practicalities of administration and enforcement. The bargaining-out of social relations along the lines suggested by the Coase Theorem is often neither feasible nor moral. The interests of marginal recalcitrants, however defined, frequently have to be ignored or suppressed in the hope that, over time, new public interest definitions will attract a consensus and even be widely regarded as efficient.[91] This seems to be what has happened to laws concerning income taxes and social security, although Medicare is still in limbo. Many useful prescriptions could be derived from theories of the second best and of workable competition,[92] relatively realistic economics theories that have hitherto played almost no role in law and economics analyses. These prescriptions would find their legal analogs in species of "equity," attempts to ameliorate the extremity of result from the strict application of the ideals of liberty or of equality.[93] The bottleneck in this process may well be the lawyers' inability to overcome one of their own false dichotomies, of liberty and equality, although they make strenuous attempts to do so. But actions in the public interest cannot await a leisurely display of academic brilliance; the perfection of legal or economic theory should not be set up as an enemy of policies which

are merely good in terms of the public interest. Finally, lawyers and economists
alike would do well to keep a legal philosopher's warning in mind: "With a little
skill (and a lack of scruple) we can reach almost any practical result from any
particular theory, so complicated are the issues that arise."[94]

APPENDIX

Readings for Law and Economics (Brietzke)

I. INTRODUCTION

    A. *Required Readings*

        R. POSNER, ECONOMIC ANALYSIS OF LAW 3–23 (2D ED. 1977).
        ECONOMIC FOUNDATIONS OF PROPERTY LAW ix–xiv (B. Ackerman,
           ed. 1975) (hereinafter Ackerman).
        J. GALBRAITH, ECONOMICS, PEACE AND LAUGHTER 50-71 (1975).
        THE ECONOMICS OF CONTRACT LAW 233-39 (A. Kronman & R.
           Posner, eds. 1979) (hereinafter Kronman & Posner).
        Hurst, *Legal Elements in U.S. History,* in *LAW IN AMERICAN HIS-*
           TORY 3 (D. Fleming & B. Bailyn, eds. 1971); *or* Friedman,
           Law, Order and History, 16 S. DAK. L. REV. 242 (1971).

    B. *Optional Readings*

        Critques of the Posner-type approach: Samuels, *Review*, 60 TEX. L.
           REV. 147 (1981) (REVIEW OF POSNER'S ECONOMICS OF JUSTICE
           (1981)); CRANSTON, *Creeping Economism*, 4 BRIT. J.L. & SOC.
           103 (1977); Liebhafsky, *Price Theory as Jurisprudence,* 10 J.
           ECON. ISSUES 23 (1976); Baker, *The Ideology of the Economic
           Analysis of Law,* 5 PHILO. & PUB. AFFAIRS (1975).
        A response: Posner, *Some Uses and Misuses of Economics in Law,*
           46 U. CHI. L. REV. 281 (1979) (plus *Comment, id.* at 307).
        An excellent overview for those with a good background in Econom-
           ics: Melvin Reder, *Chicago Economics,* 20 J. ECON. LIT. 1
           (1982).
        A fairly difficult but nontechnical article which can be contrasted to
           Galbraith's analyses: Coase, *Economics and Contiguous Disci-*
           plines, 7 J. L. STUD. 201 (1978).
        An easier and somewhat humorous treatment of the same subject
           matter: Stigler, *The Law and Economics of Public Policy,* 1 J.
           L. STUD. 1 (1972).
        A critique of efficiency concepts: Michelman, *Norms and*

Normativity in the Economic Theory of Law, 62 MINN. L. REV. 1015 (1978).

Contrasts with Posner's notion of the efficiency of the common law: Hirsch, *Reducing Law's Uncertainty and Complexity,* 21 U.C.L.A. L. REV. 1233 (1974).

An easy-to-follow analysis of macroeconomic considerations (especially fiscal and monetary policy), which can be read at V. as well: Harriss, *Basic Economic Concepts for the Lawyer,* 55 VA. L. REV. 855 (1969).

An excellent but lengthy analysis of the ideas of an influential scholar, which can be compared to Milton Friedman's ideas (pp. 77-92 in Ackerman): Samuels, *The Economy as a System of Power: The Legal Economics of Robert Lee Hale,* 27 U. OF MIAMI L. REV.261 (1973).

An historical examination of one judge's contribution: Dorfman, *Chancellor Kent and the Developing American Economy,* 61 COL. L. REV. 1290 (1961).

II. PROPERTY

A. *Required Readings*

Honore, *Ownership,* in OXFORD ESSAYS IN JURISPRUDENCE 107 (A. Guest, ed. 1961).

Anderson & Hill, *The Evolution of Property Rights: A Study of the American West,* 18 J. L. & ECON. 163 (1975).

ECONOMIC FOUNDATIONS OF PROPERTY LAW, 1-53, 69-98 (B. Ackerman, ed. 1975). The Scherer article (pp. 53-68) is more profitably dealt with in Antitrust. The Coase and Demsetz articles (pp. 17-31) are arguably the most difficult readings in the course; let us hope to clarify them in class.

Dahlman, *The Problem of Externality,* 21 J.L. & ECON. 141 (1979).

THE ECONOMICS OF CONTRACT LAW 240-44 (A. Kronman & R. Posner, eds. 1979).

Grey, *Property and Need,* 28 STAN. L. R.EV. 877 (1976).

B. *Optional Readings*

The nature and scope of property rights and the historical and socioeconomic reasons for the formalism and complexity of "inheritance" laws: Friedman, *The Law of the Living, The Law of the Dead: Property, Succession and Society,* 1966 WIS. L. REV. 340 (1966).

A difficult but superb critque of the Coase and Demsetz articles: Samuels, *The Coase Theorem and the Study of Law and Economics,* 14 NATURAL RESOURCES L.J. 1 (1974). Contrast the approaches of Coase and Demsetz with an analysis of *Miller et al. v. Schoene:* Samuels, *Interrelations between Legal and Economic Processes,* 14 J.L. & ECON. 435 (1971). Ellickson, *Suburban Growth Controls: An Economic and Legal Analysis,* 86 YALE L.J. 385 (1977) (can be read at V. as well). Can the analyses in Ackerman (especially those of Hardin and of Coase) be applied to species of property which, for technical or legal reasons, cannot be individually owned until apropriated: Friedman, *The Economics of the Common Pool: Property Rights in Exhaustible Resources,* 18 U.C.L.A. L. REV. 855 1 (1971). In 1971, Friedman was concerned about the conservation of e.g., oil reserves. Can his analysis be stood on its head to promote increased oil production today?

A more mathematical treatment of similar issues: Agnello & Donelly, *Property Rights and Efficiency in the Oyster Industry,* 18 J.L. & ECON. 521 (1975).

A practitioner-oriented analysis: Janczyk, *An Economic Analysis of the Land Title Systems for Transferring Real Property,* 6 J.L. STUD. 213 (1977).

Conventional law and economics analyses applied to conventional jurisprudential notions (especially those of Wesley Hohfeld), resulting in unconventional conclusions: Kennedy & Michelman, *Are Property and Contract Efficient?,* 8 HOFSTRA L. REV. 711-70 (1980). Pp. 739-48 are relevant to the next topic, Contracts.

An historical perspective on the actvities of governments in relation to property (relates to V. of course as well): Scheiber, *The Road to Munn,* in LAW IN AMERICAN HISTORY 329 (D. Fleming & B. Bailyn, eds. 1971).

III. CONTRACTS

A. *Required Readings*

Umbeck, *A Theory of Contract Choice and the California Gold Rush,* 20 J.L. & ECON. 421 (1977).
THE ECONOMICS OF CONRACT LAW 1-11, 26-153, 167-199 ¶ 2, 220-33, 250-67 (A. Kronman & R. Posner, eds. 1979).
R. DWORKIN, TAKING RIGHTS SERIOUSLY 90-99 (1977).

B. *Optional Readings*

The ideas of Coase and of Demsetz applied in an interesting way:

Hallahan, *The Long-Run Effects of Abolishing the Baseball Player Reserve System*, 7 J.L. STUD. 127-37 (1978).

Links between property law and contract law, via the Coase Theorem: Crocker, *Contractual Choice*, 13 NATURAL RESOURCES L.J. 561 (1973); Lowry, *Bargain and Contract Theory in Law and Economics*, 10 J. ECON. ISSUES 1 (1976).

Important links forged between contracts law and corporations law, by focusing on transaction costs and "fiduciary" relations: Anderson, *Conflicts of Interest: Efficiency, Fairness, and Corporate Structure*, 26 U.C.L.A. L. REV. 738-95 (1978) (pp. 738-62 can be read now and pp. 762-95 with reference to the next topic, Corporations).

The socioeconomic background of business contracts: Macaulay et al., *The Use of Non-Use of Contracts in the Manufacturing Industry*, 9 PRAC. LAW 13-38 (Nov. 1963).

Socioeconomic criticisms of contract law rules, which span all of the topics dealt with in Kronman and Posner: MacNeil, *The Many Futures of Contract*, 47 S. CAL. L. REV. 691 (1974); *Contracts: Adjustment of Long-Term Economic Relations.* . . . 72 NW. U.L. REV. 854 (1978). These articles are long but well worth reading.

Additional readings which relate to Kronman and Posner's Chap. 4: Kessler, *Contracts of Adhesion.* . . ., COL. L. REV. 629 (1943); Hale, *Bargaining, Duress, and Economic Liberty*, 43 COL. L. REV. 603 (1943).

Farber, *Reassessing the Economic Efficiency of Compensatory Damages for Breach of Contract*, 66 VA L. REV. 1443 (1980).

A further and better look at issues raised by Schwartz (pp. 138-42 in Kronman & Posner): Rosenn, *Protecting Contracts from Inflation*, 33 BUS. LAW. 729 (1978).

Enforcement costs, as they enter into a calculus of transaction costs: Schwartz & Tulloch, *The Costs of a Legal System*, 4 J. LEGAL STUD. 75 (1975).

A masterly historical perspective: L. FRIEDMAN, CONTRACT LAW IN AMERICA chs. 1, 5 and *passim* (1965).

IV. CORPORATIONS

A. *Required Readings*

Miller, *Legal Foundations of the Corporate State*, 6 J. ECON. ISSUES 59 (1972).

Hindley, *Capitalism and the Corporation*, ECONOMICA 26-38 (Nov. 1969).

Manne, *Our Two Corporate Systems: Law and Economics*, in *THE*

ECONOMICS OF LEGAL RELATIONSHIPS 511 (H. Manne, ed. 1975) (hereinafter Manne).

Manne, *Some Theoretical Aspects of Share Voting*, in Manne at 534.

Alchian & Demsetz, *Production, Information Costs, and Economic Organization*, in Manne at 555 (an article which can also be read first).

Hurst, *Commercial Development and Law*, in LAW AND SOCIETY 246 (C. Campbell & P. Wiles, eds. 1979).

B. *Optional Readings*

An excellent overview for those with a good background in Economics: Robin Marris and Dennis Mueller, *The Corporation, Competition, and the Invisible Hand*, 18 J. ECON. LIT. 32 (1980).

Halpern, Trebilcock & Turnbull, *An Economic Analysis of Limited Liability in Corporation Law*, 30 U. TORONTO L.J. 117 (1980).

An economic analysis of the ''race to the bottom'' among state corporation laws, the proposed federal corporate laws, and the ''optimum'' levels of shareholder protection and managerial control: Winter, *State, Law, Shareholder Protection, and the Theory of the Corporation*, 6 J. LEGAL STUD. 251-92 (1977).

Links between contracts and corporations law: Anderson, 25 U.C.L.A. L. REV. 762-95 (1978).

Rigid distinctions should not be drawn between contractual relations within and between firms: Rubin, *The Theory of the Firm and the Structure of the Franchise Contract*, 21 J.L. & ECON. 223 (1978) (an area with interesting antitrust implications).

The ways in which property rights are translated into corporate finance and power: Berle, *Property, Production and Revolution*, 65 COL. L. REV. 1 (1965); Alchian, *Corporate Management and Property Rights*, in Manne at 499.

Managerial motivations (to be explored further in Antitrust): Alchian, *The Basis of . . . the Theory of Management of the Firm*, in Manne at 487.

The economic efficiency of national stock markets and various federal regulatory schemes, particularly those governing takeover attempts: Fischel, *Efficient Capital Market Theory, the Market for Corporate Control, and the Regulation of Cash Tender Offers*, 57 TEX. L. REV. 1 (1978).

Articles by Chayes, Mason, Latham, Kaysen, & Brewster, in THE CORPORATION IN MODERN SOCIETY (E. Mason, ed. 1970).

V. POLITICS AND ADMINISTRATION

A. *Required Readings*

Buchanan & Tullock, *Simple Majority Voting*, in Ackerman at 237. *Cf.* Manne, *Some Theoretical Aspects of Share Voting, supra.*

Landes & Posner, *The Independent Judiciary in an Interest-Group Perspective*, 18 J.L. & ECON. 875 (1975).

Niskanen, *Bureaucrats and Politicians*, 18 J.L. & ECON. 617 (1975) (plus *Comments*). The mathematical formulae in the article can be analyzed or read around, as abilities dictate.

Stigler, *The Theory of Economic Regulation*, 2 BELL J. ECON. & MGT. SCI. 3 (1971).

B. *Optional Readings*

A. DOWNS, AN ECONOMIC THEORY OF DEMOCRACY (1957).

Meltzer & Vellrath, *The Effects of Economic Policies on Votes for the Presidency*, 18 J.L. & ECON. 781 (1975).

Wagner, *Economic Manipulation for Political Profit: Macroeconomic Consequences and Constitutional Implications*, 30 KYKLOS 395 (1977).

Buchanan, *The Coase Theorem and the Theory of the State*, 13 NATURAL RESOURCES L.J. 579 (1973).

A. BRETON & R. WINTROBE, THE LOGIC OF BUREAUCRATIC CONDUCT (1982).

Peltzman, *Toward a More General Theory of Regulation*, 19 J.L. & ECON. 211 (1976).

Wilson, *The Politics of Regulation*, in PERSPECTIVES ON THE ADMINISTRATION PROCESS 90 (R. Rabin, ed. 1979).

New State Ice v. Liebman, 285 U.S. 262 (1931) (especially Brandeis, J., dissenting at 280).

Kaysen, *Some Reflections on Business-Government Relations*, 51 MINN. L. REV. 64 (1966) (business attitudes which are also reflected in pressures to relax enforcement of antitrust policies).

Posner, *Taxation by Regulation*, 2 BELL J. ECON. & MGT. SCI. 22 (1971).

What induces businessmen to obey/disobey regulations: Anderson: *Public Economic Policy and the Problem of Compliance*, 4 HOUSTON L. REV. 62 (1966).

Davies, *The Efficiency of Private vs. Public Firms: The Case of Australia's Two Airlines*, 14 J.L. & ECON. 149 (1971).

Green & Nader, *Economic Regulation vs. Competition: Uncle Sam the Monopoly Man*, 82 YALE L.J. 871 (1973). (You may also wish to read the *Comment, id.* at 890.)

Connelly, *Secrets and Smokescreens: A Law and Economics Analysis of Government Disclosures of Business Data*, 1981, WIS. L. REV. 207.

ACKNOWLEDGMENTS

I would like to thank Paul Cox and David Myers for their comments on a draft of this article. Errors remain my responsibility, of course.

NOTES

1. A number of papers in a recent symposium (papers from an October 1982 conference, "The Place of Economics in Legal Education"), while not directly relevant to my topic, are cited *infra*. This symposium is an "intellectual history" of law and economics and an advanced consumer's guide to the scholarship; see the introduction by Cramton (1983). Gellhorn and Robinson (1983) and Summers (1983) proved particularly helpful to my analyses.

2. See Kelman (1983, pp. 274 and 278) ("the pop version of economics has deluded more people than it has enlightened"), and Priest (1983, pp. 437 and 439) (legal rules have anticipated objections based on standard legal thought, but the rules are vulnerable to even superficial criticisms from an economics perspective).

Reports from two of my former students are instructive here. Appearing before small-town judges who appear to be near-illiterates in economics, these lawyers nevertheless attempted to concoct law and economics policy arguments. To their (and my) surprise, the judges seemed to swallow their arguments hook, line, and sinker. It seems that the judges had heard of this "new wave" of argumentation and were eager to know more. The danger in this process was revealed in subsequent discussions: the policy arguments were of rather mediocre quality, easily rebutted by an opponent with some knowledge of the field. I attempt to circumvent this kind of misuse of law and economics by encouraging students to keep in touch after graduation.

3. For example, in the property segment of the course we investigate the rationality of the "economic man" through *Mayor of Bradford v. Pickles* [1895] A.C. 587; *Vane v. Lord Bernard* (1716) 2 Vern. 738, 23 Eng Rep. 1082; *Everett v. Paschall*, 61 Wash. 47, 111 P. 879 (1910); *Addie & Sons (Collieries) v. Dumbreck* [1929] A.C. 358; *British Ry. Bd. v. Herrington* [1972] 1 All E.R. 777; and *Miller, et al. v. Schoene*, 276 U.S. 272 (1928). See Posner (1977, p. 63 n. 9); Samuels (1971, p. 435). Similar questions are asked in the contracts segment of the course, in relation to *Hurley v. Eddingfield*, 156 Ind. 416, 59 N.E. 1058 (1901). See *The Economics of Contract Law* (1979, pp. 264-265 n.4) (hereinafter Kronman and Posner). The *Hurley* court's approach is compared with that in *Henningson v. Bloomfield Motors*, 32 N.J. 358, 161 A.2d 69 (1960). See Dworkin (1977, pp. 23-26). Notions of economic rationality and efficiency are blended when we move on to the common assertion that *Hadley v. Baxendale*, 9 Ex. 341, 156 Eng. Rep. 145 (1854), reaches an economically efficient result. See, e.g., Posner (1977, p. 94). We discuss whether this is so, and whether this efficiency carries over into subsequent applications of *Hadley: Globe Ref. Co. v. Landa Cotton Oil Co.*, 190 U.S. 540 (1903); *Kerr Steamship Co. v. Radio Corp. of America*, 245 N.Y. 284, 157 N.E. 140 (1927); *Victoria Laundry Ltd. v. Newman Indus. Ltd.* [1949] 2 K.B. 528 (C.A.); *The*

Heron II [1967] 3 All. E.R. 688 (H.L.). (These cases are familiar to my students from Contracts.) See Priest (1980, pp. 399, 413-415). See generally note 58 below.

4. Mishan (1976); and see Gellhorn and Robinson (1983, p. 248), Priest (1983, p. 459), and Stigler (1959, pp. 522, 529).

5. Meltsner (1976, p. 226) (quoting Interior Secretary Udall). Legal thinking is lumpy, discontinuous: "Not every opportunity cost is viewed as a detriment; not every expenditure saved is viewed as a benefit" (Fried, 1981b, pp. 35, 44). Courts are frequently concerned with entitlements and the wrongness of defendants' behavior, regardless of costs and benefits (*id.*). Further, through "selective inclusion or exclusion of specific costs or specific benefits, the prediction can be shaped to suit the preferences of the analyzer," particularly as "empirical guesses" are often the only ways to approximate costs and benefits. Strasser, Bard, and Arthur (1982, pp. 571, 591).

6. The last edition of the classic text in this genre is Fitzgerald (1966). Having taught both Jurisprudence and Law and Economics, I would argue that students find some of the concepts in jurisprudence more palatable and meaningful when these ideas are compared and contrasted with economics perspectives.

7. Rogers (1969, p. 17); Wildavsky (1979, p. 8); Fried (1981b, p. 35); Gellhorn and Robinson (1983, p. 250); Hansmann (1983, pp. 217, 227); Heymann (1973, pp. 797, 798-799); Kelman (1983, p. 274); Scott (1983, pp. 285, 287); Schwartz (1983, pp. 314, 335) (superior scholarship in economics can be used to refute inferior adversarial presentations); Summers (1983, pp. 342-343 n.21) (citing, *inter alia*, the Michelman Report: "the area of greatest deficiency" in law school teaching involves general theory and perspective); and *id.* at 344-345.

8. In conventional economics, these are land, labor, capital, entrepreneurship, and technology. These resources are treated as useful in the pursuit of a more or less interchangeable wealth and power. They are thus quite similar in purposes and effects to such "political" resources as coercion, legitimacy, and administrative capacities. My definitions thus tend to follow Paul Samuelson's rather than those of Milton Friedman, who defines economics as a tautologous filing system for the organizing of empirical material. See Samuelson (1964, p. 5); Veljanovski (1980, p.181) (quoting Milton Friedman). Numerous value preferences, often submerged or disguised, make economics much more than a filing system. See Boulding (1969, p. 1); Posner (1979, p. 295) (citing S. Weinberg, a physicist) ("the great thing is not to be free of theoretical prejudices, but to have the right theoretical prejudices"); and Stigler (1972, pp. 1, 5) ("an unusually disciplined economist could discuss economic policy for an hour without spending more than ten minutes on preaching").

9. See *infra* note 58; *infra* text accompanying notes 68-71, 81-92.

10. The best summary of Hale's ideas is Samuels (1973). See Flynn (1980-81, p. 364): Constraints on choice include "moral views, the media, social class, fear of punishment, hope for reward, self-perception, and coherence with values of the community in which he lives." Regardless of these constraints, there is a right to control one's body and, in some sense, one's efforts, talents, and products: The "zone around the person should be wide enough for him to have some sense of being able to move about at his discretion—in other words, he should have a right to privacy" (Fried, 1981b, p. 54). But Fried makes clear by the authority cited for this proposition (p. 54, n.62) that he has an individual political right in mind. Hale, on the other hand, contemplates the right to wherewithal sufficient to open a minimal zone of economic free choice; effective privacy often costs a great deal, as many abortion, welfare "rights," Medicare, etc., cases demonstrate.

11. And see, for example, Fatouros (1980, p. 105) ("law is based on antinomic principles— . . . coercion and freedom, efficiency and justice"); Samuels (1973) (discussing Hale's ideas); and note 79 below.

12. These are the inverse relationship between the price charged and the quantity purchased, the consumers' and producers' desire to maximize utility (their satisfactions), the measurement of the costs of consumption, production, etc., in terms of the opportunities foregone, and the tendency of resources to gravitate toward their most profitable use. Posner (1977, pp. 3-10). See Veljanovski (1980, p. 162): citing Gary Becker, the "basic concepts" are maximizing behavior, stable prefer-

ences, and opportunity costs. Compare Posner's and Becker's concepts with Kelman (1983, pp. 275-276): (1) all behavior tautologically reduces to utility maximization, which is defined simply as the observed behavior of methodologically isolated subjects [see *infra* note 21]; (2) no free lunches; (3) most goods have downward sloping demand curves; and (4) a macroeconomy does not exist "in any number of significant senses," and all resources are fully utilized.

13. The model lives and dies at the margin: thermostats are set according to the marginal cost of gas, price is determined by the marginal cost of the last unit sold, and different airplanes are marginal costs with wings (Flynn, 1980–81, p. 376).

14. See, e.g., Posner (1977, pp. 10–12). Until recently at least, "proponents of economic analysis have relied on the initial plausibility of utilitarianism in order to provide a normative basis for the various efficiency criteria" (Coleman, 1980, p. 510; part of the Symposium on Efficiency as a Legal Concern). Much of law and economics is rule-utilitarian and assumes that judges reach an efficient result based on manipulations of language, without duplicating the efficiency analyses of economists. See Moore (1981, pp. 151, 164–165). Along with a few others, Richard Posner now claims to reject a utilitarian approach to law and economics; Posner (1980, p. 487; and 1979b). Many of Posner's arguments are hastily (and perhaps poorly) constructed, however, and can be termed utilitarianism in another guise. See Bebchuk (1980), Coleman (1980), Dworkin (1980), Samuels (1981, p. 150) (problem of tautology—"any goal-directed activity can be said to constitute maximizing behavior"—can be overcome only by specifying the goal, and wealth can be specified in different ways and under different patterns of distribution), and notes 33 and 35 below.

15. These important concepts are not treated explicitly in the most widely adopted text (Posner, 1977). See, e.g., Ackerman (1975, pp. xi–xiv); Miller (1978, pp. 437–439, 441–446); Mishan (1976, pp. 386, 390, 393); Coleman (1980, pp. 520–526, 532–548); and Heymann (1973, pp. 864–866).

16. This is a major difference between my course and Professor Siegfried's. He spends four to five weeks on microeconomics before introducing its applications to legal topics. Siegfried (1981, p. 20).

17. Reder (1982) (Reder is a Chicago Business School economist). At various points in the course, we consider whether particular assumptions (in addition to those discussed elsewhere in the article) are meaningful, realistic, and essential to Chicago School efforts: a "tight" prior equilibrium which is not much affected by monopoly, government, or underutilization of the resources that are all fully mobile; shadow prices equal opportunity costs where there are no externalities, and factor and product markets are perfectly competitive; and "random disturbances" and a critical scholarship do not really contradict cherished Chicago premises. See pp. 11–13, 16–18, 20, and 25.

18. See, e.g., Mishan (1976, p. xi) (discussing the "simple and sufficient" conditions under which the "*deus ex machina*" called The Invisible Hand operates, and under which all effects relevant to individual welfare are "properly" priced); Gellhorn and Robinson (1983, p. 273); Kelman (1983, p. 275); Reder (1982, pp. 21, 25); Samuels (1982, pp. 150, 162); Tushnet (1980, pp. 1383, 1394).

19. Any academic discipline seems amenable to an anthropological treatment: "Published scientific work can be treated as artifacts of the culture under study, analogous to potsherds, and can be used to reconstruct some of its typical modes of behavior. Articles on methodology can be treated like informants' reports in work on nonliterate cultures" (Diesing, 1971, p. 19). Diesing adds that, when a substantial unity of methodology and internal cohesion is reached, a "scholastic phase" ensues. Attention is focused on smaller and smaller details, contacts with other fields decrease, and methodologist become moralists who prescribe the canons of purity for new entrants. (*Id.* at 23). While this is not now the state of affairs in law and economics, a fair number of its devotees would like to truncate the field in this manner.

20. Machlup (1978, pp. 267–301); Olson (1965, p. 105) (Marx's error in assuming that, instead of remaining apathetic, workers will be utilitarian or rational enough to see the wisdom of class action); and Reder (1982, p. 30; quoted *infra* note 66).

Economic man is best thought of as *homunculus oeconomicus*, a Weberian ideal type constructed of "meant meanings"—like Protestantism, constitutional monarchy, or oligopoly (Machlup, 1978, pp. 275, 300). The danger is, of course, that ideal types can become stereotypes in the absence of their being grounded on detailed empirical investigations (Diesing, 1971, p. 199). See *infra* note 35.

21. Becker (1976, p. 7); Flynn (1980–81, p. 367) ("Given the open-ended definition of 'utility' and the qualitatively meaningless concept of 'rationality,' the model *excludes the possibility* of describing anything a consumer does as other than rational or as maximizing one's utility."); Gellhorn and Robinson (1983, p. 249); Michelman (1983, pp. 197, 198–199) (criticizing ideas of Edmund Kitch). Posner (1981) variously terms economic rationality an analytical tool (p. 1), a conventional methodological assumption (p. 2), an accurate description of individual behavior (pp. 13, 42), an explanatory hypothesis (p. 4), and an ethical and scientific postulate (p. 13). See Samuels (1981, p. 150). But see also Becker (1976, pp. 153–156, 158, 161, 282, *passim*); Gellhorn and Robinson (1983, pp. 249–250) (rationality assumption is protean but not tautologous, and is warranted by behavior in general).

22. The following are some of the questions discussed from year to year in my course. Does economics fragment the ego, punish and reward at the lowest level—the id—and tacitly assume that most individuals will adapt to the facts of economic life by adopting a "marketplace" identity? Are mature individuals self-centered or do they sometimes seek to "grow" in ways which permit others to do the same? What is it in the psyche of many economists that prevents their accepting reports of irrational behavior at face value? Do individuals seek maximum advantage from each outcome, or do they sometimes seek harmony within and between feelings and action—to achieve the balance which many "equilibrating" economists also seek? Does economics take adequate account of: cultural influences, peer group pressures, and notions of right and wrong; envy, guile, malice, and the attendant "predatory" behavior; inertia, disorderly and inconsistent value systems, faulty calculations, and the inability to communicate wants effectively; and the differences in behavior when individuals act in groups? See, e.g., Argyris (1960, p. 10) (discussing the psychology of Sullivan, Lewin, Fromm, McDougal, May, Rogers, Maslow, Rank, and Horney); Becker (1976, pp. 278–279); Billig (1982, p. 150); Commons (1926, p. 2) (the "abstraction of self-interest gives us a shadowy phantom, an imaginary Robinson Crusoe") and (pp. 37–39) (man treated like an animal when Menger tried to use rationality to turn economics into a science; but the problem remains that, like law, economics is concerned with behavior rather than with motives); Friedman (1975, p. 63); Hummel (1977, pp. 133–136); Olson (1965, pp. 1–2, 34–35); Parsons (1969, pp. 63, 82–83) (Max Weber's theorizing handicapped by state of the psychology of his time); Schelling (1960, p. 16); Flynn (1980–81, p. 364) (economic rationality posits the primitive psychology of "You've come a long way, baby," and "Whatever turns you on"); Heymann (1973, p. 811) (citing Festinger, 1964, pp. 1–7, 152–158); Reder (1982, pp. 15, 17); and *infra* notes 23, 32. Balch (1980, pp. 35, 39) argues that: "Aggregates . . . are not simply the sum of the individuals who compose them, because the behavior of one individual in the presence of others . . . differs from that individual's behavior in isolation. Indeed, the behavior of others is the main source of 'environmental' variables which affect the individual's behavior."

23. For example, two psychiatrists persuasively argue that the many cigarette smokers are not risk-averse and, indeed, display a psychopathology rather than an economic rationality (Tamerin and Resnick, 1978). One, not very successful, riposte is that the risk of death from smoking is not a cost; this risk has already been deducted from benefits by smokers (Mishan, 1976, p. 310). So, too, most deaths amount to suicides, situations where resources are not devoted to prolonging life (Becker, 1976, p. 10). On the other hand, risk aversion has been used persuasively to explain the limited liability of corporations, the widespread use of insurance, the choice of certain contractual forms, etc.

24. In economics, altruism means "behavior actuated by a sense of others, their desires and expectations." But if economists look hard enough, they can usually find an economic self-interest in such behavior: "a *quid* for some implicit and conjectual *quo*" (Phelps, 1975, p. 2). Economists tend to "economize on love" (p. 1, quoting Sir Dennis Robertson). In the real world of transaction costs,

"the optimal degree of unselfishness cannot be determined, although it seems almost certain that the extremes, complete selfishness or complete unselfishness, would yield horrible spillovers (maybe non-survival)" (McKean, 1975, p. 30). See, e.g., Arrow (1975, p. 15) (some degrees of coercion do not eliminate the promptings of altruism); Titmuss (1970); Kennedy (1976, pp. 1685, 1713–1721, 1746–1751, 1777–1778); and notes 32, 84 below.

25. A market is "quite simply the interaction of supply and demand, . . . premised upon the broad assumptions defining consumption and firm behavior in accord with the concept of rationality" (Flynn, 1980–81, p. 372). Using "only price theory, it is possible to argue that markets are efficient, or, conversely, that they are beset by fatal imperfections" (Kitch, 1983, p. 191). As Weberian ideal-types with graphs and numbers, market theories suffer from the failings of other formalist theories. Many economists' conclusions about market behavior (and thus about the law that mimics it) are based on ambiguous information or on hopes about what will happen. Making a market more competitive is not Pareto efficient; there will be losers as well as winners. Judges must therefore make value judgments, economists and legislators having failed to provide operational criteria. Oliver (1979, p. 68); Frug (1984, p. 1361); and Stigler (1983, p. 312).

Posner and others nevertheless do well to make markets the centerpiece of our law and life. See *infra* notes 85-88 and text accompanying. Ours is a market mode of thought about the economy (Adam Smith), politics (Woodrow Wilson), morality (Ralph Waldo Emerson), and intellectual life generally (John Stuart Mill); Wills (1970, p. ix). See McCraw (1984, p. 222): Our ideas on the subject are "both profound and half-baked," and the market's return to an intellectual respectability means that "time and circumstance" are on the side of Chicagoans. This tendency has provoked much criticism. American life should not be viewed as a series of competitive games; the relevant question is not how well you play the game but whether you get to play at all. Lineberry (1978, p. 235). Under the exchange model, a citizen "who should be an active contributor, becomes instead an apathetic ingestor driven by purely personal desires" (Wildavsky, 1979, p. 117). We "convince ourselves that . . . we are currently experiencing the kind of freedom promised by the ideals of the market and democracy," rather than trying to free "ourselves from . . . truncated definitions of market and democracy" (Frug, 1984, p. 1376). See also note 54 below.

26. See Black (1973, p. 48); Dahrendorf (1959, pp. 157–164, 316); Friedman (1966, pp. 163, 166); Mayhew (1971, p. 187); Parsons (1950); Renner (1949, pp. 3–4, 48); Schubert (1974, p. 4) (problems with hypothesizing a societal homeostasis, based on a fundamental biological metaphor); Smart (1976, p. 10) (citing Alvin Gouldner, Parson's functionalism is the social theory of the market economy-society, where the state has little effect and the emphasis is on a philosophy of voluntarism) (and p. 180) (positivism seeks to reduce all social conflicts to unsolved problems in the regulation of self-governing systems); Unger (1976, p. 33) (evaluation of conduct on the basis of the consensus theory "sanctifies whatever standards happen to prevail," through an instrumentalist denial of moral points of view); Wertheim (1974, pp. 9, 105–108, 119); note 59 below.

If "legal order" is substituted for Talcott Parsons' "social system," much of his theory would be regarded as true and even as commonplace by most Western jurists (Stone, 1966, p. 41). This seems a rather strange view of a legal system in which bipolar conflicts are usually resolved coercively, on a winner-take-all basis, with little attempt to restore the parties to harmony or "equilibrium." See Chayes (1976, pp. 1282–1283). Also, many significant conflicts remain unresolved (as social problems) whether or not litigation occurs. Perhaps the most important of these, in terms of its effects on behavior, is the internal conflict between self-interest and the legal and moral duties owed to others. See Anderson (1978, pp. 738–740, *passim*). Law and economics frequently defines perceptions of the duties owed to others in terms of self-interest, defining away the conflict rather than analyzing it.

27. Anderson and Hill (1975). Entertaining and profitable comparisons with contract rights arising in a slightly different historical context are traced in discussions of Umbeck (1977).

28. Coase (1960) (read by students as abridged in Ackerman, 1975, p. 17). The Coase Theorem uses a convoluted definition of transaction costs, so as to include the purchase and sale of the right to inflict losses. The Theorem can thus can be used to examine theories of liability. Reder (1982, p. 22).

29. E.g., "Coase Theorem Symposium" (1973) *Natural Resources Journal*, Vol. 13, pp.

557ff. and (1974) Vol. 14, p. 1ff. See also Commons (1926, p. 14): An economic formula which includes group sanctions as well as individual inducements must be more complex than a formula based on an isolated self-interest.

30. Also called neighborhood effects, side effects, and spillovers, externalities are costs imposed on others. They suggest that property rights and relations do not correspond with economic reality; market prices do not measure the real costs of opportunities foregone. Mishan (1976, p. 109); Oliver (1979, p. 36).

31. I.e., individuals who cannot be excluded from consuming certain ("public" or "collect-ive") goods, even though they have not contributed to the provision of these goods. Tulloch and Wagner (1977, p. 285). In *Catch 22*, Yosarian was asked what would happen if everyone refused to fly missions. His free-riding reply: "Then I'd be a damn fool to feel any different." Frohock (1979, p. 98).

32. Mishan (1976, p. 110, and pp. 111, 115) (externalities are not deliberately produced or ab-sorbed, and are virtually unlimited); Oliver (1979, p. 38); Reder (1982, pp. 34-35) (Chicago School "thrust for endogenization" is an application of the survivor principle which increases the explana-tory power of economics, but at a cost—variables made endogenous are no longer objects of social choice and become part of the Hegelian freedom reposing in the recognition of necessity). See note 53 below.

When ethics are brought into the discussion, the question of which externalities count

> depends upon a consensus in the particular society. Though such ethical distinctions will confine the application of Pareto improvements to 'legitimate' external effects, the economist would appear justified in accepting a distinction that society consistently makes. [But] there is no lack of evidence that society does take seriously all tangible damage inflicted on people in the pursuit by others of pleasure or profit. (Mishan 1976, p. 116)

Altruistic or ethical aspects of externalities and free rider effects are the most difficult to value (in economics, to monetize or commercialize), and are thus likely to be ignored. Although experi-mental data about the nature and scope of free rider effects are inconclusive, it seems that the free rider drives a wedge between individual and group rationality; a collective maximization need not produce optimal results. Tulloch and Wagner (1977, pp. 285-287).

33. See Cox (1979, p. 267) ("efficiency" amounts to reconciling regrettably inevitable govern-ment interventions with the notions of market equilibrium); Gellhorn and Robinson (1983, p. 249); *supra* notes 3, 14, 21; and *infra* notes 84, 87-90 and text accompanying. It is "a sign of the honorific status of 'efficiency' in economics and Western culture generally that anything so labeled is prima facie justified" (Samuels, 1981, p. 156). Efficiency is grounded in notions of utilitarianism, that "product of a middle-class dominated capitalist society. 'What is the use of you?' it asked. . . ." (Farrar, 1977, p. 139). See Becker (1976, p. 8). The American "cult of efficiency" had its origin in the early 20th century scientific management movement. Kolko (1976, p. 31).

Efficiency/wealth maximization notions can lead to bizarre conclusions. E.g., Posner (1981, p. 84): "If Nazi Germany wanted to get rid of its Jews, in a system of wealth maximization it would have had to buy them out." But this is true only if Jews had "rights": see *infra* notes 48, 82-83 and text accompanying. If Jews had no rights, the Coase Theorem suggests that Jews had to buy them-selves out—as happened in some instances. In any event, it is difficult to know what to conclude from Posner's tasteless hypothetical. Was Nazi Germany not efficient/wealth maximizing? He seems to argue to the contrary elsewhere: discrimination may be efficient for the individual where it minimizes search costs or because of a willingness to pay a price for indulging "taste" (Posner, 1981, pp. 85-87, 235, 351-363). The efficiency of discrimination should not make it lawful, yet it is difficult to justify necessarily inefficient state interventions in discriminatory behavior (*id.*, pp. 363, 378, 385-386).

34. Transaction costs ultimately fix the distribution of property and contract rights, and thus the

relative burdens of negotiation. High transaction costs mean that legal changes have both allocative and distributive effects. Careful policy analyses thus require comparisons of the transaction costs of imperfect markets with the costs of imperfect governments and legal interventions.

35. Unfortunately, so central an analytical tool as transaction costs has yet to receive rigorous theoretical or empirical analysis. The typical transaction cost analysis is an "elaborate tautology," with "almost no distance between the conclusions and the premises. . . ." The "law is rationalized as efficient by assuming a configuration of transaction (and other) costs that makes it so without any attempt to investigate whether these costs exist in practice" (Veljanovski, 1980, pp. 183–184, citing Steven Cheung and Charles Fried). See *id.* pp. 170, 170 n.51.

For example, it is commonly held or assumed that transaction costs are minimized by clearly defined and certain property rights, by deploying these rights through a free and individualized bargaining, by reaching bargains which "internalize" all costs and benefits (preventing divergences between private and social costs and benefits), and by enforcing the newly created rights under a flexible set of remedies. See, e.g., Calabresi and Melamed (1975, p. 31); Ault and Rutman (1979, pp. 169–170, citing O. Johnson). While much of this is undoubtedly true in theory, it ignores many significant qualifications and practical difficulties: see, e.g., Dahlman (1979, p. 141); Farber (1980); Hale (1943); Hirsch (1974); Kennedy and Michelman (1980); Macneil (1974); Schwartz and Tulloch (1975); Trebing (1969).

36. See Goldschmid (1979) (especially articles by Victor Reinemer, Hans Augermueller, Wassily Leontief, Kenneth Scott, and Kent Greenawalt and Eli Noaom); Diamond and Rothschild (1978) (especially articles by Akerlof, Kenneth Arrow and Robert Lind, and Michael Rothschild); Connelly (1981); Maris and Mueller (1980, p. 55, citing study by Marc Porat); and Reder (1982, pp. 23–24) (Chicagoans see information as an input into productive processes which should be priced accordingly, while non-Chicagoans frequently see information as one parameter of an individual's utility function that should prima facie be "given" to the less well informed). Many of the ideas in these articles are dealt with more fully at the end of the course.

37. Posner (1981, p. 6). This thesis is justified on the basis of consent (pp. 88–94), the absence of systemic distributive effects (pp. 103–106), and the determinate and sensible results which flow from it (pp. 109–115). See Samuels (1981, pp. 147–148). As a "libertarian," Posner seeks to distance himself from Bentham's paternalism by defining wealth maximization as congruent with Calvinist virtues, p. 150. See Posner (1981, p. 68).

38. Law and economics "liberals" such as Calabresi and Michelman seek support in the Rawlsian natural law that is equally serviceable to "conservatives," who are ominously silent on distributional questions (Tushnet, 1980, p. 1390). Rawls assumes that law will define the components of income and wealth, and that taxing and welfare institutions will redistribute funds rather than general entitlements. Like Dworkin (see *infra* note 48 and text accompanying), Rawls says little about private law (Fried, 1981, p. 50) and about property law in particular. If property rights are part of Rawl's liberty principle—a question he does not seem to address—there would be very little or nothing left to redistribute under his subordinate difference principle.

39. Compare Friedman (1962, p. 7–36) with Lange (1938). These are read by students as abridged in Ackerman (1975, pp. 69–91).

40. See Grey (1976). Rogers (1969, p. 15) attacks the economists' claim that,

> given the ends, economic behavior with respect to means is unambiguously "determined." This claim fails to observe that in order to be able to reach this result even in the simplest case, the totality of the existing historical reality including every one of its causal relationships must be assumed as "given" and presupposed as known.

If we knew this much, abstract theories would be unnecessary (*id.*).

41. Nozick (1974, pp. 151, 153, 155–164) (read by students as abridged in Kronman and Posner, 1979, p. 240). Nozick contrasts patterned theories of justice (such as Rawls') with "su-

perior'' theories, those based on history and/or entitlement. He agrees with Hayek that law is not properly concerned with the particular end results sought under various patterned theories: ''from each according to his abilities. . . ,'' etc. Fried (1981b, pp. 52–53). Wildavsky (1979, pp. 155–156) adds that: ''Merit wants take away both the reality and the rationale of economics without replacing it with an intelligible politics. [B]etter a flawed economics than a bogus politics.'' For Nozick: ''Acquisition is a mark of personal development. He legitimizes self-interest and private initiative. His objection to coercive redistribution reaffirms the reluctance of the individual to submit his interests to a collective will.'' Murphy (1981, p. 137). Only a philosopher would think this an adequate basis for generating a body of laws. Fried (1981b, pp. 53–54). My own view is similar to Warren Samuels' (1981, p. 166).

42.   See Hale (1943); Samuels (1973). Macaulay and Macneil suggest that much of the reality of ''freedom'' of contract is to be found in sociability and business mores, ''relational'' interests that blanket and even displace the freedom of contract found in legal rules or a single-minded profit seeking. See Macaulay (1963); Macneil (1974, 1978). But see Friedman (1962), whose contrast between a voluntary cooperation through the market and a coercive direction of the economy by government is arguably a false dichotomy. See *infra* note 61 and *infra* text accompanying notes 60–61, 80.

43.   See Lane (1962, p. 344) (''Those who defend the *status quo* make . . . moral appeals; they call on tradition, a divine order, contractual arrangements implying individual integrity as moral sanction for the going order.''); Lewis (1977, p. 68) (''Liberal, conservative, and moderate *economists* are political actors of the first order, because they so thoroughly dominate the creation of decisional premises.''); Reder (1982, pp. 25, 31, 35); Stigler (1959, pp. 524, 527) (inherent conservatism of many economists' analyses).

44.   The order utilized is: the scope of contractual liability, unilateral contracts, implied contracts, consideration, remedies, contractual uncertainty and mistake, the insurance principle, impossibility and frustration, form contracts, duress, and unconscionability. Much of the discussion is based on Kronman and Posner (1979) pp. 1–11, 26–153, 167–199, 220–233, 250–267); and Schwartz and Tulloch (1975). See *supra* notes 34-35.

45.   Discussions focus on Alchian and Demsetz (1975); Schmid (1978, pp. 103–107); Macneil (1974, 1978); and Samuels (1973). See *infra* text accompanying notes 54–55, 71–72.

46.   26 Wis. 2d 683, 133 N.W.2d 267 (1965).

47.   Anderson (1978). Here we examine the economics of trust, my reliance on your doing right rather than on your self-interest. See Fried (1981a, p. 8). If the conventional suspicions of an arms-length bargaining can be overcome, trust becomes a capital asset. It is jointly or collectively produced and is useful for long-term planning, for reducing monitoring costs, and for resolving disputes in ways that minimize transaction costs. Repeat business or repetitive play does not by itself resolve the ''prisoner's dilemma'' actuated by self-interest, but it does increase returns to investments in trust. Breton and Wintrobe (1982, pp. 10, 48, 51, 64, 69–71, 75). In order for trust to work efficiently, the nature of the parties' expected roles must be changed and carefully defined after lengthy investigations by those who sanction breaches of trust (Heymann, 1973, p. 857). An alternative to trust, the franchise contract, is also discussed as a device blurring distinctions between infrafirm and interfirm relations (Rubin, 1978).

48.   Dworkin (1977). See Paton (1972, pp. 284-290). Utility depends on values and on expectations, the perceived probability of a net gratification. Stover and Brown (1977, p. 127). Corbin's definition of contractual justice as the compensation of reasonable expectations is thus one definition of a utility/wealth maximization. But see also Samuels (1974, p. 11): ''If rights are relative and contingent, then why are rights changes in accordance with the Coasian rules less objectionable than those in accordance with, say, the goals of egalitarian radicals? One is no more immediately paternalistic than the other.'' ''If rights do no count, then why do people want them?'' (p. 13) But see *infra* text accompanying note 90.

49.   E.g., Friedman (1962), abridged in Ackerman (1975, pp. 80-81). See Miller (1972, p. 63) (quoting Henry Carter Adams).

50.   For example, Salmond raises the conventional argument that corporate penal or punitive

liability is a denial of "natural justice" (the relevant British standard), a holding of beneficiaries (shareholders) liable for the acts of agents (management) (Fitzgerald, 1966, p. 315). If so, why look behind the legal person to worry about real persons here and not in certain other areas? Is there an economics rationale for doing so?

51. The success of corporations over time is attributed to their capacity to attract, aggregate, and discipline capital and other factors of production, on a scale impracticable for individuals and partnerships. Corporations transform property from what is often a static endowment of, for example, family status into a productive resource. We also discuss the legal ingenuity of balancing corporate desires, for a relatively permanent capital base imposing low fixed costs, with risk-averse shareholders' interests in liquidity and in limited liability. See Fitzgerald (1966, p. 308) (quoting Coke, C.J.); Dorfman (1961, pp. 1308–1310).

52. I.e., title to the monetary value of the chose in action (treated earlier in the course as a mixture of property and contractual rights) remains with the shareholders, while the use-value is transferred under contract to the corporation. Our discussions focus on Alchian (1975); Anderson (1978, pp. 784–785); Berle (1965); Hindley (1969) (a good summary of Berle and Means' theory). Property rights in a corporation are "a behavior and not a thing"; yet they are "enveloped with some mystery and taboo" (Kirshen, 1932, p. 9). As a result, corporate pluralism becomes a libertarian theory of the second best (see *infra* note 92) which contradicts Berle and Means' theory: owners have the absolute right to control their property and therefore to control the institutions they have created (Gutmann, 1983, p. 258).

53. Many economists assume the firm, whether a lemonade stand or multinational conglomerate, to be a "unified organism" incapable of decisions which do not maximize profits. Flynn (1980–81, p. 369). See *infra* notes 55, 71–72 and text accompanying. By definition, an inconsistent "satisficing" behavior becomes impossible and thus irrelevant. Examples of such behavior include the pursuit of: political and economic power and prestige, personal and employee security and welfare, and corporate social responsibility. Although the empirical evidence and the arguments for satisficing in firms' behavior are strong, current theories have too many specific assumptions to be generalizable (Maris and Mueller, 1980, pp. 39–41). But if profit maximization does not widely obtain, the argument that governmental interventions in corporate activities are necessarily inefficient loses much of its force. See Becker (1976, p. 7) (where apparently profitable steps not taken, economics tends to invent new monetary or psychic costs—an almost tautological means of completing the system); Downs (1976, p. 26) (economists pay too little attention to the nonmarket and lax-competition sectors, where firm has much discretion and the consumer has little power to punish); McDonald (1977, pp. 65–67) (profits are only the game's outcome and do not describe payoffs to particular players) (p. 70) and (p. 125) (the "Martini norm,'" drinking together frequently to promote stable relations as an alternative to adapting to economic change); Kelman (1983, p. 276) (the plethora of unrealistic assumptions underpinning profit maximization); Reder (1982, p. 17) (satisficing behavior an especially repugnant notion for Chicago School economists, for it suggests that price and marginal cost vary independently of each other and of the quantity bought and sold).

Closely related to the assumption of profit maximization is the survivor principle of Alchian and of Stigler: economic irrationality by firms is limited by budgetary constraints, and competition selects for prosperity those firms making the best decisions under conditions of uncertainty. Most economists would hold that surviving methods of production will have the lowwest cost in the long run, but the Chicago School goes further: the expected method cost is close to the least-cost method available at any given time; deviations are the result of random disturbances. Becker (1976, p. 164); Maris and Mueller (1980, p. 34); and Reder (1982, p. 24). But see Becker (1976, p. 283) (sociobiologists, whose approach is congenial to that of economics, are interested in the fact that, while self-interest has obvious survival value, altruistic people and animals also survive); Maris and Mueller (1980, p. 59) (American economic growth relies on mergers and nonprice competition, situations where there is no natural selection of the most efficient process); Reder (1982, p. 30, quoted *infra* note 66; pp. 34-35, discussed in *supra* note 32). The survivor principle lies open to all of the criticisms of any other species of Social Darwinism. The principle is deeply conservative, a variation on the

Panglossian Ethic: "Everything is for the best in this best of all possible worlds." In any event, many corporate executives are not subject to budgetary constraints because they have a more or less unfettered discretion over a fat corporate treasury.

54. Under Coase's theory of the firm, no subunit should have more than one member, if prices are efficient transmitters of information. Implicitly, then, markets are costly and imperfect information systems; costs can be reduced through an administrative integration of information-exchange, despite the other disadvantages of such a technique. Maris and Mueller (1980, p. 36). This leaves open the question of whether corporations are the cause, the effect, or most likely both, with regard to market failures. The problem with the corporation-as-market-surrogate is that resources are allocated among bureaus in ways that maximize their value *to the bureaucracy.* Competition will therefore not reveal to the sponsor (shareholder, voter, etc.) whether the bureaus are efficient or not; it reveals only the capacity for discretionary behavior (Breton and Wintrobe, 1982, p. 119).

55. Discussions focus on Posner (1977, p. 303–309, 331–334); Anderson (1978, pp. 786–793); and especially on Fischel (1978). The latter article is treated as representative of denunciations by "market" theorists, of the failure to understand the "new" corporations law. We consider whether their assumptions of a competitive capital market could ever obtain in reality. For example, does the growth of financial intermediaries mean that too many blocks of shares are in the hands of noncompeting bureaucracies? Does large size offer more protection against takeover bids, compared to high profitability? Are competitions among potential managements, as opposed to competitions among firms, adequate safeguards of corporate efficiency and other aspects of the public interest? For example, do most takeover bids amount to resources "wasted" in attempts to transfer monopoly profits from one group to another? Are mergers best explained as the maximizing of shareholder welfare, as the redeployment of capital (Oliver Williamson, J. Fred Weston), as the replacement of bad managers (Henry Manne), and/or as the result of increased cash flows, higher price-earnings ratios, and higher rates of return on shares in a buoyant economy? See Mishan (1976, p. 199); Frug (1984, pp. 1356-1357, 1358 n.291); Maris and Mueller (1979, pp. 42, 45, 55–56). Similar questions are asked later in the course, concerning other governmental disclosure requirements. Discussions then focus on Goldschmid (1979); Connelly (1981).

56. Samuels (1973, pp. 302–324) (citing Hale). See Darwall (1983, p. 57) (individual's political influence enhanced if his views coincide with those of a corporation with resources to spend in political markets, but individual's independence dubious where structure of corporate relations is hierarchical); Oliver (1979, p. 87) (widespread argument that freedom of contract essential to Pareto-efficient solutions, but there are many such solutions "and the actual outcome in a world of unequal bargaining power and information may well be one that many people would regard as 'unfair' with respect to both income distribution and resource allocation."); Flynn (1980–81, p. 374) (manifest disequilibrium can be explained as convincingly by private power as by governmental intervention).

The "economic and political natures of the corporation do not dwell apart in a Nestorian separation" (Latham, 1970, p. 218). Corporations are "lesser commonwealths" distinguished from Leviathan by their less absolute dominion (pp. 218–219, quoting Hobbes). These ideas are prominent in the philosophy of Jurgen Habermas: "Economic crisis is immediately transformed into social crisis; for in unmasking the opposition of social classes it provides a practical critique of the market's pretension to be free of power" (McCarthy, 1978, pp. 362–363, quoting Habermas). For example, to what extent do processes establishing minimum wage laws differ from the forces in other imperfect ("oligopsonistic") markets, in terms of fixing "political" wages? See note 67 below.

57. E.g., Chapman and Pennock (1983, p. xiv): In calls for a more participatory democracy, a concern "for equality renders problematic, and possibly illegitimate, the concentration of authority and power that we find in the modern corporation."

58. Rather brief discussions focus on: Buchanan and Tulloch (1975) (road repairs by local government); Cheung (1974) (effects of price controls on property rights and availability); Davies (1971); Ellickson (1971) (and cases cited therein—the impact of controls on the construction industry and such community characteristics as housing discrimination); Green and Nader (1973) (plus "Comment," p. 890—the FCC, Federal Maritime Commission, and the ICC, very briefly);

Niskanen (1975) (plus "Comments"—fire, garbage, and hospital services, and rationalizations of local governments, HUD, and the Defense Department); Posner (1971) (public utilities, very briefly). Several of these discussions revolve around property and property rights, in an attempt to round out earlier discussions.

59. See, e.g., Huntington (1981). This leading member of the political science establishment distinguishes pluralist, consensus, and Marxist schools of thought, neglecting the many points of contact between pluralists and the consensus school. He finds the interest group theories of the dominant pluralists to be fairly useful in descrribing processes during "normal" times and concerning "normal" political issues. Upheaval and moral passion are, by definition, characteristics of all significant policy issues (e.g, abortion), however, and Huntington documents the explanatory failings concerning these issues by pluralism, Marxism, and, I would add, failures by the consensus school and a pluralist/consensus law and economics. See also Olson (1965, p. 111) ("Just as Marxians glorify and magnify class action, many non-Marxian scholars glorify and magnify the pressure group."); Schubert (1962, pp. 164–173). Schubert distinguishes idealist, rationalist, and realist schools of political science. For the dominant rationalists and conservative realists (including such "due process" theorists as Frankfurter), publics rather than a public adopt an ethical relativism in an attempt to keep the boat from rocking too much (id.). See infra note 65 and text accompanying. Brief lectures are based on: Dahl (1956); Dahl and Lindblom (1976); Lowi (1969, pp. xiii, 71, passim) (interest group liberalism, a vulgarized political science pluralism, is the new public philosophy responsible for a crisis of public confidence). Much of our class discussion examines Wilson (1979) and Wagner (1977) (the most cynical treatment of interest group politics I could find, which also explores the intriguing notion of a "political business cycle").

60. At this stage, discussions are extrapolations from: Galbraith (1975, pp. 50-71), discussed in the course introduction); Macneil (1974, 1978) (discussed earlier, in relation to contracts). See infra notes 69, 72, and infra text accompanying notes 67, 71–72.

61. See Brietzke (1984); Cranston (1977, pp. 103, 106–108, 111–113); Komesar (1981, p. 1356); supra note 24 (self-interest v. altruism is arguably a false dichotomy); supra note 42 and infra note 72.

62. Rabin (1979, pp. 7, 15). See Renner (1949, pp. 47–48, 72); supra text accompanying note 9.

63. Traced briefly are the economic growth resulting from Hamiltonian (or neomercantilist) policies up to 1880, or up to Munn v. Illinois, 94 U.S. 113 (1877), the partial displacement of these policies as levels of private capital became more adequate to the task of growth, and the post-Depression realignment of privatism and intervention in a larger (primarily Keynesian but ever-changing) synthesis called the mixed economy. Students recollect discussions of Hurst (1971); Scheiber (1971); and Dorfman (1961). See Barraclough (1981, pp. 51–60); Scheiber (1980, pp. 1149, 1161–1162) (studies by Handlin about Massachusetts, Hartz about Pennsylvania, Heath about Georgia, and Scheiber about Ohio shattered the myth of an antebellum laissez faire; a "commonwealth" concept was the validating canon of "state mercantilism" and other interventions that both promoted growth and regulated economic interests).

64. These conventions are based on the Progressive/New Deal model of the extreme deference to be paid "neutral" experts. These Platonic Guardians, in effect, are seen to be "working toward an undefinable but presumptively attainable goal of the 'public interest'." (DeLong, 1982, p. 886). This model has been undermined by "the complexities of a managed economy in a welfare state, and . . . the corrosive seduction of welfare economics and pluralist political analysis" (p. 887, quoting Richard Stewart). These have given rise to "the spectre of a multitude of narrow-ended, self-regulating institutions, working at cross purposes and bound to special interests; of a system impervious to direction and leadership, incapable of setting priorities; of a fragmented and impotent polity in which the very idea of public interest is emptied of meaning" (Nonet and Selznick, 1978, p. 103) (a liberal sociologists' view).

65. Our discussions focus on Downs (1957); Buchanan and Tulloch (1975); Niskanen (1975); and Peltzman (1976). Much support for analyses by these scholars can be gleaned from literary and historical treatments of politics, especially those of local government. Given an interest in them lo-

cally (and the proximity to the Chicago School of events described!) we very briefly consider Dreiser (1925); Royko (1971); and Wendt and Kogan (1943). (Can differences between the so-called Harvard and Chicago schools of law and economics be explained in part on the basis of differences in local political environments?) Counterweights used in an attempt to balance our discussions include: Colm (1962; pp. 116–123); Komesar (1981, pp. 1357–1359); Michelman (1980, pp. 440–442); and materials discussed *supra* note 25.

66.   Reder (1982, p. 30):

> If the actions of governments are inimical to the welfare of their citizens then, by the survivor principle [see *supra* note 53], governments should be diminished as resource users. Manifestly this has not been the case . . . . Rationalizations of government growth running in terms of duped voters are unacceptable for the same reason as are explanations of consumer behavior that rest on allegations of delusion or irrationality.

> The logic of (Chicago School analysis) . . . implies that if governments are growing, they must be satisfying the demands of their consumer-voters.

Much of the literature assumes competition within the business bureaucracy and monopoly in the public bureaucracy, where a greater waste and the "quiet life" are seen to prevail. This contradicts neoclassical theory; waste cannot exist without the persistent error in choosing social institutions that is impossible under assumptions of an economically rational choice. Yet many economists are willing to assume, on the flimsiest of evidence, that Parkinson's Law (which contradicts neoclassical theory) applies to public bureaucracies. Breton and Wintrobe (1982, pp. 89–93, 157). See Becker (1976, p. 12) ("War is said to be caused by madmen and political behavior, more generally, dominated by folly and ignorance."); Breton and Wintrobe (1982, p. 24) (problems with the leading theories explaining political behavior—logrolling, bargaining, game theory); Frohock (1979, p. 92) (free rider concept—see *supra* note 35—poses a most serious challenge to interest group theories that is frequently ignored); McConnell (1966, p. 135) (Presidential "jawboning" of the steel industry, to roll back price increases, gave "support to that curious but by no means uncommon doctrine that government action can have no effect in economic affairs and that the effects of government action are always evil."); Balch (1980) (quoted in *supra* note 22); Flynn (1980–81, p. 374) (discussed in *supra* note 56); and Frug (1984, pp. 1359–1360) (insights based on an interest group pluralism are applied to political processes but frequently neglected in analyses of corporations). Coase's theory of the firm implies that, compared to markets, firms reduce costs by an administrative integration of information-exchange. See *supra* note 53. If so, why doesn't government, as the Big Firm, reduce such costs still further?

67.   One student based his analyses on the political philosophy of Jurgen Habermas, and went on to propose Habermas-style remedies. Much of Habermas is admittedly relevant to critical theories of law and economics. See, e.g., McCarthy (1978, p. 382) (quoting Habermas):

> Group needs that can expect no satisfaction from a self-regulating market tend to be regulated through the state . . . . With the interweaving of the public and private realms, not only do political authorities assume certain functions in the sphere of commodity exchange and social labor, but conversely social powers now assume political functions . . . . Large organizations strive for a kind of political compromise with the state and with one another, excluding the public wherever possible. But at the same time they must secure at least a plebiscitary support . . . through the development of demonstrative publicity.

It is not necessary to go as far as Habermas goes beyond the permissible bounds of an American discourse. Some of the most effective criticisms of contemporary theories come from scholars who are basically friends of these theories. See, e.g., Dahl and Lindblom (1976); Kennedy (1981); Michelman (1980); Reder (1982, p. 28) (normative attitudes of economic liberals, especially Chicagoans, toward suffrage and voting power are often "wobbly"; "an interaction of voting beggars with alms-offering politicians" suggests "a maleficent cobweb cycle, the outsweeping of which might require the disenfranchisement of the poor."); and Samuels (1981, p. 152) (Posner's ambivalence over social control is reflected in a confused treatment of governments' roles).

68.   See Anderson (1966); and *supra* notes 12, 58. For example, the criteria proposed by Wilson (1979) would seem to preclude regulations which spawn concentrated costs and diffuse benefits, yet this is what we have in, for example, antitrust, the FDA, and environmental and consumer protections. That these are the regulatory areas most under attack today can be attributed in part to the findings of contemporary political science and of law and economics.

69.   Niskanen (1975). See Peltzman (1976). It can be argued that "predatory" practices in the public sector—those conducive to an inefficient Big Government—receive too strict a scrutiny under analyses like Niskanen's and Peltzman's, while many other economists pay too little attention to predatory practices by private firms assumed to be attaining an efficient size in competitive markets. See *supra* text accompanying note 60. The assumptions made in such studies are too specific to add up to a general theory, and are overly influenced by the particular agencies examined. These studies oppose Max Weber's notions of a bureaucratic efficiency-by-definition with an inefficiency-by-definition. Breton and Wintrobe (1982, pp. 27–28, 33–34).

70.   Breton and Wintrobe (1982, pp. 128–129); Hummel (1977, pp. 56–57); and Olson (1982, p. 188; 1965, pp. 1–2, 6–7, 34–35). Increases in organizational rationality operate to decrease individual rationality, an unavoidable consequence of betting on organizations rather than people. Like public bureaucracies, business bureaucracies sometimes control demand in part and engage in monopolistic or discriminatory pricing, and they always have cost squeezing and capital accumulation as their categorical imperatives. Bureaucrats of both types are vulnerable to subordinates' credible explanations of inefficiency. Private and public bureaucracies each have their own folklore, and the tales are frequently adopted by economists without testing and without analyzing the behavior of one bureaucracy in terms of the other's myths. The market for managers in the public sector seems at last as competitive and efficient as that for the private sector, and job mobility is higher in the public sector, where elections are more frequent than private-sector takeover bids. Breton and Wintrobe (1982, pp. 34–35, 37, 52, 61, 93, 96–97); Hummel (1977, pp. 69, 86). Landis (1938, pp. 10–11) adds that the organization of a corporation

> would scarcely follow Montesquieu's lines . . . . Yet the problems of operating a private industry resemble to a great degree those entailed by its regulation. Rates, wages, conditions and adjudication of employee and public claims are in fact governance. [B]ecause of the rapidity and directness of their execution, the penalties that private management can impose possess a coercive force and effect that government even with its threat of incarceration cannot equal.

71.   See, e.g., Brewster (1970); Mason (1970, pp. 3–4, 16–17); and DeLong (1982, p. 888) (a marginally expert agency which has studied the matter should not be overruled by an inexpert court; the agency can be captured by clients and still articulate an adequate basis for decision—without making public all of its files). Shecky Greene's hoary joke about putting Congress on commission could be taken seriously, in light of studies concerned with minimizing monitoring costs: see, e.g., Alchian and Demsetz (1975); and Rubin (1978) (Congress as franchisor).

72.   The effects of private market controls are exaggerated, while the effects of budgeting and appropriations processes, elections, etc., are underestimated.

73.   See Simon (1957, pp. 56–57): "Democratic institutions find their principal justification as a procedure for the validation of value judgments. There is no 'scientific' or 'expert' way of making such judgments. . . ." Nevertheless, law and economics poses serious challenges to canons of politi-

:al legitimacy (see *infra* text accompanying notes 90-91) while offering no popular justification for political processes. See Murphy (1981, p. 153):

> Public authority secures the legitimate expectations of all to essential goods which it is beyond their individual power to acquire. Liberal capitalism can identify abuses of this authority. But it cannot make an effective case against its necessity. [D]emands for absolute private property are property viewed as forms of an associational selfishness.

74. See Bodenheimer (1962, pp. 206, 212); Colm (1962, pp. 116-119) (quoting Robert Dahl at 116-117); Nonet and Selznick (1978, p. 103) (quoted *supra* note 64); Wildavsky (1979, p. 392) (economists' notions of a consumer sovereignty have the effect of underemphasizing the potential roles of leadership, persuasion, and education); and Komesar (1981, p. 1357). The position most economists take is represented by Musgrave (1962, p. 108): Policy measures which come as close as possible to the results obtained under perfect competition define the public interest. Musgrave does admit (pp. 108–109) that difficulties arise when a problem cannot be solved efficiently by competition alone. But see *Bell Telephone Co. v. Driscoll*, 343 Pa. 109, 112, 21 A.2d 912, 916 (1941) (legislature entitled to determine the public interest, but this is "a concept without an ascertainable criterion"); Anderson (1979, p. 714) (different rules are used to identify problems, solutions, and evaluation criteria in law, economics, diplomacy, environmental planning, and civil engineering); and *infra* note 92. Meehan (1981, p. 200) adds that "A physicist whose rocketry program was based on gravitational forces found on an unspecified planet would be in precisely the position taken by the market-oriented economist. Neither has an intellectual apparatus that can be usefully applied to problems on earth."

Economists and most noneconomists would agree with Becker (1976, p. 37): governmental interventions are not justified where governmental imperfections exceed market imperfections. The question is, when does this occur? The selective incorporation of real-world facts into abstract theories can lead to anomalous results. One example may be the "new" antitrust/industrial organization, which holds that nongovernmental monopolies are transitory and that many of the market failures attributed to barriers to entry and predatory behavior are not significant in practice. Kitch (1983, p. 192); Reder (1982, p. 15). If these holdings are generalized to cover nonbusiness markets as well, they offer powerful arguments against intervention by "monopolizing" governments. See, e.g., Oliver (1979, p. 105): legislation redistributing property rights—concerning minimum wages and a prices and incomes policy—slows down the *tatonnement* process. This minimizing of the costs and distress of market adjustments is undesirable only *if* markets produce optimum prices and resource use (*id.*).

75. Flynn (1980–81, p. 349). See Mishan (1976, p. 407) ("The determination of the value of a project . . . by the political process . . . is either (economically) arbitrary or else . . . it arises from any other consistent body of principles. . .") and (p. 415) ("Issues over which feelings run high, and about which there is no financial complexity, can sometimes be more satisfactorily resolved by conventional voting procedures than by cost-benefit analysis."). The thoughtful Mishan may be overestimating the economists' role here; *Business Week* found that, during the 1977 American Economics Association meeting, no economist offered "anything resembling a new idea for addressing the major policy dilemmas of the West . . . . Instead, the sessions were dominated by papers seeking to refine methodologies that already have been proven ineffective. [L]ike their counterparts, the moving men, economists collect money and hours for pushing the furniture around. . . ." Kearl et al. (1979, p. 28) (quoting *Business Week*).

76. The attitude is frequently one of "macroeconomics gives us microeconomists a bad name." Kelman (1983, p. 276) (quoting Richard Zeckhauser). (Private lawyers sometimes say similar things about public lawyers.) The assumption is usually that adding up singles (micro) yields the group (macro). As in the "old" physics, the rationality of macrobodies is inferred from the rationality of microbodies. But the "new" economics, like the "new" physics, casts doubt on conventional im-

ages of rational microbodies. But see also Becker (1976, p. 161). As things stand, Keynesian macroeconomics lacks an adequate basis in microeconomics; microeconomics generally involves comparative static analyses, with no accounting for the time-paths of adjustments; and monetarists and rational expectation theorists cannot explain involuntary unemployment, and they therefore frequently imply that all unemployment is voluntary. Olson (1982, p. 8); Flynn (1980–81, p. 372); and Strasser, Bard, and Arthur (1982, p. 588).

One conclusion, frequently drawn from this incoherent jumble is that "regulation is . . . a narrow, self-contained process clearly separable from the main drift of national economic policies" (Bernstein, 1955, p. 253). This may indeed be true, but perhaps only because it is assumed true. If the assumption of narrow regulatory behavior is sufficiently widespread, the possibility of "national economic policies" evaporates. As a way around this incoherence, a 1980 study by H. Odagari, discussed in Maris and Mueller (1980, p. 46), adopts a two-sector, corporate/neoclassical model, with corporate behavior dominating the macro-equilibrium conditions of growth.

77. See *supra* text following note 75. For example, from the individual's private law, microeconomics perspective, an economic regulation is an unwelcome intrusion; from the community, public law, macro perspective, the same regulation *may* serve to correct imperfect markets in the public interest. The mainstream of law and economics barely papers over this gap by defining the relevant community perspective largely or solely in terms of the individual's vantage point. This brings us back to Myrdal's assertion (*supra* text accompanying note 20), and we discuss whether there are rational grounds for preferring the congery of value preferences derived from economics to those presently embodied in laws. See, e.g., Samuels (1974, p. 11) (quoted *supra* note 48).

78. See Frohock (1979, p. 177) (discussing need for category of quasi-public good, lying between a public good and a competitive good); Landis (1938) (quoted *supra* note 70); and Quirk (1981, pp. ix–x, 4, *passim*) (theories of "clientelism," "agency capture," and "industry protection" assume that the appointment of proindustry regulators maximizes agency budgets and their employees' opportunities for jobs in industry later). If theories mentioned by Quirk are correct, and many economists assume that they are, many of the failings of public bureaucracies can be attributed to their corruption by business bureaucracies. On their face, these problems can be solved rather easily through legislation.

79. "Legal theory stands between philosophy and political [and, I would add, economic] theory. It is thus dominated by the same antinomies." (Friedmann, 1960, p. 28) Some of these antinomies are: idealism and positivism, stability and change, subjective and objective criteria, communitarian and individualist ideals, autocracy and democracy, and nationalism and internationalism (*id.*, pp. 29–39). See Radbruch (1950, pp. 107-112) (antinomies of justice, a relativistic expediency familiar to law and economics scholars and political scientists, and a legal certainty/positivity); Fatouros (1980) (quoted *supra* note 11); and Geertz (1980) (criticizing trendy classifications of life as game theory, as drama, and as "text").

80. It is perhaps surprising that these insights come primarily from analyses of contract law. See, e.g., Macaulay (1963); Sharp (1966, p. 216). Legal analyses based on antinomies are far from an unalloyed curse, however: the "dialectical tension" between antinomies "gives law its vitality, its ability to deal with a multitude of concrete situations" (Fatouros, 1980, p. 105).

On reasoning by analogy in economics, see e.g., Wagner (1977, p. 403): Markets (and political processes) are better compared to Erector sets with wills of their own than to subatomic particles. Analogies have also figured prominently in legal reasoning. One example is the misleading 19th-century view of the corporation as "the Republic in miniature": "The shareholders were the electorate, the directors the legislature enacting general policies and committing them to the officers for execution. A judiciary was unnecessary, since the state had kindly permitted the use of its own." (Chayes, 1970, p. 39) This kind of reasoning by analogy, "the method of *successive limited comparison*," has a significant impact on bureacratic decision making: see Lindblom (1979, pp. 161–166, 174).

81. See *First National Bank v. Bellotti*, 435 U.S. 765 (1978) (commercial free speech); *United States v. Topco Associates*, 405 U.S. 596, 610 (1970) (antitrust laws are "the Magna Carta of free

enterprise," as "important to the preservation of economic freedom . . . as the Bill of Rights is to . . . personal freedoms"); *Silver v. N.Y.S.E.*, 373 U.S. 341 (1963) (nascent "commercial due process" within a self-regulating public entity); *Radiant Burners, Inc. v. People's Gas, Light, & Coke Co.*, 364 U.S. 656 (1961) (nascent "commercial due process" in a private trade association); *Appalachian Coals, Inc. v. United States*, 288 U.S. 344, 359–60 (1932) (Sherman Act "a charter of freedom," with "a generality and adaptability comparable to that . . . in constitutional provisions"). The argument runs that the law and economics, politics, etc., of antitrust, regulated industries, takings under the Fifth and Fourteenth Amendments, etc., are parts of an as yet insufficiently explored whole which cannot be readily discerned through the piecemeal, case-by-case approach presently used. See, e.g., *New State Ice v. Liebman*, 285 U.S. 262, 280 (1931) (Brandeis, J., dissenting); Hurst (1977, pp. 45–46, *passim*) (an American "constitutional ideal"); Grey (1975); and *supra* note 67. There have been attempts to deal with related matters within the framework of "policy sciences": see, e.g., Lasswell (1971, pp. 160–168) ("Bibliographic Notes"). But these attempts seem to have failed, by and large. Studies of the economic constitution should be more critical, incorporate economics insights, and focus on, for example, a great fumbling and delay in the regulation of banks and corporations, and an inability to coordinate the macroeconomic policies of Congress, the executive, its agencies, the Federal Reserve, etc. At present, the macro descriptions in much of law and economics scholarship seem inappropriately grounded in the micro assumptions of monetarism, supply-sideism, and the economics of imperfect information and rational expectations.

82. Mishan (1976, p. 390). See Frug (1984, p. 1376; quoted in part, *supra* note 25); Samuels (1981, p. 154) (quoting Veljanovski).

83. See *Myers v. United States*, 272 U.S. 52, 240, 293 (1926) (Brandeis, J., dissenting) ("The doctrine of separation of powers was adopted by the Convention in 1787, not to promote efficiency but to preclude the exercise of arbitrary power."); Posner (1981, pp. 100, 112); Frug (1984, pp. 1374–1378); and Samuels (1981, pp. 157–158), and (p. 160) ("By giving rights to the party with the maximum valuation, the state would reinforce the party whose dominance is a function of other laws, which would enable the party to be both willing and able to pay (value) more."). Summers (1983, p. 269) makes an interesting point: "The definition of due process and of individual entitlements, the legitimacy of public control of private behavior, the structure of public institutions—all involve basic value choices that transcend economics. But they transcend law as well. Do we thereby conclude that lawyers have nothing to say about such matters?" Of course not. But if legal technicalities are not allowed to dominate, economists' techniques should not dominate either.

84. Mishan (1976, pp. 382–386); Reder (1982, p. 25); Summers (1983, p. 343) (citing Gellhorn and Robinson, 1983); Horowitz (1980); Trebilcock (1983). See Bernstein (1955, p. 270); Strasser, Bard, and Arthur (1982, p. 580; and p. 583) (bias in law and economics in favor of presently wealthy and productive individuals); Tushnet (1980, p. 1389); and *supra* note 43. Compare Murphy (1981, pp. 126–127, 141–142) (liberalism) with Stigler (1959, pp. 524, 527–528) (economists' conservatism), and compare Darwall (1983, p. 60) with Reder (1982, p. 31).

Harry Johnson's definition of the purpose of economics, "as guarding against waste of time in ideological polemics," reminds one of a "nineteenth century Briton's comment, 'I wish I was as certain about anything as Macaulay is about everything' " (Cox, 1979, p. 267). One of the few economists who does not adopt a Wicksellian approach finds that: "Any individualistic conception of 'the State' is a gross aberration . . . [and] nothing but a blind ideology of shopkeepers and street hawkers" (Olson, 1965, p. 101, quoting Hans Ritschel). Ritschel goes on (*id.*) to describe the "fundamental power" of the communal spirit, which is based not on market relations but on love, sacrifice, solidarity, and generosity. Understanding this spirit can lead to meaningful explanations of the state economy and even of coercion, as means of putting this spirit into effect. Ritschel's arguments are no less ideological than Posner's, of course. But *as ideology* they seem no less convincing. See, e.g., *supra* note 24.

85. Posner (1977, pp. 404, 439–441); Komesar (1981, p. 1356); Michelman (1979, p. 308) (paraphrasing Posner fairly). But see Priest (1980) (an effective critique); Reder (1982, p. 34) (Posner's, Becker's, and Stigler's argument that pre-20th-century common law allocated liability to

persons with the lowest costs of loss-prevention is an example of the "thrust for endogenization"—see *supra* note 32); Samuels (1981, p. 149) (Posner approximates Marx's view by finding that the common law assumes its modern shape in the 19th century, when economic values were an important part of the prevailing ideology) and (p. 171) (in *The Economics of Justice* (1981), Posner "does not say that every decision by a court makes legal, philosophical or economic (wealth maximizing) sense; but that is the gravamen of his argument"); and *supra* note 14 and *infra* note 90.

    86.   Cardozo (1947, pp. 107, 135, 150–153, 177, 182). See Davis et al. (1962, pp. 126–127) (O. W. Holmes saw the social utility of the rule as the "inarticulate major premise" of judicial decisions); and Komesar (1981, p. 1364) ("'conflicts over the distribution of scarce resources should be resolved by reference to the needs and values of the members of society, and . . . the weight assigned to these . . . should reflect the intensity of the feeling of . . . individuals'").

    87.   The Chicago School is preoccupied with the "supposed virtues of (largely judge-made) private law, while showing little inclination to explore the affirmative functions of public law" (Hansmann, 1983, p. 225). See *id.* Clearly, there are some differences in approach. One (overdrawn) distinction has it that the "judge addresses himself to standards of consistency, equivalence, predictability, the legislator to fair shares, social utility and equitable distribution" (Hayek, 1973, p. 124, quoting Paul Freund). Federal, state, and local legislatures grind out 150,000 new laws each year, each requiring an average of ten new regulations (Tribe, 1979). This mess could hardly be efficient, but neither is the current explosion in litigation that turns on private as well as public laws. With all due respect to Posner, it is hard to spot any drift toward efficient case law, now or earlier.

    88.   The burden of proof typically required is one of showing that "a rearrangement is 'efficient,' i.e., if someone gains while no one loses. Recently, even this has been criticized as overlooking gain or loss from change in relative position" (Musgrave, 1962, p. 110). Of course, this assumes the congruence of efficiency and the public interest. But see *supra* text accompanying notes 73–74; *infra* notes 90–92. The historical basis for this argument is exceedingly fragile: see Diesing (1971, p. 11); *supra* note 63. Law and economics "always begins with a historically given state of the law. . . . It has no way of explaining or criticizing the law's state . . . , except to trace it back to some . . . prior stage of law, about which nothing of economic relevance can be said. . . ." (Michelman, 1980, p. 445) In other words, law and economics is presently unable to trace a law back to the economic constitution (Michelman's "foundations of the underlying *corpus juris*," pp. 445–446) or forward as a coherent and consistent part of that evolving constitution. A more likely explanation is that judges exercise social judgment, while choosing one suboptimal outcome rather than another (Oliver, 1979, p. 39).

    89.   Gellhorn and Robinson (1983, p. 248, quoting Solow) (economic analysis is influential because it demonstrates rigor and ways of accounting for the interplay of facts, values, and theories); Reder (1982, p. 35) (great impact of Chicago School scientific and expository talent on an intellectually bankrupt conservativism); and *supra* notes 6–7, 48. Jurisprudence is sometimes so open-minded as to make the analyst seem a credulous bubblehead. Economics properly insists that analyses be tighted up, but this can be at the expense of a dogmatism and a narrower focus: too many variables which lawyers would like to analyze are treated as "given." See Breyer (1983, p. 304); Loevinger (1968, p. 179) (jurisprudence "is based on speculation, supposition and superstition," and is "concerned with meaningless questions"); Reder (1982, p. 21).

    For the future, jurisprudence must openly and honestly make and defend value judgments, to identify those ends to which efficiency remains a viable means. To purport to eliminate value judgments about ends is to eliminate the very subject matter of social science. Jurisprudence must maintain and extend a humane and humanistic element in legal discourse. It must show that law is not always dependent, parasitic, and amenable to reduction into something else. The shadings and qualifications that the real world imposes on theory must be identified, along with the limits of an economic orthodoxy and of its trendy new movements. See Robinson (1970, p. 122); Fried (1981b, p. 46) (concepts such as entitlement, fault, property, and responsibility are insoluble in the medium of economic discourse); Michelman (1983, p. 192); Priest (1983, p. 438); Summers (1983, p. 344); Scheiber (1980, p. 1189); and *supra* notes 7, 73 and text accompanying. For example, capital is separate from the capitalist and land from the owner, but labor is not separate from the laborer (Mishan, 1976, p. 69).

Many economists tacitly ignore this distinction while, for example, treating high levels both of unemployment and of idle capital as equally "voluntary." Such a perspective could foster the "alienation" of labor, in both the sociologists' and the economists' sense. Economists report but seldom experience unemployment, the experience of "rising in the morning with fading hope to a day committed to desultory inquiries, new deprivations, numbing frustrations, humiliation, and a growing apathy" (Lane, 1962, p. 417).

90.   Posner (1979, p. 292–293). This is a milder (or revisionist) Posner who admits that evidence for the efficiency of the common law, "the only positive theory of the common law . . . in contention at this time," is not of such strength as to encourage complacency (pp. 291, 294). See *supra* note 14.

91.   One reason why theory seems so potent is that it divorces such ideals as efficiency, liberty, and equality from the social structures and practices that give these ideals their practical effect. The need to sacrifice a theoretical potency to an administrative practicality is manifest in, for example, antitrust laws (see Sullivan, 1977, pp. 1, 8, 12), and race relations. The mainstream of law and economics (apart from Posner) rests content with declaring both racism and reverse discrimination to be economically inefficient. Professorial demonstrations of an economic irrationality are unlikely to knock out a larger and stronger irrationality, however. For a political economy concerned with the legitimacy of public policy and aware that a failure to act ratifies the status quo, the relevant question is: which recalcitrant minority—racists or blacks—is the law to succor, and in which circumstances? Once these decisions are made, and altered from time to time, the more or less uncaring majority is deeply influenced by the way the law lies. In economics terms, policy shifts in race relations since the 1960s (and until recently at least) illustrate the application of theories of the second best and of workable competition, especially through attempts to eliminate barriers to entry and predatory practices in housing, education, and job markets. See Grey (1976, p. 886) (discussed *infra* note 93); *infra* note 92.

More general performance goals under the economic constitution are rather easy to state; low unemployment, reasonable price stability, adequate economic growth, avoiding artificially contrived income inequalities, and a reasonably healthy environment. See, e.g., Bain (1968, p. 13); Colm (1962, p. 124). Dissensus over the best means to these goals is manifest, however, particularly as these means have required painful trade-offs among goals. Innovative new approaches seem called for, in light of the signal failures of the old means in recent years.

92.   There are many reasons why all of the numerous assumptions law and economics scholars make concerning pure competition within a general equilibrium (or concerning a Pareto optimality) cannot be realized in the real world. (In economic theory, these reasons include: economies of scale, barriers to entry, externalities, unanticipated risks resulting from imperfect information, complicated horizontal and vertical relationships in a modern economy, and the desire for real and apparent variety that spawns product differentiation.) Empirical findings are incomplete and often inconclusive. The theory of the second best thus asserts that it is by no means certain that public policy should come as close as possible to the results attainable in theory under pure competition. This amounts to a counsel of despair, and it is at this point where the theory of workable competition can usefully take over. It attempts more of a macro perspective, relating particular problems to general performance goals (see *supra* note 91) rather than treating them in isolation—in a piecemeal fashion, frozen in time. The effects of labor and government are treated, as well as those of business, under the theory of workable competition, and particular emphasis is placed on the adaptability of institutions to changed circumstances. There is a rather surprising near-consensus over the relevant ingredients of competition among theorists of a workable competition, whose policy prescriptions turn on a detailed knowledge of the circumstances peculiar to a particular problem. The theory of workable competition has been approved in such antitrust cases as: *United States v. Dupont (Cellophane)*, 351 U.S. 377 (1956); *F.T.C. v. Cement Institute*, 333 U.S. 683 (1948); *American Tobacco Co. v. United States*, 306 U.S. 208 (1939); *United States v. United Shoe Mach.*, 110 F. Supp. 295, 344 (D. Mass. 1953). See Bain (1968, pp. 13–15, 464–467); Koch (1974, pp. 53, 314, 322, 347); Miller (1978, pp. 445–446); Markham (1963, pp. 79–81); Scherer (1970, pp. 22–25). But see Musgrave (1962, pp. 108–109) (discussed *supra* note 74) and (p. 110) (quoted *supra* note 88); and *supra* notes 12-15.

For examples of the kinds of analyses that could be carried out under theories of workable competition and the second best, see DeLong (1982, p. 888) (discussed *supra* note 71); Gutmann (1983) (discussed *supra* note 52); Heymann (1973, pp. 864–866) (ways of striking a balance between the costs of discussion and stalemate and the costs of having individual and group preferences overriden); Olson (1965, pp. 113–118) (discussing studies by Otto von Gierke, F. W. Maitland, John Dewey, Emile Durkheim, G. D. H. Cole, John R. Commons, Thorsten Veblen, John M. Clark, J. K. Galbraith, and Earl Latham); Strasser, Bard, and Arthur (1982, p. 590) (consumers of law and economics must identify potential qualifications on ostensibly unqualified analyses—circumstances where individuals do not behave as rational maximizers, where markets are not perfectly competitive, and where private exchanges will not roughly approximate socially optimal results); and *supra* notes 47, 82-83 and text accompanying.

93.   See, e.g., Ginsberg (1965, pp. 41, 99–117); Grey (1966, p. 886) ("weak but coherent" property concept tolerating redistribution—tending toward equality and social cohesion—where supported by a consensus in which the coercion of marginal recalcitrants is permitted); McKean (1975, p. 34); Majone (1975, p. 52) (practical impossibility of separating equity and efficiency illustrates the importance of devising second best or merely better policies). McKean (1975, p. 34) emphasizes social cohesion through participation: "[E]ach person need not benefit each time or in the very short run in order for social contracts to be viable. It is important, though, for each person to anticipate that his turn will come and that he will receive a stream of net benefits during [his life]."

94.   Paton (1972, p. 409). See Kitch (1983) (quoted *supra* note 25); Olson (1982, p. 96) ("The range of statistical techniques available to the modern econometrician is so wide that the zealous advocate can often 'torture the data until it confesses'.") and (p. 183) (the skill and cunning of the protagonists is such that logical errors are not the basis for disagreement in macroeconomics; most differences occur over judgments about inconclusive empirical evidence); Stigler (1959, p. 531) ("The apparatus of economics is very flexible: without breaking the rules of the profession . . . a sufficiently clever person can reach *any* conclusion he wishes on any *real* problem."); Strasser, Bard, and Arthur (1982, p. 591) (quoted *supra* note 5).

REFERENCES

Ackerman, Bruce, ed. (1975) *Economic Foundations of Property Law*, Boston, Little, Brown.
Alchian, Armen. (1975) "Corporate Management and Property Rights," p. 499 in H. Manne, ed., *The Economics of Legal Relationships*, St. Paul, West.
———— and Harold Demsetz. (1975) "Production, Information Costs and Economic Organization," p. 555 in H. Manne, ed., *The Economics of Legal Relationships*, St. Paul, West.
Anderson, Alison. (1978) "Conflicts of Interest: Efficiency, Fairness and the Corporate Structure," *U.C.L.A. Law Review*, Vol. 25, p. 738.
Anderson, Charles. (1979) "The Place of Principles in Policy Analysis," *American Political Science Review*, Vol. 73, p. 711.
Anderson, James. (1966) "Public Economic Policy and the Problem of Compliance," *Houston Law Review*, Vol. 4, p. 62.
Anderson, Terry, and P. S. Hill (1975) "The Evolution of Property Rights," *Journal of Law and Economics*, Vol 18, p. 163.
Argyris, Chris. (1960) *Understanding Organizational Behavior*, Homewood, Ill., Dorsey Press.
Arrow, Kenneth (1975) "Gifts and Exchanges," p. 13 in E. Phelps, ed., *Altruism, Morality and Economic Theory*, New York, Russell Sage.
Ault, David, and Gilbert Rutman. (1979) "The Development of Individual Rights to Property in Tribal Africa," *Journal of Law and Economics*, Vol. 22, p. 163.
Bain, Joe. (1968) *Industrial Organization*, 2d ed., New York, John Wiley.
Balch, George. (1980) "The Stick, the Carrot, and Other Strategies," *Law and Policy Quarterly*, Vol. 2, p. 35.

Barraclough, Geoffrey. (1981) *An Introduction to Contemporary History*, Harmondsworth, England, Penguin.

Bebchuk, Lucian. (1980) "The Pursuit of a Bigger Pie," *Hofstra Law Review*, Vol. 8, p. 671.

Becker, Gary. (1976) *The Economic Approach to Human Behavior*, Chicago, University of Chicago Press.

Berle, Adolf. (1965) "Property, Production and Revolution," *Columbia Law Review*, Vol. 65, p. 1.

Bernstein, Marver. (1955) *Regulating Business by Independent Commission*, Princeton, Princeton University Press.

Billig, Michael. (1982) *Ideology and Social Psychology*, Oxford, Basil Blackwell.

Black, Donald. (1973) "The Boundaries of Legal Sociology," p. 41 in D. Black and M. Mileski, eds., *The Social Organization of Law*, New York, Seminar Press.

Bodenheimer, Edgar. (1962) "Prolegomena to a Theory of the Public Interest," p. 205 in C. Friedrich, ed., *Nomos V: The Public Interest*, New York, Atherton Press.

Boulding, Kenneth. (1969) "Economics as Moral Science," *American Economic Review*, Vol. 59, p. 1.

Breton, Alfred, and Ronald Wintrobe. (1982) *The Logic of Bureaucratic Conduct*, Cambridge, Cambridge University Press.

Brewster, Kingman. (1970) "The Corporation and Economic Federalism," p. 72 in E. Mason, ed., *The Corporation in Modern Society*, New York, Atheneum.

Breyer, Stephen. (1983) "Economics for Lawyers and Judges," *Journal of Legal Education*, Vol. 33, p. 294.

Brietzke, Paul. (1984) "Public Policy," *Valparaiso University Law Review*, Vol. 18, p. 741.

Buchanan, James, and Gordon Tulloch. (1975) "Simple Majority Voting," p. 237, B. Ackerman, ed., *Economic Foundations of Property Law*, Boston, Little, Brown.

Calabresi, Guido, and A. D. Melamid. (1975) "Property Rules, Liability Rules, and Inalienability," p. 31 in B. Ackerman, ed., *Economic Foundations of Property Law*, Boston, Little, Brown.

Cardozo, Benjamin. (1947) "The Nature of the Judicial Process," p. 107 in M. Hall, ed., *Selected Writings of Benjamin Nathan Cardozo*, New York, Fallon.

Chapman, John, and J. R. Pennock. (1983) "Preface," p. xiii in J. Chapman and J. Pennock, eds., *Nomos XXV: Liberal Democracy*, New York, University Press.

Chayes, Abram. (1976) "The Role of the Judge in Public Law Litigation," *Harvard Law Review*, Vol. 89, p. 1281.

————. (1970) "The Modern Corporation and the Rule of Law," p. 39 in E. Mason, ed., *The Corporation in Modern Society*, New York, Atheneum.

Cheung, Steven. (1974) "A Theory of Price Control," *Journal of Law and Economics*, Vol. 17, p. 53.

Coase, Ronald. (1960) "The Problem of Social Cost," *Journal of Law and Economics*, Vol. 3, p. 1.

Coleman, Jules. (1980) "Efficiency, Utility, and Wealth Maximization," *Hofstra Law Review*, Vol. 8, p. 509.

Colm, Gerhard. (1962) "The Public Interest," p. 115 in C. Friedrich, ed., *Nomos V: The Public Interest*, New York, Atherton.

Commons, John. (1926) "Anglo-American Law and Economics," unidentified mimeo, available in Yale Law Library.

Connelly, Mark. (1981) "Secrets and Smokescreens," *Wisconsin Law Review*, Vol. 1981, p. 207.

Cox, Robert. (1979) "Ideologies and the New International Economic Order," *International Organizations*, Vol. 33, p. 257.

Crampton, Roger. (1983) "Introduction," *Journal of Legal Education*, Vol. 33, p. 183.

Cranston, Ross. (1977) "Creeping Economism," *British Journal of Law and Society*, Vol. 4, p. 103.

Dahl, Robert, and Charles Lindblom. (1976) *Politics, Economics, and Welfare*, Chicago, University of Chicago Press.

————. (1956). *A Preface to Democratic Theory*, Chicago, University of Chicago Press.

Dahlman, Carl. (1979) "The Problem of Externality," *Journal of Law and Economics*, Vol. 22, p. 141.

Darwall, Stephen. (1983) "Equal Representation," p. 51 in R. Pennock and J. Chapman, eds., *Nomos XXV: Liberal Democracy,* New York, New York University Press.

Davies, David. (1971) "The Efficiency of Private vs. Public Firms: The Case of Australia's Two Airlines," *Journal of Law and Economics,* Vol. 14, p. 149.

Davis, F., et al. (1962) *Society and the Law,* New York, Free Press.

DeLong, James. (1982) "Review," *Michigan Law Review,* Vol. 80, p. 885.

Diamond, Peter, & Michael Rothschild, eds. (1978) *Uncertainty in Economics,* New York, Academic Press.

Diesing, Paul. (1971) *Patterns of Discovery in the Social Sciences,* New York, Aldine.

Dorfman, Joseph. (1961) "Chancellor Kent and the Developing American Economy," *Columbia Law Review,* Vol. 61, p. 1290.

Downs, Anthony. (1957) *An Economic Theory of Democracy,* New York, Harper and Row.

Downs, George. (1976) *Bureaucracy, Innovation and Public Policy,* Lexington, Mass., Lexington Books.

Dreiser, Theodore. (1925) *The Titan,* Garden City, N.J., Garden City Publishing.

Dworkin, Ronald. (1980) "Why Efficiency?", *Hofstra Law Review,* Vol. 8, p. 563.

_____ . (1977) *Taking Rights Seriously,* London, Duckworth.

Ellickson, Robert. (1977) "Suburban Growth Controls: An Economic and Legal Analysis," *Yale Law Journal,* Vol. 86, p. 385.

Farber, Daniel. (1980) "Reassessing the Economic Efficiency of Compensatory Damages for Breach of Contract," *Virginia Law Review,* Vol. 66, p. 1443.

Farrar, John. (1977) *Introduction to Legal Method,* London, Sweet and Maxwell.

Fatouros, A. A. (1980) "The Law of the New International Economic Order," *Willamette Law Review,* Vol. 17, p. 93.

Fischel, Daniel. (1978) "Efficient Captial Market Theory, the Market for Corporate Control, and the Regulation of Cash Tender Offers," *Texas Law Review,* Vol. 57, p. 1.

Fitzgerald, P. J. (1966) *Salmond on Jurisprudence,* 12th ed., London, Sweet and Maxwell.

Flynn, John. (1980-81) "Appendix: Definitions and Assumptions of Economic Analysis," *Southwestern University Law Review,* Vol. 12, p. 361.

Fried, Charles. (1981a) *Contract As Promise,* Cambridge, Harvard University Press.

_____ . (1981b) "The Artificial Reason of the Law," *Texas Law Review,* Vol. 60, p. 35.

Friedman, Lawrence. (1975) *The Legal System,* New York, Russell Sage.

_____ . (1971) "Law, Order and History," *South Dakota Law Review,* Vol. 16, p. 242.

_____ . (1965) *Contract Law in America,* Madison, University of Wisconsin Press.

Friedman, Milton. (1962) *Capitalism and Freedom,* Chicago, University of Chicago Press.

Friedman, Wolfgang. (1960) *Legal Theory,* 4th ed., Toronto, Carswell.

Frohock, Fred. (1979) *Public Policy,* Englewood Cliffs, N.J., Prentice-Hall.

Frug, Gerald. (1984) "The Ideology of Bureaucracy in American Law," *Harvard Law Review,* Vol. 97, p. 1277.

Galbraith, John. (1975) *Economics, Peace and Laughter,* Harmondsworth, England, Penguin.

Geertz, Clifford. (1980) "Blurred Genres," *American Scholar,* Vol. 49, p. 165.

Gellhorn, Ernest, and Glen Robinson. (1983) "The Role of Economic Analysis in Legal Education," *Journal of Legal Education,* Vol. 33, p. 247.

Ginsberg, Morris. (1965) *On Justice in Society,* Baltimore, Penguin.

Goldschmid, Harvey, ed. (1979) *Business Disclosure: Government's Need to Know,* New York, McGraw-Hill.

Green, Mark, and Ralph Nader. (1973) "Economic Regulation vs. Competition," *Yale Law Journal,* Vol. 82, p. 871.

Grey, Thomas. (1976) "Property and Need: The Welfare State and Theories of Distributive Justice," *Stanford Law Review,* Vol. 28, p. 877.

_____. (1975) "Do We Have an Unwritten Constitution?" *Stanford Law Review*, Vol. 27, p. 703.

Gutmann, Amy. (1983) "Is Freedom Academic?" p. 257 in R. Pennock and J. Chapman, eds., *Nomos XXV: Liberal Democracy*, New York, New York University Press.

Hale, Robert Lee. (1943) "Bargaining, Duress, and Economic Liberty," *Columbia Law Review*, Vol. 43, p. 603.

Hansmann, Henry. (1983) "The Current State of Law-and-Economics Scholarship," *Journal of Legal Education*, Vol. 33, p. 217.

Hayek, Frederick. (1973) *Law, Legislation, and Liberty*, Vol. 1, London, Routledge and Kegan Paul.

Heymann, Philip. (1973) "The Problem of Coordination," *Harvard Law Review*, Vol. 86, p. 797.

Hindley, Brian. (Nov. 1969) "Capitalism and the Corporation," *Economica*, p. 426.

Hirsch, Werner. (1974) "Reducing Law's Uncertainty and Complexity," *U.C.L.A. Law Review*, Vol. 21, p. 1223.

Horowitz, Morton. (1980) "Law and Economics," *Hofstra Law Review*, Vol. 8, p. 905.

Hummel, Ralph. (1977) *The Bureaucratic Experience*, New York, St. Martin's Press.

Huntington, Samuel. (1981) *American Politics*, Cambridge, Belknap Press.

Hurst, J. Willard (1977) *Law and Social Order in the United States*, Ithaca, Cornell University Press.

_____. (1971) "Legal Elements in U.S. History," p. 3 in D. Fleming and B. Bailyn, eds., *Law in American History*, Boston, Little, Brown.

_____. (1970) *The Legitimacy of the Business Corporation*, Charlottesville, University Press of Virginia.

Kearl, J. R., et al. (1979) "A Confusion of Economists?" *American Economic Review*, Vol. 69, p. 28.

Kelman, Mark. (1983) "Misunderstanding Social Life," *Journal of Legal Education*, Vol. 33, p. 274.

Kennedy, Duncan. (1981) "Cost-Benefit Analysis of Entitlement Problems," *Stanford Law Review*, Vol. 33, p. 387.

_____ and Frank Michelman. (1980) "Are Property and Contract Efficient?," *Hofstra Law Review*, Vol. 8, p. 711.

_____. (1976) "Form and Substance in Private Law Adjudication," *Harvard Law Review*, Vol. 89, p. 1685.

Kirshen, H. B. (1932) "Essays in Legal Economics," *Maine Bulletin*, Vol. 35, p. 7.

Kitch, Edmund. (1983) "The Intellectual Foundations of 'Law and Economics'," *Journal of Legal Education*, Vol. 33, p. 184.

Koch, James. (1974) *Industrial Organization and Prices*, Englewood Cliffs, N.Y., Prentice-Hall.

Kolko, Gabriel. (1976) *Main Currents in Modern American History*, New York, Harper and Row.

Komesar, Neil. (1981) "In Search of a General Approach to Legal Analysis," *Michigan Law Review*, Vol. 79, p. 1350.

Kronman, Anthony, and Richard Posner, eds. (1979) *The Economics of Contract Law*, Boston, Little, Brown.

Landis, James. (1938) *The Administrative Process*, New Haven, Yale University Press.

Lane, Robert (1962) *Political Ideology*, Glencoe, N.Y., Free Press of Glencoe.

Lange, Oscar. (1938) *On the Economic Theory of Socialism*, B. Lippincott, ed., Minneapolis, University of Minnesota Press.

Lasswell, Harold. (1971) *A Pre-View of the Policy Sciences.*

_____. (1936) *Politics: Who Gets What, When, How.*

Latham, Earl. (1970) "The Body Politic of the Corporation," p. 218 in E. Mason, ed., *The Corporation in Modern Society*, New York, Atheneum.

Lewis, Eugene. (1977) *American Politics in a Bureaucratic Age*, Cambridge, Winthrop.

Lindblom, Charles. (1979) "The Science of Muddling Through," p. 160 in R. Rabin, ed., *Perspectives on the Administrative Process*, Boston, Little, Brown.

Lineberry, Robert. (1978) *American Public Policy*, New York, Harper and Row.

Loevinger, Lee. (1968) "Jurimetrics," p. 178 in R. Simon, ed., *The Sociology of Law*, San Francisco, Chandler.

Lowi, Theodore. (1969) *The End of Liberalism*, New York, Norton.

McCarthy, Thomas. (1978) *The Critical Theory of Jurgen Habermas*, Cambridge, MIT Press.

McConnell, Grant. (1966) "The Steel-Price Controversy," p. 127 in R. Ripley, ed., *Public Policies and Their Politics*, New York, Norton.

McCraw, Thomas. (1984) *Prophets of Regulation*, Cambridge, Belknap Press.

McKean, Roland. (1975) "Economics of Trust, Altruism and Corporate Responsibility," p. 29 in E. Phelps, ed., *Altruism, Morality and Economic Theory*, New York, Russell Sage.

Macaulay, Stewart. (Nov. 1963) "The Use and Non-Use of Contracts in the Manufacturing Industry," *Practical Lawyer*, Vol. 9, p. 13.

Machlup, Fritz. (1978) *Methodology of Economics and Other Social Sciences*, New York, Academic Press.

Macneil, Ian. (1978) "Contracts," *Northwestern University Law Review*, Vol. 72, p. 854.

—————— . (1974) "The Many Futures of Contract," *Southern California Law Review*, Vol. 47, p. 691.

Majone, Giandomenico. (1975) "The Feasibility of Social Policies," *Policy Science*, Vol. 6, p. 49.

Maris, Robin, and Dennis Mueller. (1980) "The Corporation, Competition, and the Invisible Hand," *Journal of Economic Literature*, Vol. 18, p. 32.

Markham, Jesse. (1963) "Workable Competition and Antitrust," p. 79 in J. Markham, ed., *The American Economy*, New York, George Braziller.

Mason, Edward. (1970) "Introduction," p. 1 in E. Mason, ed., *The Corporation in Modern Society*, New York, Atheneum.

Mayhew, Leon. (1971) "Stability and Change in Legal Systems," p. 187 in B. Barker and A. Inkeles, eds. *Stability and Social Change*, Boston, Little, Brown.

Meehan, Eugene. (1981) *Reasoned Argument in Social Science*, Westport, Greenwood Press.

Meltsner, Arnold. (1976) *Policy Analysts in the Bureaucracy*, Berkeley, University of California Press.

Michelman, Frank. (1983) "Reflections on Professional Education, Legal Scholarship, and the Law-and-Economics Movement," *Journal of Legal Education*, Vol. 33, p. 197.

—————— . (1980) "Constitutions, Statutes and the Theory of Efficient Adjudication," *Journal of Legal Studies*, Vol. 9, p. 431.

—————— . (1979) "Comment," *University of Chicago Law Review*, Vol. 46, p. 306.

Miller, Arthur Selwyn. (1972) "Legal Foundations of the Corporate State," *Journal of Economic Issues*, Vol. 6, p. 59.

Miller, Roger. (1978) *Intermediate Microeconomics*, New York, McGraw-Hill.

Mishan, E. J. (1976) *Cost-Benefit Analysis*, new ed., New York, Praeger.

Moore, Michael. (1981) "The Semantics of Judging," *Southern California Law Review*, Vol. 54, p. 151.

Murphy, Cornelius. (1981) "Liberalism and Political Society," *American Journal of Jurisprudence*, Vol. 26, p. 125.

Musgrave, R. A. (1962) "The Public Interest," p. 108 in C. Friedrich, ed., *Nomos V: The Public Interest*, New York, Atherton.

Myrdal, Gunnar. (1954) *The Political Element in the Development of Economic Theory*, P. Streeten, trans.

Niskanen, William. (1975) "Bureaucrats and Politicians," *Journal of Law and Economics*, Vol. 18, p. 617

Nonet, Phillippe, and Philip Selznick. (1978) *Law and Society in Transition: Responsive Law*, New York, Harper and Row.

Nozick, Bernard. (1974) *Anarchy, State, and Utopia*, Oxford, Basil Blackwell.

Okun, Arthur. (1975) *Equality and Efficiency: The Big Tradeoff,* Washington, Brookings Institution.

Oliver, J. M. (1979) *Law and Economics,* London, George Allen and Unwin.

Olson, Mancur. (1982) *The Rise and Decline of Nations: Economic Growth, Stagflation, and Social Rigidities,* New Haven, Yale University Press.

_____. (1965) *The Logic of Collective Action,* Cambridge, Harvard University Press.

Parsons, Talcott. (1969) "Methodology of Social Science," p. 63 in R. Rogers, ed. in part, *Max Weber's Ideal Type Theory,* New York, Philosophical Library.

_____. (1950). *The Social System,* London, Routledge and Kegan Paul.

Paton, George. (1972) *A Textbook of Jurisprudence,* 4th ed., Oxford, Clarendon Press.

Peltzman, Sam. (1976) "Toward a More General Theory of Regulation," *Journal of Law and Economics,* Vol. 19, p. 211.

Phelps, Edmund. (1975) "Introduction," p. 1 in E. Phelps, ed., *Altruism, Morality and Economic Theory,* New York, Russell Sage.

Posner, Richard. (1981) *The Economics of Justice,* Cambridge, Harvard University Press.

_____. (1980) "The Political and Ethical Basis of the Efficiency Norm in Common Law Adjudication," *Hofstra Law Review,* p. 487.

_____. (1979a) "Some Uses and Misuses of Economics in Law," *University of Chicago Law Review,* Vol. 46, p. 281.

_____. (1979b) "Utilitarianism, Economics, and Legal Theory," *Journal of Legal Studies,* Vol. 8, p. 103.

_____. (1977) *Economic Analysis of Law,* 2nd ed., Boston, Little, Brown.

_____. (1971) "Taxation by Regulation," *Bell Journal of Economics and Management Science,* Vol. 2, p. 22.

Priest, George. (1983) "Social Science Theory and Legal Education," *Journal of Legal Education,* Vol. 33, p. 437.

_____. (1980) "Selective Characteristics of Litigation," *Journal of Legal Studies,* Vol. 9, p. 399.

Quirk, Paul. (1981) *Industrial Influence in Federal Regulatory Agencies,* Princeton, Princeton University Press.

Rabin, Robert. (1979) "Introduction," p. 1 in R. Rabin, ed., *Perspectives on the Administrative Process,* Boston, Little, Brown.

Radbruch, Gustav. (1950) "Legal Philosophy," p. 43 in K. Wilks, transl., *The Legal Philosophies of Lask, Radbruch and Dabin,* Cambridge, Harvard University Press.

Reder, Melvin. (1982) "Chicago Economics," *Journal of Economic Literature,* Vol. 20, p. 1.

Renner, Karl. (1949) *The Institutions of Private Law,* London, Routledge and Kegan Paul.

Robinson, Joan. (1970) *Freedom and Necessity,* London, Allen and Unwin.

Rogers, Rolf. (1969) *Max Weber's Ideal Type Theory,* New York, Philosophical Library.

Royko, Mike. (1971) *Boss: Mayor Richard J. Daley of Chicago,* London, Barrie and Jenkins.

Rubin, Paul. (1978) "The Theory of the Firm and the Structure of the Franchise Contract," *Journal of Law and Economics,* Vol. 21, p. 223.

Samuels, Warren. (1981) "Review," *Texas Law Review,* Vol. 60, p. 147.

_____. (1974) "The Coase Theorem and the Study of Law and Economics," *Natural Resources Law Journal,* Vol. 14, p. 1.

_____. (1973) "The Economy as a System of Power," *University of Miami Law Review,* Vol. 27, p. 261.

_____. (1971) "Interrelations between Legal and Economic Processes," *Journal of Law and Economics,* Vol. 14, p. 435.

Samuelson, Paul. (1964) *Economics,* 6th ed., New York, McGraw-Hill.

Scheiber, Harry. (1980) "Public Economic Policy and the American Legal System," *Wisconsin Law Review,* Vol. 1980, p. 1149.

_____. (1971) "The Road to *Munn,*" p. 329 in D. Fleming and B. Bailyn, eds., *Law in American History,* Boston, Little, Brown.

Schelling, Thomas. (1960) *The Strategy of Conflict,* Cambridge, Harvard University Press.

Scherer, F. M. (1970) *Industrial Market Structure and Economic Performance*, Chicago, Rand McNally.

Schmid, A. Allan. (1978) *Property, Power and Public Choice*, New York, Praeger.

Schubert, Glendon. (1974) *Judicial Policy Making*, rev. ed., Glenview, Scott, Foresman.

_____ .. (1962) "Is There a Public Interest Theory?" p. 162 in C. Friedrich, ed., *Nomos V: The Public Interest*, New York, Atherton.

Schwartz, Warren, and Gordon Tulloch. (1975) "The Costs of a Legal System," *Journal of Legal Studies*, Vol. 4, p. 75

Scott, Kenneth. (1983) "Answers are More Needed than Perspectives," *Journal of Legal Education*, Vol. 33, p. 285.

Sharp, Malcolm. (1966) "Reflections on Contract," *University of Chicago Law Review*, Vol. 33, p. 211.

Siegfried, John. (1981) "Factors Affecting Student Performance in Law School Economics Courses," *Journal of Legal Education*, Vol. 31, p. 19.

Simon, Herbert. (1957) *Administrative Behavior*, 2nd ed., New York, Macmillan.

Smart, Barry. (1976) *Sociology, Phenomenology and Marxian Analysis*, London, Routledge and Kegan Paul.

Stigler, George. (1983) "What Does an Economist Know?" *Journal of Legal Education*, Vol. 33, p. 311.

_____ . (1972) "The Law and Economics of Public Policy," *Journal of Legal Studies*, Vol. 1, p. 1.

_____ . (1971) "The Theory of Economic Regulation," *Bell Journal of Economics and Management Science*, Vol. 2, p. 3.

_____ . (1959) "The Politics of Political Economists," *Quarterly Journal of Economics*, Vol. 73, p. 522.

Stone, Julius. (1966) *Law and the Social Sciences*, Minneapolis, University of Minnesota Press.

Stover, Robert, and Donald Brown. (1977) "Understanding Compliance and Noncompliance with Law," p. 121 in S. Nagel, ed., *Policy Studies Review Annual*, Vol. 1, New York, Russell Sage.

Strasser, Kurt, Robert Bard, and H. T. Arthur (1982) "A Reader's Guide to the Uses and Limits of Economic Analysis with Emphasis on Corporations Law," *Mercer Law Review*, Vol. 33, p. 571.

Sullivan, Lawrence. (1977) *Antitrust*, St. Paul, West.

Summers, Robert. (1983) "The Future of Economics in Legal Education," *Journal of Legal Education*, Vol. 33, p. 337.

Tamerin, J. S., and H. L. P. Resnick. (1978) "Risk-Taking by Individual Option," p. 3 in P. Diamond and M. Rothschild, eds., *Uncertainty in Economics*, New York, Academic Press.

Trebilcock, Michael. (1983) "The Prospects of 'Law and Economics'," *Journal of Legal and Education*, Vol. 33, p. 288.

Trebing, Harry. (1969) "Government Regulation and Modern Capitalism," *Journal of Economic Issues*, Vol. 3, p. 87.

Tribe, Lawrence. (April 1979) "Too Much Law, Too Little Justice," *Atlantic Monthly*, p. 25.

Tulloch, Gordon, and Richard Wagner. (1977) "Introduction," *Policy Studies Journal*, Vol. 5, p. 280.

Tushnet, Mark. (1980) "Post-Realist Legal Scholarship," *Wisconsin Law Review*, Vol. 1980, p. 1383.

Umbeck, John. (1977) "A Theory of Contract Choice and the California Gold Rush," *Journal of Law and Economics*, Vol. 20, p. 421.

Unger, Roberto. (1976) *Law in Modern Society*, New York, Free Press.

Veljanovski, Cento. (1980) "The Economic Approach to Law," *British Journal of Law and Society*, Vol. 7, p. 158.

Wagner, Richard. (1977) "Economic Manipulation for Political Profit: Macroecnomic Consequences and Constitutional Implications," *Kyklos*, Vol. 30, p. 395.

Wendt, Lloyd, and Herman Kogan. (1943) *Lords of the Levee,* Indianapolis, Bobbs-Merrill.

Wertheim, W. F. (1974) *Evolution and Revolution,* Harmondsworth, Penguin.

Wildavsky, Aaron. (1979) *Speaking Truth to Power,* Boston, Little, Brown.

Wills, Gary. (1970) *Nixon Agonistes,* Boston, Houghton Mifflin.

Wilson, James Q. (1979) "The Politics of Regulation," p. 90 in R. Rabin, ed., *Perspectives on the Administrative Process,* Boston, Little, Brown.

ON THE GROWTH OF GOVERNMENT AND THE POLITICAL ECONOMY OF LEGISLATION

William F. Shughart II and Robert D. Tollison

ABSTRACT

This paper investigates the causes of governmental growth by examining the factors that influence the output of legislation. The growth of government and legislative output are linked because the legislature must approve the taxing, spending, and regulatory initiatives that lead to increases in the size of the public sector. Using data on the legislative activities of the U.S. Congress from 1789 through 1980, we find a positive and statistically significant ceteris paribus relationship between real government spending per capita and the number of public and private

Research in Law and Economics, volume 9, pages 111–127.
Copyright © 1986 by JAI Press Inc.
ISBN: 0-89232-657-3

bills enacted into law. We then estimate a production function for legislation, finding evidence consistent with the predictions of the interest-group theory of government. An important finding is that on- and off-budget government are substitutes. A theory of what drives legislation over time is a theory of the growth of government, and this paper sheds additional light on this question.

I. INTRODUCTION

Few doubt that at least since World War I, government at all levels has absorbed increasing proportions of domestic wealth. The causes and consequences of this trend, which accelerated in the post-World War II era, have been the subject of much scholarly debate. Several hypotheses about governmental growth have been advanced in this literature.[1] First, exogenous events such as war are given to cause once-and-for-all increases in the size of the public sector. Second, some version of Wagner's "Law"—that the demand for government services is an increasing function of income—is supposed to operate in the context of an explicit or implicit market for public goods wherein demand and cost conditions determine the level of spending. Other explanations center on the expansionist motives of politicians and bureaucrats, on "unbalanced growth" by a labor-intensive public sector, and on the information costs faced by voters.[2]

Recent contributions key on the redistributive elements in governmental activity. For example, Peltzman (1980, p. 285) finds wide empirical support for the proposition that "the *leveling* of income differences across a large part of the population—the growth of the 'middle class'—has in fact been a major source of the growth of government in the developed world over the last fifty years" (emphasis in original). In contrast, Meltzer and Richard (1981) develop a theoretical model which suggests that an increase in income differences, due to the extension of the franchise to groups with relatively low incomes, raised the demand for redistribution and, hence, led to more government.

In the main, the growth-of-government literature has used either public employment or government spending as a percent of gross domestic product as a proxy for the size of the public sector. However, this approach does not capture the full scope of governmental activity. Many of government's intrusions into economic life (e.g., minimum wage laws, nonprice trade barriers, antitrust exemptions, and price-entry regulations, to name a few) are off-budget. That is, taxing and spending activities are just the tip of the government iceberg.

In this paper we investigate the growth of government by examining the event necessary to generate a public sector of given size, the enactment of a body of laws. To do so we analyze the legislative output of the U.S. Congress from its first session in 1789 through the 96th assembly, which ended in 1980. The paper has two main threads. First, after outlining our theory, in Section III we relate the legislative output series to the growth of government, and find a positive and statistically significant ceteris paribus relationship between real government spending per capita and the enactment of public and private laws. That the output of legislation affects spending is not surprising. What is important, however, is that when we relate the mix of public and private bills to overall expenditures, we find evidence that the two are substitutes. This result strongly implies that off-budget government is not a monotone transformation of on-budget government. In Section IV, we go behind the legislative output series and develop a production function for enacted laws. Combining our results leads to the conclusion that the empirical determinants of congressional output—the size and characteristics of the legislature, the enactment of the income tax, and the demand for wealth transfers, among others—explain a large proportion of the secular growth of government. Section V contains some closing remarks.

II. THE INTEREST-GROUP THEORY OF GOVERNMENT

The U.S. Congress is the body that authorizes the taxing, spending, regulatory, and other initiatives that lead to increases in the size of the public sector. Our approach to the growth-of-government issue therefore focuses on the factors that influence the output of such legislation. In particular, we draw upon the interest-group theory of government for a model that assigns to the legislature the function of brokering wealth transfers among the various interest groups that exist within the polity (see, e.g, Stigler, 1971; Peltzman, 1976). Our main point is that legislative output and governmental growth are both driven by the benefits and costs citizens face in utilizing the machinery of the state to increase their wealth.

In the interest-group setting, each legislator/broker searches over his constituency, identifies those groups that are net demanders of wealth transfers and those that are net suppliers, and develops a legislative agenda—a level and pattern of wealth transfers—that maximizes his political majority. This choice is constrained by the fact that while a transfer of wealth to one group leads the beneficiaries to provide political support (votes) for the incumbent, it also draws opposition from those interests called upon to supply the wealth.

Obviously, not all representatives can secure passage of their preferred agendas. The final outcome on a given bill is delimited by such considerations as the necessity of obtaining majorities in committee and on the floors of two legislative chambers. Moreover, the identity of the winners and losers will generally change from issue to issue. It is the role of the legislature to resolve these conflicts, that is, to clear the market for wealth transfers.

McCormick and Tollison (1981) suggest that the institutional characteristics of the legislature—principally its size and degree of bicameralism—are important to the determination of legislative outcomes. In particular, total legislature size

(House plus Senate membership) has opposing effects on the costs to interest groups of obtaining votes in Congress. On the one hand, increases in the number of legislators could result in lower costs of lobbying because of additional competition among the vote suppliers. With a larger legislature, each legislator/broker's vote has a smaller relative influence; he accordingly commands a smaller brokerage "fee." Furthermore, if larger legislatures are associated with fewer voters per legislator, it will be cheaper for voters to monitor their representatives. Such considerations suggest that legislative output will increase as the size of the legislature rises. On the other hand, however, the cost of obtaining a particular legislative outcome may rise if larger legislatures make it increasingly difficult for the brokers to reach agreement on a set of wealth transfers that is consistent with overall political equilibrium. In this case, legislative output would be predicted to fall as total membership grows (McCormick and Tollison, 1981, pp. 33–34). Thus, the effect of changes in legislature size on the output of enacted laws is an empirical question whose answer is dependent upon the relative strengths of the factors described above. (We offer evidence on this issue in Section IV.)

In addition to total legislature size, McCormick and Tollison (pp. 44–45) argue that the relative size of the two legislative chambers—the House-Senate ratio—plays an important role in determining the cost of lobbying. Under the assumption that the cost of influencing votes increases at an increasing rate in each house, the cost of obtaining an additional vote in the larger chamber will exceed the saving from buying one less vote in the smaller house. Thus, the cost of obtaining a majority in both houses will be less the more equal the two chambers are in size.

The interest-group theory of government suggests that the political process is one of interplay between demanders and suppliers of wealth transfers, with a brokerage function provided by the elected representatives of these groups. Within this theory, the demand for wealth transfers translates into a demand for legislation, and the amount of legislation ultimately supplied depends in part on the institutional characteristics of the legislature itself. Our contribution is to suggest that governmental growth is part and parcel of this process. Because legislative authorization is necessary for expansions in the size of the public sector, factors that lead to increases in the output of laws (wealth transfers) will also tend to increase the size of government as measured by government spending. In the remainder of this paper, we test this proposition.

III. LEGISLATIVE OUTPUT
AND THE GROWTH OF GOVERNMENT

That the growth of government is a relatively recent phenomenon is illustrated dramatically in Figure 1 which shows real government spending per capita from 1789 to 1980. The series reaches a peak during World War II when the 78th

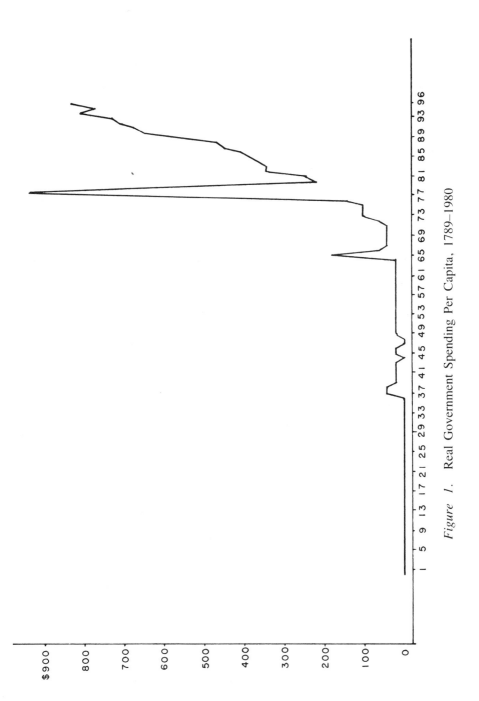

Figure 1. Real Government Spending Per Capita, 1789–1980

115

Congress (1943–44) authorized expenditures of $941 per person (in 1910–14 dollars). Spending declined as the war effort ended, but beginning with the 85th Congress (1957–58), the federal budget again took off, and by the 96th Congress (1979–80), peacetime expenditures per capita nearly equaled the World War II high. Over the entire 1789–1980 period, real spending by each biennial congress averaged $129 for every person residing in the United States.

The corresponding time series of bill introductions and bill enactments are displayed in Figures 2 and 3, respectively. Of particular interest are the two strong peaks in bill introductions shown in Figure 2, the first occurring during the 61st Congress (1909–10), the second during the 90th and 91st Congresses (1967–70). An average of 11,388 bills were introduced in each congress; slightly less than one quarter of these measures were enacted into law.

We also calculated several alternative measures of legislative output. These were bills passed per legislator, BPL; bills passed per session-day, BPDAY; and the ratio of private to public laws enacted, SPINT.[3] Descriptive statistics are given in Table 1.[4]

As our earlier discussion indicated, recent contributions to the growth-of-government literature have sought to explain the rise in government spending as a percent of GNP. A wide variety of alternative explanations have been put forward. Our approach is to model the production of legislation necessary to run a government of given size. To do so we employ a single-equation regression that posits government spending to be a function of the legislative output of the U.S. Congress.[5]

Our government spending equation is of the following form:

$$RGOVPC_t = a_0 + a_1Q_t + a_2TAXDUM_t + a_3DUM20_t + a_4DUM46_t + v_t, \tag{1}$$

where $RGOVPC_t$ = real government spending per capita,
Q_t = legislative output,
$TAXDUM_t$ = income tax amendment dummy variable,
$DUM20_t$ = 20th amendment dummy variable
$DUM46_t$ = 1946 Reorganization Act dummy variable, and
v_t = the regression error term.

TAXDUM, set equal to unity for the years 1913 and beyond, and zero otherwise, denotes ratification of the 16th amendment to the constitution which gave Congress the power to lay and collect taxes on incomes. DUM20 denotes ratification in 1933 of the 20th Amendment which established January 3 of the year following elections as the beginning and end of congressional terms, and DUM46 controls for the effects of the 1946 Legislative Reorganization Act.[6]

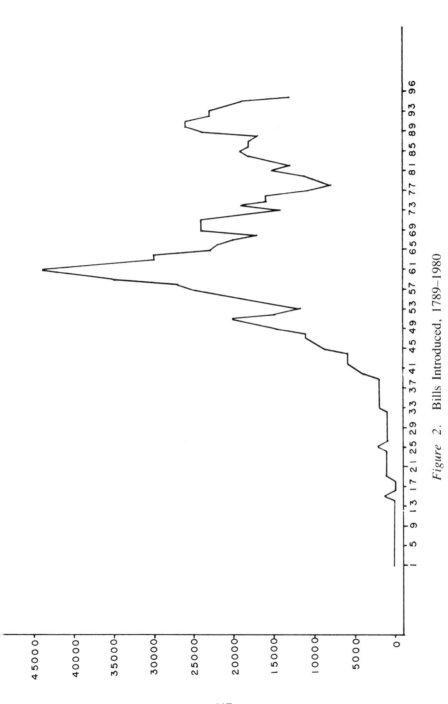

Figure 2. Bills Introduced, 1789–1980

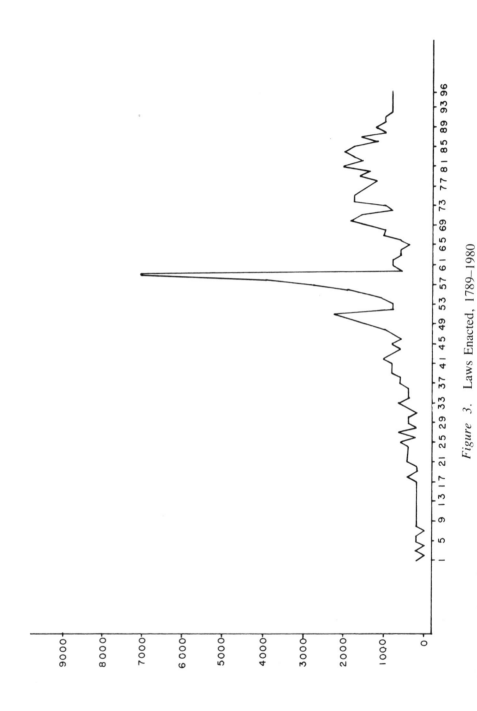

Figure 3. Laws Enacted, 1789–1980

Table 1.   Descriptive Statistics for
Legislative Activity Variables, 1789-1980

Variable		Mean	Standard Deviation	Coefficient of Variation
AGENDA	Bills introduced	11,388.29	10,944.4	0.96
ACTPAS	Bills enacted	910.48	924.7	1.02
PASSRATE	Bills passed/bills introduced	0.23	0.2	0.87
BPL	Bills passed per legislator	2.15	1.8	0.84
BPDAY	Bills passed per session-day	2.39	3.0	1.26
SPINT	Private/Public bills passed	1.06	1.2	1.13

We estimated the regression equation using our alternative measures of legislative output, Q_t. The continuous variables were transformed logarithmically, and the specification was estimated by the method of instrumental variables, where we used as instruments the predicted values from the legislative output regressions reported below. The results for Eq. (1) are reported in Table 2.

Table 2.   Two-stage Least Squares
Regression Results

Dependent Variable: Log of Real Government
Spending per Capita
1789-1980

C	−7.1714	−6.1996	0.9756
Log of ACTPAS	1.4451 (8.19)***		
Log of BPL		2.0952 (5.12)***	
Log of BPDAY			1.8653 (5.55)***
Log of SPINT	−0.9181 (−4.68)***	−0.7274 (−2.67)***	−1.2947 (−3.69)***
TAXDUM	0.2759 (0.87)	1.2805 (3.73)***	0.2002 (0.42)
DUM20	1.7146 (6.01)***	1.2737 (3.19)***	2.1224 (4.82)***
DUM46	0.5489 (2.12)**	0.7842 (2.17)**	0.6942 (1.82)*
R²	0.924	0.858	0.847
D-W	1.21	1.19	1.01

Notes: t-statistics in parentheses. D-W is the Durbin-Watson d-statistic. Asterisks denote significance at the 1 percent (***), 5 percent (**), and 10 percent (*) levels.

The estimates suggest a positive and significant relationship between legislative output and the size of government. For example, over the 1789–1980 period, a 1 percent increase in the number of legislative matters enacted into law led to a 1.4 increase in government spending per person, other things equal. Moreover, government expenditures per capita were raised more than proportionately by increases in laws passed per legislator and per session-day.

A second result of interest is that as the mix of legislative output shifts toward private bills (see note 3 *infra*), government spending per person tends to decline. This finding has important implications for the growth-of-government literature because it suggests that not all governmental activities are a monotone transformation of budgetary expenditures. In fact, just the opposite is the case. A significant category of wealth transfers—waivers of indebtedness to government, grants of citizenship outside the law, and so forth—are off-budget. This result tends to support Peltzman's (1980, p. 209) admission that his use of budgetary expenditures as a proxy for the size of the public sector was "obviously wrong," though unavoidable because of data limitations. The private-public bill ratio result may also indicate that there is an overall burden-of-taxation constraint on government such that on- and off-budget spending are substitutes.

Government spending per capita was raised further by the ratifications of the 16th and 20th amendments to the constitution, and by passage of the 1946 Legislative Reorganization Act.[7] Each of these results has a straightforward interpretation. That is, one would expect the size of government to be increased by the tapping of a new revenue source, by a lengthening of the time during which legislators remain in session, and by organizational changes which streamline the legislative process.[8]

The results reported in Table 2 imply that the factors which tend to raise the output of laws also tend to increase the size of government, and vice versa. In the next section, we investigate the underlying production function for legislation.

IV. LEGISLATION AND WEALTH BROKERING

In estimating the relationship between the growth of government and the legislative activities of the U.S. Congress, we used as regressors the predicted values from a legislative production function. In this section, we outline how the predicted output values were obtained. The results reported herein also provide evidence on the underlying causes of governmental growth.

Empirical tests of the interest-group theory of government using data from state legislatures by McCormick and Tollison (1981), Crain (1979), and Crain and Tollison (1980) support a legislative production function of the following form:

$$Q_t = b_0 + b_1 SIZE_t + b_2 HSRATIO_t + b_3 AGENDA_t$$
$$+ b_4 TAXDUM_t + b_5 DUM20_t + b_6 DUM46_t + b_7 DUM70_t + e_t. \quad (2)$$

Equation (2) hypothesizes that the output of laws in any given Congress is a function of legislature SIZE (house plus senate membership); the ratio of house size to senate size, HSRATIO; the number of bills introduced during the two sessions, AGENDA; and four dummy variables.

As described earlier, the sign of the coefficient on SIZE must be determined empirically. That is, b_1 will be positive if increases in legislature size result in lower costs to interest groups of obtaining votes in Congress. In contrast, if larger legislatures make it more difficult for legislators to reach agreement, b_1 will be negative.

The interest-group theory of government unambiguously predicts b_2 to be less than zero. Specifically, as HSRATIO rises (the two legislative chambers become more disparate in size), the cost of obtaining a majority in both houses increases. Such increased costs should be associated with fewer bills enacted, ceteris paribus.

AGENDA controls for the scale of legislative operations. As with the legislature size variables, opposing effects can be identified. First, the number of bills introduced can be interpreted as representing the demand for legislative output. If legislators respond systematically to demand conditions, we would expect $b_3 > 0$. Second, however, an increase in bill introductions places the legislators in the position of having to clear more margins. Each legislator must search over more bills to identify those which are consistent with political equilibrium. On this account, $b_3 < 0$. Thus, the sign of the coefficient on AGENDA is indeterminant a priori.

The four dummy variables control for events which altered either voters' costs of monitoring representatives or Congress' costs of supplying legislation. As before, TAXDUM denotes ratification of the 16th amendment to the constitution, DUM20 the 20th amendment, and DUM46 the 1946 Legislative Reorganization Act. DUM70 controls for the effects of the Reorganization Act of 1970, which provided further structural changes in the Congress, and required that teller votes on the House floor be recorded individually rather than tabulated without identifying individual members' votes (Congressional Quarterly Inc., 1976, p. 60).

Because of the simultaneous-equations bias arising from the nonindependence between bills introduced and bills passed, we specified an additional structural equation with AGENDA as the dependent variable:

$$AGENDA_t = c_0 + c_1 SIZE_t + c_2 PASSRATE_{t-1} + c_3 TAXDUM_t$$
$$+ c_4 DUM20_t + c_5 DUM46_t + c_6 DUM70_t + u_t. \quad (3)$$

All variables are defined as before, but in addition we employ the previous period's ratio of bills enacted to bills introduced, $PASSRATE_{t-1}$, as an explanatory variable. Under the de novo rule of 1790, all bills not enacted into law die at the end of each session (Congressional Quarterly Inc., 1976, p. 72). In consequence, the higher the previous pass rate, the smaller the number of bill introductions one would expect in the following Congress.

A fourth structural equation accounts for Stigler's (1976) finding that population is an important determinant of legislature size:

$$SIZE_t = d_0 + d_1 POP_t + d_2 DUM29_t + z_t, \qquad (4)$$

where POP_t is the total resident U.S. population at the beginning of each Congress, and DUM29 controls for the 1929 congressional decision to limit the House of Representatives to 435 members. Prior to that time, the size of the House had been increased in census years to accommodate population growth as well as additions to the number of states. Except for the dummy variables, all data were transformed logarithmically before estimating the system of regression equations. This allows us to gauge directly the elasticity of legislative output with respect to the continuous explanatory variables.

A. The Results

Using our alternative measures of legislative output, we estimated the four structural equations by two-stage least squares. The results for Eqs. (2)–(4) are reported in Table 3.

The estimates presented in the table provide broad support for the propositions derived from the interest-group theory of government. Specifically, increases in legislature size lead to more than proportional increases in legislative output, ceteris paribus. (SIZE was omitted as an independent variable when BPL was used as the measure of output to prevent it from appearing on both sides of the regression equation.) For example, a 1 percent increase in the number of congressmen results in a more than 5 percent rise in bills enacted, ACTPAS, and a more than 7 percent increase in the ratio of private to public laws passed, SPINT. At the mean each additional congressman was responsible for the passage of 13 more bills.

The coefficients on SIZE in the output regressions suggest that in the U.S. Congress the effect on competition of larger legislatures more than offset the tendency for transactions costs to rise as more members were added. That is, on balance interest groups found it easier to obtain legislation in a growing Congress.

In general, an increase in the disparity of House and Senate sizes, HSRATIO, reduced the output of laws. The coefficient of HSRATIO is negative and significantly different from zero at the 5 percent level in two regressions, ACTPAS and BPDAY, and negative but insignificant in the other two, SPINT

Table 3. Two-stage Least Squares Regression Results, 1789-1980

Dep. Var.	C	SIZE	HSRATIO	Log of POP	AGENDA	PASSRATE(-1)	TAXDUM	DUM 20	DUM 29	DUM 46	DUM 70	R^2	D-W
Log of ACTPAS	-15.4550	5.3987 (3.31)***	-2.5619 (-2.48)**		-0.6847 (-1.91)*		-0.8551 (-3.39)***	0.0815 (0.23)		0.1345 (0.46)	-0.6588 (-2.12)**	0.697	0.98
Log of BPL	-1.3439		-0.2053 (-0.55)		0.2753 (9.15)***		-0.5788 (-3.68)***	0.6280 (3.19)***		-0.1130 (-0.60)	-0.6558 (-3.10)***	0.558	1.23
Log of BPDAY	-25.3378	6.6837 (3.24)***	-3.0022 (-2.30)**		-1.0139 (-2.23)**		-1.0955 (-3.43)***	-0.2883 (-0.65)		0.1113 (0.30)	-0.7014 (-1.78)*	0.504	0.81
Log of SPINT	-30.2500	7.5414 (4.38)***	-1.7499 (-1.51)		-1.3038 (-3.46)***		-2.1149 (-6.92)***				-1.0335 (-2.82)***	0.467	1.03
Log of AGENDA	-11.8830	3.3298 (14.92)***				(-0.5037) (-5.70)***	-0.6278 (-3.69)***	-0.1075 (-0.50)		0.2912 (1.52)	-0.3983 (-1.74)*	0.951	0.70
Log of SIZE	4.4338			0.3880 (33.21)***					-0.1322 (-4.24)***			0.949	0.38

Notes: See Table 2

123

and BPL. The overall results imply that the cost to interest groups of obtaining a majority in both chambers rises as the degree of bicameralism increases. The magnitude of the effect on output of changes in House-Senate disparity is roughly half that of changes in total legislature size.

An increase in the demand for wealth transfers, represented by AGENDA, lowers legislative output. Each 1 percent increase in bill introductions causes approximately a 1 percent decrease in new laws. This suggests that as the legislature's agenda expands, the costs to legislators of searching for political equilibrium increase.

The results indicate that legislative output was reduced significantly by passage of both the income tax amendment to the constitution and the Reorganization Act of 1970. The former suggests that the invention of the income tax as a source of general revenue mitigated the necessity for legislators to target specific groups of wealth suppliers through the passage of legislation; the latter suggests that recording individual member's votes raised wealth-brokering costs. In contrast, neither the 1946 Legislative Reorganization Act nor ratification of the 20th Amendment had a perceptible effect on the number of measures enacted into law. Overall, the regressions explain between 47 percent (SPINT) and 70 percent (ACTPAS) of the variation over time in bill enactments.[9]

V. CONCLUDING REMARKS

In this paper we have examined the growth of government by analyzing the event necessary to generate a public sector of given size, the enactment of a body of laws. As Bennett and Johnson (1980, p. 97) observe, neither expenditures by nor employment in the government can increase without legislative appropriations. Moreover, our approach allows us to capture government's off-budget intrusions into the economy.

In relating the legislative output series to the growth of government spending per capita, we found that the factors which tend to raise the output of laws also tend to increase the size of government, and vice versa. More importantly, however, we found that not all governmental activities are a monotone transformation of budgetary expenditures. A significant category of wealth transfers—those put into operation by the passage of private bills—are off-budget, and these laws apparently substitute for on-budget spending. Explanations of the growth of government which focus solely on taxing and spending thus tell only a part of the story.

We then went behind the legislative output series to estimate a production function for enacted laws. Basing our work on the interest-group theory of government, and analyzing the legislative output of the Congress from its first session in 1789 through the 96th assembly ending in 1980, we found evidence that the enactment of bills over time depends on factors influencing the demand for and supply of legislation. For example, an increase in the degree of bicameralism reduced the output of laws. That is, as the sizes of the House of Representatives and Senate became more disparate, the cost to individuals and groups of obtaining a majority in both chambers rose.

Our results, in total, carry a message for growth-of-government theorists. First, government does not grow uniformly across the board. There is an effective constraint on wealth transfers that makes political trade-offs imperative. To argue that one captures the essence of off-budget developments by looking only at on-budget empirical proxies is to commit a fallacy of composition. Second, government in a democracy grows because the legislature passes laws and the executive signs them. Spending and taxes are ultimately a reflection of legislation. A theory of what drives legislation over time *is* a theory of the growth of government. This means that the proper focus of a theory of governmental growth is at one stage removed from spending and taxes and that it is the ability of individuals and groups to use the legislative process to attain their ends, noble or otherwise, that causes government to grow or decline.

APPENDIX

Table A1.   Two-Stage Least Squares
Regression Results

Dependent Variable: Log of Real Government Spending per Capita
1789-1899 and 1909-1980

C	− 15.3698	− 6.1579	− 6.0568
Log of	1.6563		
ACTPAS	(9.14)***		
Log of		2.1606	
BPL		(5.00)***	
Log of			2.3308
BPDAY			(6.42)***
Log of	− 1.1137	− 0.6691	− 1.6434
SPINT	(− 5.68)***	(− 2.51)**	(− 4.66)***
TAXDUM	− 0.0640	1.2541	− 0.3720
	(0.20)	(3.65)***	(− 0.74)
DUM20	1.7588	1.2017	2.2284
	(6.06)***	(3.04)***	(4.92)***
DUM46	0.5367	0.8263	0.7585
	(2.05)**	(2.34)**	(1.93)**
R^2	0.924	0.868	0.843
D-W	1.21	1.15	1.06

Notes: See Table 2.

ACKNOWLEDGMENTS

We benefited from the comments of two anonymous referees. Any remaining errors are our own.

NOTES

1. For a useful survey, see Bennett and Johnson (1980, pp. 59–95).

2. Representative discussions of these hypotheses can be found in Buchanan and Tullock (1962), Downs (1957), Tullock (1967), Baumol (1967), and Buchanan and Wagner (1977).

3. Private legislation includes those measures passed for the relief of individual persons or firms. Illustrative private bill categories are refunds of payments made to government or waivers of such indebtedness, the payment of tort claims, and private immigration and naturalization bills. See Congressional Quarterly Inc. (1976, pp. 303–306).

4. With the exception of lengths of congressional sessions, all data were obtained from U.S. Department of Commerce (1975) and from U.S. Department of Commerce (1971–81). The session-length data are from Congressional Quarterly Inc. (1976). Nominal values were deflated by the all-commodities wholesale price index (1910–14 = 100). We would be happy to supply our data set on request.

5. Obviously, not all laws are created equal. The amount of support or opposition generated will not be uniform across pieces of legislation, that is, each bill will in general carry a separate "price." However, this consideration should not complicate the relationship between changes in the output of laws over time and changes in the institutional characteristics of the legislature.

6. Among other provisions, the 1946 Legislative Reorganization Act reduced the number of standing committees in both houses, prohibited the introduction of certain categories of private bills (those for the payment of pensions or tort claims, the construction of bridges, and the correction of military records), and authorized each standing committee to appoint four professional and six clerical staff members (Congressional Quarterly Inc., 1976, p. 53).

7. The effects of TAXDUM may be obscured by the fact that the 17th amendment, providing for the popular election of senators, was also ratified in 1913.

8. We also estimated the government spending equation for a subperiod, 1869-1980, during which observations on gross national product were available. The regression results were dominated by a positive and significant relationship between the supply of wealth transfers, real GNP per capita, and government spending per capita. All legislative output variables retained the signs reported in Table 2, but the estimated coefficients were generally not different from zero at standard significance levels.

As a further check on our results, we ran the government spending equation excluding four outlying observations occurring in the legislative output series around the turn of the twentieth century (57th through 60th Congresses). The results, which are reported in the appendix, indicate that our original findings are not dependent on this episode.

9. To explore these results further, we estimated the four-equation system for the 1869-1980 subperiod, using the logarithm of real GNP per capita as a proxy for the amount of wealth available for transfer. In general, the estimates were not as supportive of the interest-group-theory hypotheses as were the results reported in Table 3. Although all of the coefficients on SIZE in the output regressions were positive, only half were different from zero at standard levels of significance. Moreover, none of the coefficients on HSRATIO retained their previous significance levels.

The overall weakness of the results when real GNP per capita is added as an explanatory variable is due by and large to the fact that the variances of both SIZE and HSRATIO are much smaller in this data subset than in the entire 1789-1980 series. Between 1869 and 1980, the number of members of

Congress rose by about 70 percent (from 309 to 539) and the House-Senate ratio increased by 23 percent (from 3.5 to 4.35). The majority of these changes took place between 1869 and 1913, at which time the House of Representatives reached its present membership of 435, and there were 96 senators. In contrast, between 1789 and 1980, congressional membership rose from 91 to 535, and HSRATIO increased from 2.5 to 4.35.

In spite of this data problem, several of our previous results did hold up. In particular, legislative output for the 1869–1980 period was reduced significantly by growth in the legislature's agenda and by ratification of the income tax amendment. Furthermore, bill introductions fell as a result of ratification of the 20th amendment, and passage of the Reorganization Act of 1970 tended to reduce enactments of private laws relative to public bills. Interestingly, however, passage of the 1946 Legislative Reorganization Act led to a greater number of bill introductions.

REFERENCES

Baumol, William J. (June 1967) "Macroeconomics of Unbalanced Growth," *American Economic Review*, Vol 57, pp. 415–426.

Bennett, James T., and Manuel H. Johnson. (1980) *The Political Economy of Federal Government Growth: 1959–1978*, College Station, Center for Education and Research in Free Enterprise, Texas A&M University.

Buchanan, James M., and Gordon Tullock. (1962) *The Calculus of Consent*, Ann Arbor, University of Michigan Press.

Buchanan, James M., and Richard E. Wagner. (1977) *Democracy in Deficit*, New York, Academic Press.

Congressional Quarterly Inc. (1976) *Congressional Quarterly's Guide to Congress*, 2nd ed., Washington, D.C.

Crain, W. Mark (June 1979) "Cost and Output in the Legislative Firm," *Journal of Legal Studies*, Vol. 8, pp. 607–621.

Crain, W. Mark and Robert D. Tollison. (January 1980) "The Sizes of Majorities," *Southern Economic Journal*, Vol. 46, pp. 726–734.

Downs, A. (1957) *An Economic Theory of Democracy*, New York, Harper.

McCormick, Robert E., and Robert D. Tollison. (1981) *Politicians, Legislation, and the Economy: An Inquiry into the Interest-Group Theory of Government*, Boston, Martinus Nijhoff.

Meltzer, Allan H., and Scott F. Richard. (October 1981) "A Rational Theory of the Size of Government," *Journal of Political Economy*, Vol. 89, pp. 914–927.

Peltzman, Sam. (August 1976) "Toward a More General Theory of Regulation," *Journal of Law and Economics*, Vol. 19, pp. 211–240.

————. (October 1980) "The Growth of Government," *Journal of Law and Economics*, Vol. 23, pp. 209–287.

Stigler, George J. (January 1976) "The Sizes of Legislatures," *Journal of Legal Studies*, Vol. 5, pp. 17–34.

————. (Spring 1971) "The Theory of Economic Regulation," *Bell Journal of Economics*, Vol. 2, pp. 3–21.

Tullock, Gordon. (1967) *The Politics of Bureaucracy*, Boston, Little, Brown.

U.S. Department of Commerce, Bureau of the Census. (1971–81) *Statistical Abstract of the United States*, Washington, D.C., U.S. Government Printing Office.

————. (1975) *Historical Statistics of the United States, Colonial Times to 1970*, 2 vols., Washington, D.C., U.S. Government Printing Office.

TAXICAB REGULATION:
AN ECONOMIC ANALYSIS

Mark W. Frankena and Paul A. Pautler

ABSTRACT

The rationale for regulations imposed on taxicabs in virtually all large cities in the 1930s has recently been called into question by regulatory reform in over a dozen cities and by antitrust complaints brought against two cities by the Federal Trade Commission based on their taxicab ordinances. This paper provides a comprehensive survey of the economic issues involved in taxicab regulation. This review leads to the conclusion that there is no persuasive economic rationale for restrictions on the total number of taxicabs or on the minimum level of fares.

I. INTRODUCTION

The taxicab industry is heavily regulated, mainly by local governments. However, a number of cities have recently deregulated entry, fares, and some aspects of service. In addition, the Supreme Court has decided that municipal govern-

Research in Law and Economics, volume 9, pages 129–165.
Copyright © 1986 by JAI Press Inc.
All rights of reproduction in any form reserved.
ISBN: 0-89232-657-3

ment activities are subject to the antitrust laws,[1] and the Federal Trade Commission has issued complaints against two municipalities on the grounds that their regulation of taxicabs involves antitrust violations.[2] These actions indicate that the pervasive regulation of the taxicab industry may be weakening.

This paper focuses on the economic rationales for taxicab regulation. It also presents a theoretical model of a taxicab market and summarizes a longer report that provides a detailed discussion of the forms and effects of regulation and the experiences of cities that have deregulated (Frankena and Pautler, 1984).

The principal conclusion of this paper is that no persuasive economic rationale is available for some of the most important taxicab regulations. Restrictions on the total number of firms and vehicles and on minimum fares waste resources and impose a disproportionate burden on low-income people.[3] Similarly, there is no economic justification for regulations that restrict shared-ride service.

By contrast, potential market failures and "second best" considerations might provide a credible theoretical rationale for some other regulations, including fare ceilings, requirements relating to vehicle safety and liability insurance, prohibitions on service refusal, requirements to offer service at certain times or places, or minimum levels on the number of cabs operated by each firm. However, the fact that a theoretical justification can be offered for a certain form of regulation does not imply that regulations of this type, particularly those actually observed in the real world, could pass a cost-benefit test.

II. THE TAXICAB INDUSTRY

A. Industry Patterns

The taxicab industry provides a significant fraction of urban public transportation services. Gilbert et al. (1982) estimate that nationwide in 1981 taxis produced 1.7 billion passenger trips, or 27 percent as many as did urban transit. These taxi trips generated consumer expenditures of $3.4 billion, or 4 percent less than transit. The taxi industry employed 192,000 people, slightly more than the transit industry.[4]

It is useful to distinguish between four taxicab market segments, because they differ in the probable benefits and costs of various forms of regulation, and because the regulations imposed on them differ: radio-dispatched cabs that respond to telephone requests, cabs that wait at stands, cruising cabs, and cabs that provide service under contracts. Radio-dispatch and contract services involve parcels as well as passengers.

Cruising is important only in the central areas of a few large, dense cities including New York, Chicago, and Washington, D.C. With these exceptions, in large cities radio-dispatch typically accounts for 60-75 percent of taxi trips, cab stands for 15-30 percent, and contracts for 10-20 percent. In small cities, radio-dispatch accounts for over 85 percent of taxi trips.

Taxi service is provided by fleets and independent cabs. Independents generally operate in the cruising and stand segments while fleets operate in all market segments.

B. Regulations

Since about 1930, the taxicab industry has been characterized by pervasive government regulation, although a number of cities have relaxed regulations in the last five years. In general, the extent of regulation increases with city size, and a substantial majority of large cities have strict controls over entry, fares, and service. By contrast, some small communities have virtually no taxicab regulations other than safety and insurance requirements. Regulations governing contract services and package delivery are often less restrictive than those applying to other taxi services.

Although at least 10 states regulate entry and/or fares in the taxicab industry, most regulation is done by municipal governments. In addition, airport authorities often regulate taxicabs.

1. Entry Regulation

In a survey of 103 cities with populations of 50,000 or more, Shaw et al. (1983, v. 1, pp. 29-32) found that 70 percent had explicit entry restrictions: 30 percent had a fixed number of licenses; 9 percent had a fixed ratio of licenses to population; 25 percent required a showing of public convenience and necessity to obtain a license; and 6 percent had franchise requirements. Another 17 percent had minimum service requirements, some of which may be intended to impede entry.[5]

In some major cities, the number of licenses has changed little, if at all, since entry barriers were imposed in the 1930s. A few cities have a significant number of unlicensed cabs operating illegally, principally in minority neighborhoods. The fact that entry restrictions are effective in limiting the number of cabs is evident from positive medallion values.[6]

2. Fare Regulation

Shaw et al. (1983, v.1) found that 77 percent of the sample cities regulated fares: 50 percent set fare levels and 27 percent set fare ceilings. A few of the cities that set ceilings also set floors.

3. Service Regulation

Taxi firms in many jurisdictions are prohibited from providing certain types of service. Pickrel and Rogers (1978, p. 42) report that 70 percent of the 50 largest cities had ordinances that restricted shared-ride service. In some cities, taxis are prohibited from cruising or picking up passengers who hail them on the street.

Taxi firms are often required to provide service to all customers within the jurisdiction who call for or hail their cabs, regardless of origin or destination. Sometimes they are also required to have 24-hour-a-day radio-dispatch facilities. A number of cities require that taxi firms operate at least some minimum number of cabs and/or that each cab operate at least a certain number of hours or miles. Some cities set standards for how fast cab firms must respond to calls.

4. Quality Regulation

Most cities impose minimum standards on vehicle condition, driver qualifications, and insurance coverage.

III. THEORETICAL MODEL

This section explains a theoretical model of a cruising cab market that is useful in analyzing several issues, including some of the potential market failures discussed in Section IV and some of the effects of regulation evaluated in Section V.[7] Although, the model is used primarily in analyzing the cruising segment, it is useful in analyzing some regulatory issues in the radio-dispatch and other segments as well, for example, effects of regulation on number of cabs, waiting times, medallion values, and efficiency.

The principal characteristic that distinguishes this model from those used for other competitive markets is the role of waiting time. For consumers, particularly in a cruising market, expected waiting time is an important consideration in deciding whether to take a cab. We incorporate expected waiting time on the demand side of the model as though it were a quality variable. A reduction in expected waiting time increases the demand for taxi service. However, from the point of view of each individual cab firm, expected customer waiting time is different from the quality of the typical product. In most markets where quality is a variable, each firm can decide what quality to produce. In the cruising market, expected waiting time depends on the total number of vacant cabs. An individual firm cannot offer customers an expected waiting time different from that offered by other firms, although a large firm may be able to affect expected waiting time.

Some of the basic assumptions underlying the model are: (1) Expected waiting time depends on the total number of vacant cabs. (2) All other aspects of cab service quality are exogenously determined and uniform. (3) The number of taxi rides demanded depends on the expected fare and the expected waiting time. (4) The cost of operating a cab is a constant per hour. (5) In the absence of regulations limiting entry, in equilibrium cab firms earn zero profits, that is, a normal rate of return. In order to complete the model, we will need assumptions concerning how individual cabs set fares and how individual riders respond to them. We will return to these matters in Section IV below. In the remainder of the present section, for expositional purposes we will assume that the government imposes a uniform fare.

It follows from these assumptions that, within a certain range, at each fare that the government might impose, a unique number of cab hours of service would be supplied. The level of service would be such that revenues and costs per cab hour of service would be equal. The various possible zero-profit fare and service combinations for a cruising market are summarized by the "zero-profit locus" in Figure 1, where the fare (F) and the total number of cab hours of service (S) are on the axes.[8] F_{min} and F_{max} are the lowest and highest fares at which cabs could break even; outside this range, no service would be offered.

The various combinations of fare and service that would result in any given number of cab rides can be represented by an "iso-rider" line, two of which are drawn in Figure 1. The number of rides along R^1 is greater than that along R^0.

Given the breakeven constraint, the number of cab hours of service would be maximized at point D; the number of cab rides would be maximized at point B; and the average waiting time would be minimized at a point between D and G, such as E.

At fare-service combinations to the left of the zero-profit locus, such as H, taxi firms would earn positive economic profits. If entry were restricted and the right to operate a taxi could be sold or leased, medallions would command a price or rental equal to the present discounted value of these profits.

If the government imposed a mandatory fare equal to F* but did not impose entry restrictions, firms would enter the industry until profits were zero, at C. If the government limited the maximum number of cabs and hence the maximum

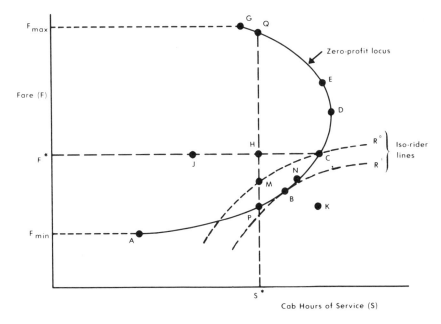

Figure 1. Model of a Taxi Market in Fare-Service Space

number of cab hours of service per hour to S*, the industry would operate along line APMHQG; the point at which it would operate would depend on the fare. If the government limited the maximum number of cabs to S* and set the fare at F*, the taxi industry would operate with fare and service combination H.

From the point of view of the taxi industry, there is some fare-service combination such as J at which joint profits would be maximized. If the government gave a single taxi firm a monopoly franchise and did not control the fare or service level, the firm would operate at J. If there were more than one firm, the firms might try to get the government to impose entry and fare regulations that would move the industry away from the zero-profit locus toward point J.

From the point of view of the economy as a whole, the efficient allocation would be to the right of the zero-profit locus, at a point such as K. Such a point is not attainable by the industry without a subsidy. A competitive taxi industry would not expand to the efficient level because there is an external economy. A simultaneous, equal percentage increase in the number of taxis in service and the number of passengers would increase the number of vacant cabs and hence reduce the average waiting time for all riders and the average social cost for rides. When there are a number of taxi firms and one of them adds a cab, that firm cannot capture all the social benefits of the addition in capacity. As a result, given the efficient fare, there will be less than the efficient amount of service in the absence of a subsidy. This "waiting time externality" is discussed further in Section IV.[9]

In the absence of a subsidy, the industry would be constrained to operate on the zero-profit locus and the "second best" efficient allocation would be at a point such as B.[10]

Figure 1 illustrates the theoretical model of a taxi market in fare-service (F, S) space. For some purposes it is more revealing to use a diagram in which cab hours of service (S) and number of taxi rides (R) are on the axes, as in Figure 2.[11] Points in (F, S) space can be mapped to points in (S, R) space, and the same letters (without and with prime signs) are used to designate corresponding points in Figures 1 and 2.

In Figure 2, suppose that J' is the point of joint profit maximization for the taxi industry. Around J' one can draw a family of iso-profit contours, such as the three solid elliptical contours that pass through M', B', and K'. The profit level is constant along each contour and declines as one moves to contours farther from J'. Thus, suppose that profits are positive along the contour through M', zero along the contour through B', and negative along the contour through K'. Along the zero-profit contour, B' is the point where number of taxi rides is maximized, D' is the point where number of cab hours of service is maximized, and E' is the point where average waiting time is minimized. If entry is unrestricted, the industry will operate along the zero-profit contour. If entry is limited, the industry will typically operate at a point such as H' or M', where profits are positive.

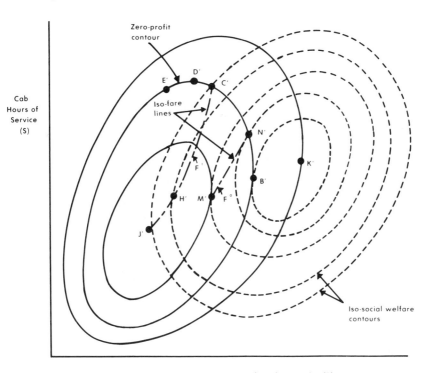

Figure 2. Model of a Taxi Market in Service-Rides Space

Suppose that the efficient allocation of resources from society's point of view is at K′, where the industry would operate at a loss. Around K′ one can draw a family of iso-social welfare contours, such as the five dashed elliptical contours that pass through B′, N′, M′, H′, and C′. The social welfare level is constant along any given contour and declines as one moves to contours farther from K′. Figure 2 has been drawn so that B′ is "second-best" efficient, that is, on the highest iso-social welfare contour along the zero-profit constraint.

If the fare is held constant and service is increased, the number of cab rides will increase. For a given fare, the relationship between service and ridership is represented by an "iso-fare" line, two of which are shown in Figure 2. F^1 represents a fare higher than F^0.

Suppose the government were to set the fare at the second-best efficient level but not limit entry. In that case, the taxi industry would operate at point B′. If the government chose a fare above the second-best efficient level and did not restrict entry, the industry would operate at a point along the zero-profit locus such as N′, C′, D′, or E′. If the fare was set so that the industry would operate at N′, a restriction on the maximum number of taxis would move the industry to a point such as M′, on the same iso-fare line where both cab hours of service and ridership would be lower. If the fare was set higher so that the industry was operating at C', a restriction on the maximum number of taxis to the same level as at M' would move the industry to H'.

Suppose now that the government initially imposes fare and entry regulations so that the taxi industry is operating at H'. There would be an efficiency gain if the government reduced the fare to the second-best efficient level and eliminated entry restrictions, since the industry would then move to B', which is on a higher iso-social welfare contour. In this case, there would be a smaller efficiency gain if the fare were reduced even if the entry restriction were not changed, since the industry would move from H' to a point such as M' on a higher iso-social welfare contour.

By contrast, eliminating of the entry restriction without a reduction in the fare might reduce social welfare. Starting from point H', such a policy change would move the industry to point C', which is on a lower iso-social welfare contour. In this case, the cost of the additional cabs exceeds the benefit of reduced waiting time. While such a result is possible, it is not necessary. If the industry started at M' (which corresponds to a lower fare level) rather than H', eliminating entry restrictions without a fare reduction would move the industry to N', which is on a higher iso-social welfare contour. This issue is discussed further in Section IV.

IV. POTENTIAL SOURCES OF MARKET FAILURE

In the absence of market imperfections, the forces of supply and demand produce an efficient allocation of resources. In order to justify government taxicab regulations, one must begin by identifying imperfections in taxicab markets that would lead to market failure. The market failure might take the form of over- or underproduction of various taxicab services, production of the wrong quality of service, or an unnecessarily high cost for a given output. One must then demonstrate that government intervention would in fact produce net benefits.

This section provides a discussion of nine imperfections that might occur in markets for taxicab services as well as a proposed rationale for entry restrictions based on enforcement costs for other regulations. We consider whether each imperfection would partially justify some kind of government intervention.

One of the principal conclusions of this section is that the probable benefits and costs of taxicab regulations vary among the four taxi market segments. Some possible sources of market failure that might be important in the cruising or stand segments do not appear to be important in the radio-dispatch or contract segments.

A. Impediments to Price Competition

In presenting the theoretical model of a cruising cab market in Section III, we assumed for the sake of exposition that the government imposed a uniform fare.

In this section we will remove that assumption and consider how the fare and level of service would be determined simultaneously if there are neither entry nor fare restrictions.

Standard models of competitive markets assume that each firm faces a demand curve that is perfectly elastic at the market price. Such firms maximize profits by producing the level of output at which marginal cost equals price, which is efficient. If firms face demand curves that are not perfectly elastic, they maximize profits by charging prices above marginal cost, and industry output is inefficiently low. In this case, a government price ceiling might increase efficiency.

The demand curves facing individual taxi firms will not be perfectly elastic with respect to price, even when each firm is small relative to the market, if potential riders cannot costlessly select the cab with the lowest fare. If it is not worthwhile for potential riders to incur the search costs required to find and use cabs offering lower fares, or if lack of information or opportunity would prevent riders from doing so, cabs will not have an incentive to offer lower prices. No such problems would arise in the radio-dispatch or contract market segments, since users can easily obtain comparative price information and use the firm with the lowest price.[12] However, such impediments to price competition might arise and provide a possible rationale for fare ceilings in the cruising segment and at airport stands.[13]

1. Cruising Cabs

Consider a model of a cruising market similar to that in Section III but without government-imposed fares. Suppose that each cruising cab is owned by an independent firm, that cabs are free to choose any fare system, and that cabs commit themselves to a fare structure prior to making contact with potential riders. Once a contact is made, the rider has a choice between taking this cab, waiting for another cab, or withdrawing from the cruising market segment (e.g., taking a bus or phoning for a cab).

Consider first the rider's choice between taking the first cab and waiting for another. A rider will accept the first cab as long as the excess of its fare over the expected fare that would be paid after waiting is less than the value of the expected waiting time. Suppose that initially all cabs charge a uniform fare that is low enough so that the average waiting time for a cruising cab is significant. In this situation, each cab would have an incentive to raise its fare since a small fare differential would not cause the loss of riders to other cruising cabs. No cab would have an incentive to cut its fare, since a rider would not turn down a cab that charged that uniform fare in order to wait for another cab.

In this situation, there would be an incentive to raise fares until average waiting time is small. At some point, the fraction of riders who have more than one vacant cab in sight might become significant, and further price increases would be deterred by the resulting loss of riders.

Schreiber (1975) has argued that the outcome would be an inefficiently high fare in the cruising segment unless the government imposed a fare ceiling. There would be too many cruising cabs and too few trips produced.[14]

Cruising cab fare increases would, however, be limited by competition with other forms of taxi service that are not subject to the same problems of achieving workable price competition and with public transit. Coffman (1977) and Williams (1980a,b) point out two ways that taxis could offer lower-priced services. First, taxis offering lower prices could wait at stands, where riders could find them at the cost of some additional walking. Second, radio-dispatched taxis offering lower prices could be summoned by telephone, at the cost of some additional waiting.[15]

The problems caused by search costs in the cruising segment might also be limited by formation of fleets of distinctively marked cruising cabs. Because its cabs could be identified easily, a fleet would reduce search costs for riders looking for a lower fare. In addition, the larger the number of cabs charging a lower fare, the lower the expected cost to riders who turn down higher-priced cabs. Finally, a fleet might attract to the cruising segment a group of riders who are unwilling to pay the higher fare charged by other cabs and who will wait until a fleet cab appears. As a result, even if an individual cab would not be able to do so, a fleet could get more riders by charging a lower fare.

2. Taxi Stands

Price searching and competition might also be limited at stands at locations such as airports for three reasons. First, at airports many riders are from other cities. As long as most cities regulate fares, many riders might not be aware that fares are not uniform in a city that does not regulate fares. Second, stands designed for a first-in-first-out allocation system, which makes sense when fares are set by the government, might not allow price shopping, Third, where permitted by law, some hotels sell exclusive service contracts to taxi firms.

Evidence on fare deregulation in Section V suggests that problems stemming from limited price competition have occurred at airports. These problems might justify fare-posting requirements, fare ceilings, or redesign of taxi allocation systems at airports so that consumers would be able to locate the lowest-priced cab. For example, airports with cab holding areas could send the lowest-priced cabs to the terminal rather than send cabs on a first-come basis.[16]

B. Bargaining over Price

The preceding subsection considered the cruising and stand segments under the assumption that cabs commit themselves to a fare structure before making contact with riders. However, cabs might bargain. It has been suggested that fares should be regulated in order to deal with two problems that might arise in the cruising and stand segments if cabs negotiate fares. These problems probably would not be significant in the radio-dispatch and contract segments, where repeat purchasing should make search costs and exploitation unimportant.

First, with negotiated fares riders and drivers would have an incentive to devote resources to gathering information about fares, searching for low fares (in the case of riders) or high fares (in the case of drivers), and bargaining. Palmer (1983, ch. 3, pp. 2-3) and Gallick and Sisk (1984) have argued that one rationale for regulating fares is to reduce these transactions costs. However, to the extent that these activities do occur, one can conclude that the impediments to price competition discussed in the preceding subsection are exaggerated.

Second, drivers might exploit riders in bargaining. Fare ceilings would prevent such exploitation. This argument is based on the assumption that the driver might be in a position to extract an unreasonably high fare, either because the rider might be faced with a high cost of finding another cab, or because a significant share of taxi riders are visitors who would not have the information necessary to bargain effectively. However, Beesley and Glaister (1983) note that the rider might be in a position to impose a low fare because the driver would be faced with the cost of finding another rider.

C. Economies of Scale

Economies of scale exist when average cost declines as a firm's output increases. If the output range over which average cost declines is large relative to the size of the market, the number of firms in the industry may be small and firms may charge prices above marginal cost without inducing entry. If so, industry output will be inefficiently low, and a price ceiling that prevents firms from exercising market power could increase efficiency.

There appear to be no important economies of scale for cruising or stand taxis.[17] Where these segments are significant and entry is not limited, independently owned cabs generally operate in large numbers.[18] In New York City, some medallions are reserved for fleets while others are reserved for independents. The fact that the price of independent cab medallions is 20 percent higher than that for fleet cab medallions[19] suggests that scale economies are not important for cruising cabs.

On the other hand, there are significant economies of scale in radio-dispatch. First, economies arise because of indivisibilities in inputs used in dispatching, management, and advertising.[20] Second, a larger fleet would be able to provide service with less customer waiting time and less vacant cab hours or miles, because a rider calling a random cab company would be more likely to call one with a cab nearby if fewer dispatch systems controlled a given total number of cabs.[21] There are also economies of scale in negotiating for and providing contract services.

Economies of scale in radio-dispatch and contract operations would be more likely to cause problems of market power in small urban areas than in large ones.[22] In any event, market power would not be a significant concern in areas where "hit and run" entry from neighboring jurisdictions is feasible or where close substitutes, such as good public transit, exist.[23]

D. Underpricing of Taxi Trips

A number of the preceding subsections have suggested rationales for fare regulation. An attempt to regulate fares may price some categories of trips so low that they would involve losses for taxi firms. Firms would have an incentive to refuse service in such cases even though most of the riders involved might be willing to pay enough to make the service profitable. This problem could be used as an argument against fare regulation, but if fares are regulated it provides a possible rationale for prohibitions against service refusal and for requirements to provide service at certain places or times.

While some mispricing of this sort may be unintentional, as a matter of social policy cities may deliberately set unprofitably low fares (or avoid surcharges) for certain categories of trips, for example, during periods and at places where demand is low.

The efficient policy would be to permit (or impose) fare surcharges for the unprofitable categories of trips. If this is not done, a second-best policy would be to provide an explicit subsidy for the services in question. A prohibition against service refusal or a requirement to provide certain services involves a cross-subsidy, that is, a tax on some categories of trips to finance a subsidy for other categories, and would be (at best) a third-best policy.

It is sometimes argued that a prohibition against service refusal or a requirement to provide certain services would not be effective without a requirement that firms operate fleets. This argument is most relevant to the cruising and stand market segments, where independents commonly operate. However, it might also be relevant to the radio-dispatch segment, since independent cabs can operate in that segment by subscribing to dispatch service. Suppose a city has adopted a fare structure that makes off-peak service unprofitable. If there are no restrictions on entry by independent cabs, it might be difficult to get any firm to offer the unprofitable off-peak service. First, it might be costly to enforce a requirement that independent cabs operate at unprofitable times, since it would be difficult to monitor the times that independent cabs operate. Second, if independent firms are free to operate only at high demand times, they will drive profits down to a normal level at these times. As a result, it would not be possible to induce larger firms to provide service at unprofitable times because they would not be able to balance the resulting losses with above-normal profits at any other time.[24]

This rationale for preventing entry by independent cabs is weakened by the fact that requirements to provide service may not be effective even with such a barrier. Complaints about service refusal are common in regulated cities. In some cases low-income, minority neighborhoods are not served by licensed cabs and depend on unlicensed, gypsy cabs.[25]

E. Inefficiently High Taxi Fares

Taxi fares might be inefficiently high for two reasons. First, they might be set at a high level by regulation. Second, in the absence of a fare ceiling at the efficient level, some of the potential sources of market failure discussed above might lead to high fares. As a result, high fares might be an important distortion in taxi markets, and efficiency gains from reducing fares might be large. However, if inefficiently high fares must be taken as given, then (as we have seen in Section III) restrictions on the number of taxicabs could conceivably increase efficiency.[26]

Consider the situation that prevails at some airports. Taxi fares are set at very high levels. At these fares, cabs are willing to wait a long time to get a passenger. Entry is restricted, and hence cabs earn an above-normal rate of return. Nevertheless, the number of cabs is sufficient that passenger waiting times are zero. Removal of entry restrictions without a reduction in fares would lead to a lengthening of the taxi line and a drop in the occupancy rate until average revenue equals average cost per hour. From society's point of view, costs would increase, but there would be no benefits. Thus, given the high fare, an entry restriction would be second-best efficient.

A less extreme version of this problem could conceivably arise in the cruising and radio-dispatch segments. Suppose the government sets the fare well above the efficient level in the latter market segments. In the absence of entry barriers, cabs will enter until profits are zero, even if the cost of additional cabs is greater than the willingness of consumers to pay for the resulting reduction in waiting time. Given the fare, an entry restriction that would prevent dissipation of rents could be second-best efficient. Although consumers would unambiguously gain from removal of such an entry barrier because waiting time would decline, owners of taxi firms would lose more than consumers would gain.

Tolley et al. (1984, pp. 28-31) report simulations that suggest that under some assumptions deregulation of entry without a reduction in fares might reduce efficiency in each of the major taxi market segments (cruising, dispatch, and airport). Further simulations suggest that the problem is likely to occur at airports, is conceivable but by no means certain in the cruising segment, and is unlikely in the radio-dispatch segment.[27]

F. Overpricing of Public Transit

If two goods are close substitutes in consumption and the first is priced above marginal cost, then efficiency may be increased by pricing the second above marginal cost as well. The inefficiently high price for the first good would encourage inefficiently low consumption of the first good and inefficiently high consumption of the second, and these misallocations might be reduced if the latter's price was raised.

It has been argued by Schreiber (1975) that taxi and transit rides are close substitutes and that transit rides are priced above short-run marginal cost. If this is true, transit use would be too low and taxi use would be too high. The efficient policy would be to reduce transit fares. A second-best policy might be to raise taxi fares above marginal cost. If neither of these policies is adopted, a restriction on the number of taxis might increase efficiency.

It is unlikely that on average, for the various categories of transit rides, fares are above marginal costs. Where transit fares do not vary with time of day, transit rides during off-peak periods when the transit system is not congested probably are priced above marginal cost. However, transit rides during peak periods when the transit system is congested probably are priced below marginal cost. And where transit passes are used, all rides for passholders are priced below marginal cost. This suggests that transit fares are below as often as they are above marginal costs, and that it would not be efficient to restrict taxi service on the grounds that transit is mispriced.[28]

G. Congestion and Pollution Externalities

1. Congestion

Taking the level of nontaxi traffic as given, the operation of cabs on congested streets and at stands slows down other road users, increasing their travel time and the money costs of travel. The economics literature dealing with congestion suggests that passenger cars impose marginal congestion costs of over $.25 per mile when they use congested urban streets.[29] If road users are not charged for the marginal congestion costs they impose, the use of congested streets will be inefficiently high. Economists have suggested that in theory the most efficient form of government intervention to correct this market failure would be imposition of road user charges that would vary with the extent of congestion. For a variety of political and economic reasons, governments do not in fact impose such congestion charges. The question is whether efficiency would be increased in this situation by restrictions on the number of taxicabs and/or on cruising without restrictions on other types of road vehicles.

A limitation on the number of taxicabs or on cruising would probably reduce the amount of congestion cabs themselves cause, but there are several reasons to doubt that the benefits of such restrictions would outweigh the costs.[30] Such restrictions would increase travel costs for potential taxi riders. Off-setting benefits might be negligible. First, while there would be an inefficiently large number of private automobiles in the absence of government intervention, it is not clear that there would be an inefficiently large number of cabs or excessive cruising. Another market imperfection, discussed below in the subsection on waiting time externalities, would cause underproduction of taxicab services, particularly by cruising cabs. The market failure due to waiting time externalities would at least partially offset any market failure due to congestion externalities. Second, a restriction on the number of cabs or on cruising would lead to an increase in road use by private automobiles. This would cause an at least partially offsetting increase in congestion.

In any event, the extreme version of the congestion argument, namely, that free entry would lead to downtown areas clogged with taxicabs, is refuted by the experience of cities such as Washington, D.C., and London, which have not restricted entry, and of the 14 or more U.S. cities that opened entry in 1979–1984.[31] However, if a city does conclude that the number of cruising cabs is inefficiently high, the appropriate policy would be a reduction in the maximum fare, not a restriction on entry.

The preceding discussion has been concerned with general congestion of urban streets. A different, local congestion problem arises at cab stands at some airports and rail stations. In such cases, cabs impose delays on each other and on other traffic, and occasionally cabbies use force to allocate limited space.[32] Sometimes the origin of the problem is high fares, which attract a large number of cabs. In these cases, the efficient policy would be to reduce fares, not to restrict entry. In some cases, the problem is that a scarce resource, space for taxicabs, is not priced. In these cases, the efficient policy might be to charge user fees at congested cab stands, not to restrict entry.

2. Air Pollution

Schreiber (1975) argues that air pollution provides a justification for restrictions on the number of taxis and on cruising similar to that provided by congestion. The arguments are similar, except that the marginal pollution damage per vehicle mile is considerably less than the marginal congestion cost on busy streets.[33] Also, it makes little sense to restrict road use, particularly by one category of users, to deal with air pollution. A more efficient approach would be to reduce the amount of pollution per vehicle mile or hour through emission standards or charges.[34] However, air pollution standards are already imposed on automobiles, and additional measures might reduce efficiency.[35]

H. Waiting Time Externalities

Passenger requests for taxi service are random in time, space, and length. As a result, models of passenger waiting time, vehicle occupancy rates, and trip generation use queuing theory. Queuing models commonly have an increasing returns to scale property at what in this case amounts to the industry (rather than firm) level. In particular, if the number of passenger requests for service and the number of taxis in service are simultaneously increased by the same percentage, the average passenger waiting time and therefore the average social cost of production for rides declines.[36]

In this situation, if the taxi industry has a competitive structure, the return to a firm adding a cab is less than the marginal social benefit, that is, there is an externality. As a result, even without barriers to entry, there would be less than the efficient amount of service.[37] One solution to this potential market failure would be to subsidize taxi service.[38] In the absence of subsidies, the existence of waiting time externalities provides an argument against restrictions on the number of cabs and on cruising.

I. Informational Problems

It may be difficult or impossible for riders to judge some aspects of cab service quality before they ride. This might be true of driver behavior, driver qualifications, and some aspects of vehicle condition. Some of these aspects of quality can be judged by a rider on the basis of experience, however. Even for a single trip, drivers have an incentive to supply these aspects of quality because riders can adjust the size of the tip; see Gallick and Sisk (1984, p. 7). Also, provided that a significant share of riders are repeat users or are able to learn about reputations, there will be an incentive to form fleets and to supply some of these aspects of quality.

There are other aspects of quality that even regular riders might find difficult to judge, however, such as vehicle safety. Other aspects might take a large effort for riders to determine, such as liability insurance coverage. In these cases, regulations governing quality might reduce information costs and/or prevent inefficiently low quality service.

J. Enforcement of Regulations

Preceding subsections have suggested that some taxicab regulations, including fare ceilings, prohibitions on service refusal, and insurance and vehicle quality requirements, might be justified on efficiency grounds. It has been suggested that additional regulations may be justified because they reduce the cost of enforcing these regulations.

Gallick and Sisk (1984) suggest that entry barriers that enable incumbent taxi firms to earn above-normal returns, particularly transferable medallions, would reduce the cost of enforcing other regulations. They argue that it would be less costly for the government to obtain compliance by firms that depend on license renewals to continue earning above-normal profits than to obtain compliance by firms that stand to lose little if their violations cause them to be excluded from the industry. It might also be suggested that regulations that would reduce the number of taxi firms, including franchise and minimum size requirements, would reduce the costs of enforcing taxi regulations.

There are three problems with this argument that lead us to conclude that it does not justify entry restrictions. First, some cities with entry restrictions and high medallion values do not use suspension or revocation of licenses to enforce other policies.[39] Second, it seems likely that the benefits of increased cab service and competition that result from open entry would greatly exceed any benefits from reduced enforcement costs under a restricted entry system. Third, the alleged enforcement advantages attributed to restricted entry could be achieved if cab firms were required to post bonds that would be forfeited in the event of their violation of taxi regulations.

K. Conclusion

Because of market imperfections, certain regulations might increase efficiency, particularly in the cruising and stand segments: requirements that cabs post fares, fare ceilings, and minimum standards affecting the quality of service. In addition, if fares are regulated in such a way that certain categories of service are unprofitable, prohibitions against service refusal, requirements to provide service, and requirements that firms operate some minimum number of cabs may be second-best efficient. However, restrictions on entry, minimum fare controls, and restrictions on ride sharing (including dial-a-ride and jitney service) reduce rather than increase efficiency in all market segments.

V. REGULATION IN PRACTICE

Although theoretical justifications can be offered for some taxicab regulations, there are four reasons for skepticism concerning whether such regulations would generally increase efficiency in the real world. First, regulation has administrative costs for governments and cab companies, for example, costs involved in changing regulated fares.

Second, the analytical and informational problems involved in determining the efficient levels of the relevant policy variables are great. Many of the agencies that regulate taxis (e.g., police departments) have no economic expertise.[40]

Third, regulations impose an inefficient uniformity. For example, it might be efficient to have different qualities of cab service available at different fares. However, fare or quality regulations might lead to a homogeneous service. Also, regulations interfere with the market's ability to reallocate resources in response to changes in costs and demand.

Fourth, the agencies that regulate taxis may not be motivated primarily by concern for market failure and efficiency. This is evident from the fact that a number of common regulations (e.g., restrictions on entry and minimum fares) have no persuasive efficiency justification. The following subsection discusses some of the apparent motivations behind taxi regulations other than prevention of market failure.

A. Motivations for Regulation

1. Protection of Transit and Taxis

An important motivation for taxi regulation, particularly for restrictions on entry and the range of services, has been protection of public transit and existing taxi firms from competition.[41] Entry restrictions enable taxi owners to earn a return greater than that available in other activities. This conclusion is supported by the review of the history of taxi regulation in Section V.B and by the existence of high medallion prices.

2. Promotion of City Image

Regulations may have been used to artificially create taxi systems that appeal to high-income business people and tourists visiting the city, as well as to high-income local residents. There is some evidence that reregulation of taxicabs in Atlanta and San Diego following open entry may have been supported mainly by nontaxi businesses concerned with the convention trade.[42]

3. Self-Interest of Regulators

The nature of taxi regulations may have been influenced by the self-interest of regulators. For instance, Eckert (1973) hypothesizes that the form of taxi regulation will be different when there is a permanent regulatory agency run by career bureaucrats (e.g., a police department) than when there is a regulatory commission consisting of unpaid members appointed for limited terms. He argues that career bureaucrats will have more incentive to increase their salaries, and hence the sizes of their bureaucracies and the amount of regulation, while appointed commissioners will have more incentive to simplify their jobs and hence reduce the number of taxi firms they deal with. Empirically, he finds that regulatory commissions are more likely to grant monopoly franchises, to set up exclusive cab stands, to impose uniform rates, and to prohibit leasing of cabs. These regulations limit the number of parties commissions must deal with.[43]

4. Quality of Taxi Service

It is sometimes argued that a combination of minimum fare regulations and entry barriers is justified to raise the quality of taxi service.[44] The argument is that this combination would increase profits per taxi trip but prevent the dissipation of profits through entry. If cabs were not fully utilized, cab firms would allegedly increase the quality of their vehicles and drivers in order to attract more riders.

There are serious problems with this argument. It would apply only to aspects of quality that riders can evaluate and only to taxi market segments in which cabs compete on quality, for example, vehicle appearance in the radio-dispatch segment. However, there is no reason to expect an unregulated market to undersupply quality in these cases. If the regulations considered here did in fact increase quality, one would expect such increases to be inefficient. [45] In addition, these regulations would do nothing to deal with the two potential quality problems we identified earlier (when fixed fares and search costs limit quality competition and when riders cannot readily evaluate quality).

In any event, it is obvious from the high market prices of medallions that a large share of the excess taxi profits that result from entry barriers are not used to increase the quality of service, even when there are minimum fare regulations. [46]

B. History of Taxi Regulation

Prior to 1929, three major types of government regulations affected taxis: (1) maximum fare regulations; (2) consumer protection regulations requiring posting of fares and/or use of meters, [47] licensing of drivers, and insurance coverage; and (3) restrictions on jitney operation, including prohibitions against ride sharing, which were imposed around 1915 to protect streetcars from competition. [48] There were few (if any) direct restrictions on entry into the taxicab industry or minimum fare requirements that would have limited price competition. [49]

This situation changed dramatically between 1929 and 1937. Many cities established commissions to regulate taxis and imposed restrictions on entry and minimum fares. By 1932, eight states had authorized their commerce commissions to regulate taxicabs as common carriers.

This movement began during the late 1920s, before the Depression, following taxi fare reductions and a number of fare wars. The trend accelerated during the early 1930s, when both car prices and wages dropped. Unemployed workers entered the taxi industry using rented cars, and fares, occupancy rates, and revenues per cab declined. Pressure for restrictions on taxis came from the American Transit Association, transit firms, the National Association of Taxicab Owners, and established taxi fleets.

State and local regulation of entry and minimum fares in the taxi industry coincided with the extension of federal regulations to interstate transportation. [50] The Motor Carrier Act of 1935 imposed federal regulation on entry, routes, and rates in the trucking and intercity bus industries, and the Civil Aeronautics Act of 1938 imposed federal regulation on the airline industry.

In 1932–36, there were 93 U.S. cities with populations in excess of 100,000. Table 1 shows how the number of these cities with three types of taxi regulations increased between 1932 and 1936. In addition, as of April 1932 at least 53 cities with populations over 25,000 required taximeters (Gilbert and Samuels, 1982, p. 71). They note (p. 73): "The taximeter requirement made the taxi operators pro-

Table 1.   Taxi Regulations in 93 U.S. Cities with Populations over 100,000

| | Number of Cities | |
Type of Regulation	Jan. 1, 1932	Jan. 1, 1936
Taxis licensed only after proof that public convenience and necessity require additional service	33	57
Fixed ceiling on number of permits	•2	n.a.
Minimum fare regulation	20	34
Taxis required to have insurance or be bonded	66	73*

n.a.: not available
*Four more granted certificates of public convenience and necessity only to financially responsible operators.
Sources: Transit Journal (January 1936, p. 23); Gilbert and S amuels (1982, p. 71).

viders of exclusive-ride service. Unable to provide shared-ride service, taxis could no longer compete with mass transit modes. This was welcomed by the mass transit operators.''[51]

The discussions of the early 1930s emphasize that the motivation behind the regulations was "to drive many cut-throat cabs, operating without authority, from the streets" and to enable the organized cab fleets and transit companies to increase their profits.[52] Restriction of entry was not motivated by a concern for congestion or pollution (Transportation Center, 1958, pp. 61-63).

C. Effects of Regulation

The theoretical model and empirical evidence from cities with and without regulation indicate that the typical regulatory regime has a number of important effects on resource allocation and income distribution.[53]

1. Effects on Industrial Structure

A number of taxicab regulations contribute to increased concentration and market power in the taxi industry. (1) Franchise requirements create monopolies or limit the number of firms. (2) Restrictions on the number of taxicabs make it possible for one firm or a few firms to acquire a significant share of licenses and to exercise market power. (3) Requirements that new taxi firms operate at least a certain number of cabs act as barriers to entry. (4) Policies that allocate new licenses to existing firms make entry of new firms impossible even if the industry expands.

According to statistics presented by Gilbert et al. (1982, p. 14), in 1981 over 35 percent of cities with taxi service had only one taxi firm; 32 percent more had one firm that operated 50 to 99 percent of all cabs. One indication that taxi firms in some cities exercise market power is that they leave a significant share of their licenses idle even though the positive price of medallions indicates that there are economic profits.

Table 2.   Entry by New Radio-Dispatch
Fleets with 10 or More Cabs
following Open Entry

City	Firm	Number of Cabs
Oakland	Bay Area*	74
	St. Francis	17
	Goodwill	14
Berkeley	Bay Area*	25
Sacramento	Capitol	27
Jacksonville	Gator	26
Tucson	Allstate	20
Portland	Portland	15
Charlotte	Queen City	14
Phoenix	5 companies	10 or more each

*The same firm entered Oakland and Berkeley using the same cabs.
Sources: Knight et al. (1983), Gelb (1982) p. 34), Paratransit Services (1983) Figure 6), Teal et al. (1983, pp. 8, 19).

In virtually all cities that deregulated entry, the number of taxi firms increased and the market shares of the largest firms decreased. In more than half the cities, new radio-dispatch fleets entered (see Table 2), and in most cities there was a significant increase in the number of independents.

2. Effects on Industry Performance

a. Fare level.   In the absence of mandated fares or binding ceilings, one would expect restrictions on the number of firms, the number of cabs, and shared-ride service and regulations that raise costs to lead to higher fares. However, since most cities regulate fares, this effect is not automatic. Fare regulations could divert the impact of other regulations on to waiting time. Also, a city could mandate a high or low fare without having other taxi regulations. It seems likely that regulations have generally raised fares but that this effect varies substantially among cities. Washington, D.C., has open entry, low, regulated fares and a very large number of cabs. The fact that service is good, at least in areas where drivers can expect to obtain a return trip, suggests that fares are not inefficiently low on average. Fares in large cities with entry barriers range from marginally higher than those in Washington to over twice as high (see Table 3). Some of the difference among fares seems to be a systematic difference between West Coast and other cities. Cities on the West Coast generally have higher fares than other cities, perhaps because costs are higher due to higher wages or lower density of demand for taxi trips. Thus, fares in Seattle and San Diego, which deregulated entry and fares in 1979, are above those of many non-West Coast cities that have entry barriers and fare regulations. Nevertheless, it seems plausible to argue that in the absence of regulation radio-dispatch fares would generally be somewhat lower.[54]

Table 3.   Fares in Washington, D.C., and Eight Other Cities, 1984*

Description of Trip				
Origin	RFK Stadium	Japanese Embassy	Japanese Embassy	Capitol
Destination	Wisconsin and M	Capitol	White House	White Hous
Zone lines crossed	3	1	1	0
Airline distance	5.21	3.07	1.59	1.54
(mi.)				
Fare ($)				
Washington, D.C.**†	3.90	2.45	2.45	1.70
Los Angeles	9.10	6.10	3.90	3.90
San Diego	7.40	4.80	3.00	3.00
Seattle	7.20	4.60	2.80	2.80
Minneapolis	6.75	4.35	2.75	2.55
New Orleans	6.30	4.10	2.50	2.50
New York	5.60	3.70	2.40	2.30
Chicago	5.60	3.60	2.30	2.30
Baltimore	4.10	2.80	1.90	1.90

*Fares for other cities are meter rates for airline distance.
**Add $.65 for phone hails.
†Washington's zone system can cause trips of equal length to be priced differently if a different number of zone lines a crossed. This accounts for the difference in the price of the 1.54 mile ride versus the 1.59 mile ride.
Sources: D.C. fare and zone data: District of Columbia, Public Service Commission, Taxicab Zone Map.
          New Orleans: FTC Survey
          Baltimore: ITA Rate Sheet, May 1983
          Other Cities: J. M. Chernow, Houston, Texas

This expectation is supported by evidence from Seattle and Milwaukee. Using a private transportation index to proxy taxicab costs, Zerbe estimated that in 1984, five years after Seattle deregulated entry and fares, fares in the radio-dispatch segment were 17 to 20 percent lower than they would have been if regulation had continued. By contrast, non-radio-dispatch fares were 4 percent higher.[55] A similar calculation for Milwaukee, which deregulated entry but not fares in 1979, indicates that in 1984 fares were 12 percent lower than they would have been if entry regulation had continued.[56]

b. Number of cab hours of service.   Entry restrictions reduce the number of cabs in service, at least during peak periods, and the exercise of market power that they permit has led to a further reduction in cab service in some cities.

Cities without entry restrictions prior to the recent series of deregulations (Atlanta between 1965 and 1981, Honolulu, and Washington, D.C.) had substantially higher ratios of taxicab licenses per resident in 1970 than did cities with entry restrictions. The same is true for Washington, D.C., in 1983 (see Table 4).[57]

The number of cabs increased in a large majority of the cities that recently switched to open entry. The range of the increase was wide, presumably reflecting the extent to which entry restrictions were binding prior to deregulation and the extent of deregulation. The median increase in the number of cabs for 14 cities that opened entry was 21 to 30 percent (see Table 5). Although percentage increases were generally higher for independents than for fleets, they were also significant for fleets. There is evidence that the number of cab hours of service per day increased by a smaller percentage than the number of cabs, perhaps because the entry barriers were not binding in off-peak periods.

c. Waiting time. Taxi regulations, particularly entry restrictions, have probably led to an increase in average customer waiting time. The increase in the number of cabs and fleets in cities that have deregulated has probably reduced waiting time. In the first two years following regulatory reform in San Diego, there was a 20 percent drop in average waiting time in the radio-dispatch segment.[58] There are also reports that waiting times for radio-dispatch service declined significantly in Seattle.[59] On the other hand, there is a report that waiting time did not change in Oakland and Berkeley in spite of an increase in the number of cabs and firms (Knight et al., 1983).

d. Number of trips. Since taxicab regulations have apparently increased fares and/or waiting times, they have presumably reduced the number of taxi trips. Kirby et al. (1974, p. 284) report that the number of taxi rides per capita in Washington, D.C., where entry is not restricted and fares are low, is more than four times as high as in San Francisco, a city of comparable size, where entry is restricted and fares are higher.

e. Quality of service. Regulations concerning driver qualifications, vehicle safety, and insurance coverage presumably increase the quality of taxi service. Moreover, in cities that have deregulated other aspects of the taxi industry, quality regulations have seldom been relaxed and sometimes have been tightened.

The effects on quality of other regulations are ambiguous. On the one hand, high regulated fares combined with entry restrictions could encourage radio-dispatch firms to compete for customers by offering higher quality service, for example, more comfortable cabs. On the other hand, maximum fare regulations could lead to lower quality in the cruising cab and airport stand market segments, where quality competition would be limited. Also, inefficiently low mandatory fares could lead to low quality service. In any event, there are about equal numbers of reports of quality improvement and deterioration following deregulation of entry and fares in various cities.[60]

f. Costs. The effect of regulation on vehicle and driver costs per passenger mile is ambiguous. On the one hand, several regulations would increase these costs. Quality regulations increase input levels. Some requirements reduce utilization rates: for example, requirements to provide a certain number of hours of service; or restrictions forcing cabs from one jurisdiction that drop of passengers in another jurisdiction to return empty.

On the other hand, entry restrictions that reduce the number of cabs would increase the utilization rate and hence reduce vehicle and driver costs per passenger mile, unless they were accompanied by a large fare increase.

Table 4. Taxicab Licensing

City	1980 Population[a]	1970 Licensing Policy[b]	1983 Number of Vehicle Licenses	1970 Licenses/1970 Population	1983 Licenses/1980 Population[c]	1983 Licenses/1977 Hotels[d]	1983 Licenses/1977 Hotel Receipts[e]	1983 Licenses/1982 Air Passengers[f]
New York	7,072	N	11,787	1.5	1.7	31.9	16.6	677
Chicago	3,005	N	4,600	1.4	1.5	21.0	12.5	275
Los Angeles	2,967	C	1,500	0.4	0.5	4.0	6.3	93
Philadelphia	1,688	C	1,600	0.9	0.9	30.2	22.9	417
Miami (Dade)	1,626	N	1,528	1.3	0.9	2.7	4.3	155
Houston	1,595	C	1,829	0.4	1.1	10.7	10.2	216
Detroit	1,203	N	1,310	0.9	1.1	12.8	24.2	274
Dallas	904	C	900	0.6	1.0	7.2	6.2	92
San Diego	876	n.a.	900	0.4	1.0	5.1	6.2	329
Phoenix	790	C	325	0.2	0.4	2.6	4.2	82
Baltimore	787	N	1,100	1.3	1.4	33.3	n.a.	579
San Antonio	786	n.a.	480	0.8	0.6	4.5	7.7	288
Indianapolis	701	n.a.	326	0.6	0.5	4.0	n.a.	26
San Francisco	679	N	711	1.1	1.0	3.1	2.2	68
Memphis	646	n.a.	300	0.6	0.5	3.5	4.6	137
Washington, D.C.	638	Open	8,600	11.3	13.5	98.8	38.7	1,206
Milwaukee	636	N	400	0.6	0.6	9.5	11.2	256
San Jose	629	n.a.	150	n.a.	0.2	4.3	6.3	100
Cleveland	574	C	240	0.7	0.4	4.7	5.7	95
Columbus	565	C	390	0.7	0.7	7.8	7.7	317
Boston	563	N	1,525	2.5	2.7	46.2	16.4	215

152

City		Licensing policy	Population (thousands)					
New Orleans	558	C	1,608	2.5	2.9	18.1	9.8	564
Jacksonville, Fla.	541	n.a.	225	0.5	0.4	3.5	7.0	230
Seattle	494	C	570	0.6	1.2	6.4	8.0	124
Denver	492	n.a.	507	0.6	1.0	4.8	5.3	45
St. Louis	453	C	1,500	2.0	3.3	35.7	37.7	261
Kansas City, Mo.	448	N	530	1.1	1.2	8.0	7.4	206
Atlanta	425	Open	1,450	3.8	3.4	21.0	9.3	84
Pittsburgh	424	C	500	1.1	1.2	25.0	n.a.	109
Oklahoma City	403	n.a.	231	n.a.	0.6	3.2	4.9	183
Cincinnati	395	n.a.	380	n.a.	1.0	15.2	n.a.	238
Ft. Worth	385	n.a.	185	n.a.	0.5	4.3	6.5	38
Minneapolis	371	N	248	0.6	0.7	6.5	n.a.	48
Portland, Ore.	366	n.a.	250	n.a.	0.7	3.1	n.a.	135

n.a.: not available

aPopulation in thousands for the political jurisdiction, i.e., the central city, except Dade County. In New York City, licensed cabs are concentrated in Manhattan, which had a population of 1,428 thousand.

bN: Number of vehicles restricted

C: Franchise requirement, possibly with restriction on total number of vehicles

cLicenses per 1,000 population

dLicenses per hotel, motor hotel, and motel (establishments with payrolls)

eLicenses per million dollars in hotel, motor hotel, and motel receipts (all establishments)

fLicenses per million enplaned air passengers

Sources:

Population: U.S. Department of Commerce, Bureau of Census Statistical Abstract of the United States: 1982-83 (1982), Table 26. Data are for 1980.

Licensing policy: Kirby et al. (1974, p. 77). Data circa 1970.

Number of vehicle licenses: International Taxicab Association. Rate Sheet, May 1983; District of Columbia Public Service Commission. Data are for 1983.

Number of hotels, motor hotels, and motels and hotel, motor hotel, and motor receipts: U.S. Department of Commerce, Bureau of the Census, 1977 Census of Service Industries

Enplaned air passengers: U.S. Civil Aeronautics Board, Airport Activity Statistics of Certified Route Carriers. Data are for 1982.

Table 5. Changes in Total and Fleet Cabs Following Open Entry

City	Year of Observation		Total Cabs			Fleet Cabs[a]		
	Before	After	Before	After	Change(%)	Before	After	Change(%)
Cities in which the number of cabs increased								
Atlanta	1965	1983	700[b]	1538	120	n.a.	n.a.	n.a.
Portland	1978	1981	226	244	8	226	244	8
San Diego	1978	1983	409	915	123	384	439	14
Seattle	1979	1981	421	511	21	369	433	17
Oakland	1979	1983	224[c]	329	47	207	309	49
Berkeley	1979	1983	75[d]	91	21	64	82	28
Milwaukee	1979	1983	380	425	12	n.a.	n.a.	n.a.
Phoenix	1981	1983	250	325	30	250	290	16
Tucson	1982	1984	60	110	83	60	85	42
Sacramento	1982	1983	110	168	53	110	155	41
Charlotte	1982	1984	75	105	40	75	105	40
Jacksonville	1983	1984	107	n.a.[c]	n.a.	107	n.a.[c]	n.a.
Cities in which the number of cabs decreased								
Indianapolis	1972	1974	502	466	-7	492	309	-37
Fresno	1979	1981	70	50	-29	65	n.a.	n.a.
Spokane	1980	1983	100	80	-20	96	57	-41

n.a.: not available

[a]Cabs in fleets of four or more, except in the case of Indianapolis, where data are for cabs in fleets of two or more. The increase in the number of fleet cabs in Table5 is less than the size of new fleets in Table 2 in Berkeley and Phoenix because incumbent fleets decreased in size.

[b]Plus a large but unknown number of unlicensed cabs.

[c]Only about 100 were active.

[d]Many of these were not active.

Sources: Gelb (1982, p.34; 1983a, p. 54; 1983b, p. 30); Gilbert and Gelb (1980, p. 9); Knight et al. (1983); Paratransit Services (1983, pp. 9, 10, 17, 36, 37, and

[e]By 1984, one new fleet with 26 cabs and 17 to 19 independent cabs had entered.

Figs. 5, 6, 7, 10; Teal et al. (1983, p. 9).

154

Taxi regulations also involve administrative costs for city councils that deal with entry applications and requests for fare increases. There are also enforcement costs for quality regulations, but these costs may be reduced by entry restrictions that reduce the number of firms and vehicles that must be dealt with.

g. Allocation of cabs. In regulated cities, there are complaints about refusals of short-haul service in situations where cabs wait in long queues, and complaints that cabs may refuse to pick up passengers who they think will give small tips or who want to go to areas where cabs are unlikely to find a return fare or that are not safe.[61] These problems can generally be attributed to inefficient fare structures, for example, inefficiently high fares that lead to long cab lines or inefficiently low fares for certain categories of service as a result of requirements to use the same meter fares for all trips. Many cities prohibit service refusals.

The typical deregulation evidently has not solved service refusal problems, for two reasons.[62] First, limitations on fare competition at cab stands may have left such fares inefficiently high, and hence queues are still long. Second, even when fares are deregulated, cities have continued to require the use of meters, and hence some trips are priced below cost.

h. Types of service. Many cities prohibit, or impose regulations that effectively eliminate, shared-ride service, including dial-a-ride and jitney service. These restrictions may be significant in large, densely populated cities. However, in spite of the fact that several West Coast and Sun Belt cities legalized shared-ride and jitney service in the process of deregulating the taxi industry, such services were not introduced except in San Diego. This may be a result of the relatively low density of these cities.

3. Effects on Efficiency

There is virtually unanimous agreement among economists that existing restrictions on entry into the taxi market, mimimum fares, and ride sharing are inefficient; however, see Gallick and Sisk (1984). Some of the ways in which the allocation of resources under existing regulations is inefficient include: (a) the number of taxi rides taken is inefficiently low because of regulations that raise fares, restrict the level of taxi service, and increase waiting times; (b) the cost of producing taxi trips is unnecessarily high because of regulations that prevent ride sharing or that increase deadheading and the length of taxi lines; and (c) there are shortages of certain types of service because of the incentives provided by fare structures.

There are, however, few empirical estimates of the welfare loss due to regulation. Beesley and Glaister (1983, p. 611) calculate the welfare effects of reducing the regulated fare and restricting the number of cabs in London. They estimate that a 10 percent reduction in the fare with continued free entry would have produced a net social gain of $721 (at the 1984 exchange rate) per hour in 1978. They estimate that a 20 percent reduction in the number of cabs below the free entry level would have caused a net social loss of $2,744 per hour. Assuming these two effects occur 10 hours per day, 250 days per year, the annual amounts would be $1.8 million and $6.9 million, respectively.

4. Effects on the Distribution of Well-Being

The principal losers from regulation are consumers of the services whose prices and/or waiting times increase. Data indicate that in many cities consumption of taxi rides per capita is higher for lower-income people (Allred et al., 1978). In addition, taxi regulations restrict employment opportunities for low-income and minority urban workers. Thus, taxi regulation imposes a disproportionate burden on low-income people.

The principal gainers from regulation are the people who obtained licenses and franchises at prices below their market values. Many of these people have already sold their medallions or shares in taxi companies, and hence many current owners have not gained from regulation (Tullock, 1975).

D. Regulatory Reform

In a survey of 103 U.S. cities, Shaw et al. (1983) found that during the past five years 24 cities made major changes in entry and fare regulation. Sixteen cities relaxed entry controls while three tightened them. Seventeen cities relaxed fare regulations, with 13 eliminating controls over fares and four moving from mandatory to maximum fares. [63]

Overall, there has been a number of favorable effects and no widespread significant problems related to open entry in radio-dispatch market segments. The problems that have been observed could be dealt with through driver qualification and vehicle safety requirements without restrictions on the total number of cabs.

By contrast to the radio-dispatch segment, there have been many problems in the cab stand segment, principally at airports. Such problems have been documented in some detail for Seattle, San Diego and Phoenix, and there are brief reports of problems in Atlanta, Spokane, and Sacramento.

Airport taxis have charged high and/or different fares following deregulation, evidently because of the difficulty of achieving a workable degree of price competition at taxi stands that continue to operate on a first-in-first-out basis. Higher fares have led to inefficient lengthening of cab lines and shorthaul refusals. Attempts by drivers to circumvent the queue and holdups in the queue when consumers have not accepted the first cab have contributed to disputes among drivers. The increased number of cabs and the resulting incentive to avoid the queue have increased administrative costs for airport authorities. Consumers have complained about vehicle quality, driver behavior, and all the other problems just described.

These problems do not provide an argument in favor of entry restrictions. Rather, they suggest that there would be significant efficiency gains from redesigning airport cab stands to increase fare competition or from imposing or lowering fare ceilings on airport taxi service.[64] Fare ceilings could be reduced until the taxi queue shortened to the desired length. In fact, some airports (San Diego, Seattle) have responded by imposing fare ceilings. It is not necessary to respond, as have some airports, such as Phoenix, by limiting the number of taxis that can pick up passengers, or, as have other cities (Atlanta, San Diego) by abandoning open entry in the entire city.

VI. CONCLUSION

Although a number of cities have recently deregulated, entry, fares, service, and quality in the taxi industry remain heavily regulated in most cities.

There is no persuasive economic rationale for some of the most important regulations. Restrictions on the total number of firms and vehicles and on minimum fares waste resources and impose a disproportionate burden on low-income people. Similarly, there is no economic justification for regulations that restrict shared-ride, dial-a-ride, and jitney service.

However, potential market failures provide a credible theoretical rationale for some other types of regulations, including fare ceilings and regulations dealing with vehicle safety and liability insurance.

Finally, some regulations might conceivably be justified on efficiency grounds because of distortions created by other taxi regulations. Fare regulations that underprice certain categories of trips might provide a second-best rationale for prohibitions on service refusal, requirements to offer service at certain times or places, or minimum levels on the numbers of cabs operated by firms. However, surcharges for unprofitable services would be more efficient than such service requirements.

Experience with open entry and fare competition in the radio-dispatch market segment has generally been favorable. This is particularly true in Seattle, Oakland, Berkeley, Sacramento, Charlotte, and Jacksonville. This is important because typically about 75 percent of taxi trips are produced by radio-dispatched cabs.

The favorable effects of open entry in the radio-dispatch segment include increases in the number of taxi firms and decreases in the market shares of the largest firms, increases in the number of cab hours of service, reductions in fares and response times, and reductions in the amount of time city councils devote to licensing and fare setting.

Overall, there have been no widespread significant problems related to open entry in radio-dispatch market segments. While an increase in customer complaints was recorded in Indianapolis and Fresno, these can best be dealt with through driver qualification and vehicle safety requirements rather than restrictions on the total number of cabs.

In marked contrast to the radio-dispatch segment, there have been many problems at airport cab stands following regulatory reform as a result of lengthening of the cab queues. These problems do not provide an argument in favor of entry restrictions, however. Rather, they suggest that there would be significant efficiency gains from either increasing fare competition at airports by altering the queue system or imposing or lowering fare ceilings on airport taxi service.

ACKNOWLEDGMENTS

The analysis and conclusions are the responsibility of the authors and do not necessarily reflect the views of other members of the Federal Trade Commission staff or the Commission itself. The authors would like to thank Denis Breen, Edward Gallick, Robert Lande, William MacLeod, Jerry Philpott, David Scheffman, Richard Zerbe, and an anonymous referee for comments on earlier drafts and other assistance.

NOTES

1. *Community Communications Co. v. City of Boulder*, 455 U.S. 40 (1982); *City of Lafayette v. Louisiana Power and Light Co.*, 435 U.S. 389 (1978).

2. *FTC v. City of New Orleans*, Dkt. 9179, complaint filed May 10, 1984, withdrawn January 3, 1985; *FTC v. City of Minneapolis*, Dkt. 9180, complaint filed May 10, 1984. There are also several private antitrust actions challenging the authority of cities to preclude entry. See *Red Top Sedan Services, Inc. v. Dade County*, Civil Action No. 84-0701 (S.D. Fla., March 20, 1984); *Campbell v. City of Chicago*, 1983-2 CCH Trade Cas. ¶65,684 (N.D. Ill., E.D. 1983).

3. Restrictions on entry and minimum fares are the only regulations challenged in the FTC complaints cited in note 2.

4. Transit data are for 1980 and come from American Public Transit Association (1981).

5. For example, New Orleans requires that new taxi firms operate a minimum of 125 cabs while a number of existing firms do not meet that requirement and operate under a grandfather clause.

6. For example, medallion values for a few major cities are: New York City, $50,000—$60,000; Boston, $32,000; San Francisco, $15,000—$20,000.

7. Versions of this model can be found in Orr (1969), Douglas (1972), De Vany (1975a), Schreiber (1975), Abe and Brush (1976), Beesley and Glaister (1983), and Tolley et al. (1984). Similar models appear in the public transit literature, e.g., Frankena (1981, 1982, 1983). See also De Vany (1975b, 1976), and De Vany and Saving (1977).

8. Mathematically, the zero-profit locus gives the solutions to the equations $FR - cS = 0$, $R = f(F, V)$, and $V = S - bR$, where F is the fare, R is the number of rides, c is the cost per cab hour of service, S is the total number of cab hours of service, $f(\cdot)$ is the demand function, V is the number of vacant cab hours of service, and b is the fraction of an hour required to produce a ride. The zero-profit locus in fare-service space would be roughly elliptical, and hence for a given fare there would be two equilibrium service levels. However, the lower service level would be unstable (Frankena, 1981, p. 339, n. 10). Figure 1 shows only the stable equilibrium portion of the zero-profit locus.

9. The model discussed here does not consider the external diseconomy involved in road congestion. In theory, a negative congestion externality could at least partially offset a positive waiting time externality, in which case the efficient point would lie to the left of K. However, in Section IV we suggest that consideration of congestion externalities would not have much effect on the location of the efficient point, in which case the efficient allocation would not lie to the left of the zero-point locus when both congestion and waiting time externalities are taken into account.

10. In this discussion, B happens to be the point at which the number of rides is maximized as well. In general, the two points need not coincide. For a discussion of some of the assumptions that determine the relationship between efficiency and ridership maximization, see Frankena (1983).

11. This figure is adapted from Sheshinski (1976), and Frankena (1982, Appendix C).

12. Wainwright (1984) notes that following deregulation of fares in San Diego and Seattle, fleets concentrating on radio-dispatch service charged lower fares than did independent cabs concentrating on street-hail and stand service.

13. If fares are regulated but quality is not, a similar argument might apply to quality competition. That is, firms serving the cruising and stand market segments might be able to reduce quality below the efficient level without causing riders to turn down the first cab. In this case, driver and vehicle quality regulations might increase efficiency. See Gallick and Sisk (1984). Of course, this could be considered as an argument against fare regulation.

14. Similarly, Douglas (1972) suggests that, because of high cost to consumers of searching for lower fares, fare competition would be limited and the equilibrium fare would be inefficiently high, for example, where the level of vehicle hours of service is maximized (point D in Figure 1). Other models make alternative assumptions to determine the fare-service equilibrium uniquely. Orr (1969) assumes arbitrarily that there is a ''normal'' ratio of engaged passenger miles to vehicle hours of taxi service. Beesley and Glaister (1983) simply assert that the equilibrium would coincide with the most efficient allocation along the zero-profit constraint (point B in Figure 1). For a similar conclusion in another model, see De Vany and Saving (1983).

15. Even if taxi stand and radio-dispatch service limit cruising cab fares, one might still argue that a price ceiling for cruising cabs could increase efficiency since it might obviate this replacement of the cruising cab market.

16. Quality competition would still be difficult, and minimum quality standards might be efficient.

17. Turvey (1960, p. 86), Meyer et al. (1965, p. 356), Eckert (1970, p. 431), De Vany (1977, p. 35), Beesley and Glaister (1979, p. 3 and footnote 3) and Palmer (1983, ch. 3, p. 3). Brown (1973) concluded that larger firms can obtain lower prices for inputs such as gas, oil, and tires. However, independent taxis can obtain the same prices by organizing purchasing cooperatives. Two other potential market imperfections might provide an incentive to organize fleets. First, in the absence of fare regulation there might be an incentive for cruising cabs to form fleets offering lower prices. Second, fleets could develop reputations and overcome potential problems arising from imperfect information about quality.

18. In New York City in 1930, prior to entry restrictions, 47.5 percent of cabs were independents; Schreiber (1975, p. 273). In cities that have deregulated recently and in Washington, D.C., independents are important in the cab stand and (where it exists) the cruising segment.

19. Gilbert and Samuels (1982, p. 92). One source attributes the price difference to the higher cost of labor to fleets due to unionization. *Regulation* (1982), p. 36.

20. Indivisibilities exist when there are minimum feasible quantities for inputs, e.g. one dispatcher or one phone line. Palmer (1983, ch. 3, p. 31) reports that cab firms in Toronto and London, Ontario, had one dispatcher per 60 to 90 cabs in peak periods. Taxi firms also provide phone lines at hotels, hospitals, stores, and bars.

21. Gelb (1983b, p. 96) reports that average response times and service refusal rates for radio-dispatch service in Seattle varied inversely with fleet size. See also Schroeter (1983, p. 89).

22. Palmer (1983, ch. 3, p. 10ff). Palmer suggests that a city with 250,000 people can support only two or three radio-dispatch/contract taxi firms.

23. Where there is market power, it may be efficient to impose a price ceiling on the service for which there are economies of scale. In the case of taxis, this would be dispatching, management, and advertising. Where fleets are not vertically integrated, the prices that should be subject to maximum controls are those charged by the fleet organization to owner-drivers. However, maximum fares for taxi rides may achieve similar results.

24. In their study of cities in England, Coe and Jackson (1983, p. 11) found that there was no shortage of cabs at any time of day in five out of six districts without entry barriers. Thus, entry barriers do not appear necessary to ensure service in off-peak periods.

25. There are unlicensed cabs in New York City, Chicago, Cleveland, Pittsburgh, and Toronto.

26. Very brief statements of this argument appear in De Vany (1975a, pp. 93-94) and Schroeter (1983). A longer exposition appears in Tolley et al. (1984, pp. 27-32).

27. Additional simulations were carried out by George Tolley and Charles Kahn under a Federal Trade Commission contract. There is another, somewhat different second-best argument against elimination of entry restrictions. Elimination of entry restrictions and hence above-normal profits might induce regulatory authorities to raise regulated fares to inefficiently high levels in an effort to maintain a target rate of return above the competitive level. Douglas and Miller (1974a,b) suggest that regulation of airline fares without restrictions on flight frequencies had this effect, which they called the "ratchet effect." The behavior of regulated fares in Washington, D.C., and Milwaukee under open entry does not support this argument, however.

28. For a discussion of efficient transit fares and the closely related issue of transit subsidies, see Frankena (1982).

29. For a summary of the literature on congestion costs, see Frankena (1979; 1982, ch. 2). See also Zerbe and Croke (1975, pp. 76-81).

30. Stelzer (1980, p. 5) suggests that some cruising might represent an inefficiently high quality service provided because of competition for riders at inefficiently high fare levels. In this case, deregulation of entry and fares might lead to lower fares, a shift from cruising to cab stands, and less congestion.

31. Kirby et al. (1974, p. 97). Palmer (1983, ch. 3, p. 79) notes that free entry works well in Sarnia and Windsor, Ontario, which have populations of 50,000 and 250,000, respectively.

32. Palmer (1983, ch. 3, p. 2) reports that in Los Angeles in the 1920s cab drivers fought over waiting space in front of certain buildings. Zerbe (1983b, p. 46) reports that following a switch to open entry at the Seattle Amtrak station in 1979: "Long taxi lines developed, taxis spilled out of the assigned areas, some drivers left their cabs (blocking access for Amtrak employees and passengers, as well as fellow cabbies), and some loitered in the station aggressively seeking passengers. Independent drivers clashed with drivers of the lower-priced 'major' cab fleets." However, similar problems have been reported at the Chicago airport, which does not have open entry. *Chicago Tribune*, March 7, 1984.

33. Frankena (1982, ch. 2) cites three studies that estimate average air pollution costs at 1 cent per vehicle mile or less in current dollars in the mid-1970s.

34. See Zerbe and Croke (1975, pp. 58–61) for a discussion of the benefits and costs of retrofitting pollution control devices on taxis.

35. Langenfeld (1983) concludes that the costs exceed the benefits from existing automobile air pollution standards.

36. Glaister (1981, p. 102). See also Manski and Wright (1976), and Tolley et al. (1984).

37. This point is made by Beesley and Glaister (1983) and by Tolley et al. (1984, p. 22). By contrast, De Vany and Saving (1983) present a model in which there is no such economy of scale at the industry level and in which the competitive equilibrium capacity is found (pp. 995–996) to be efficient.

38. A similar argument is widely accepted as a justification for public transit subsidies; Mohring (1972) and see also Douglas and Miller (1974b).

39. Kitch et al. (1971, pp. 292–297) report that cab companies violated Chicago ordinances requiring use of 75 to 90 percent of licenses and prohibiting service refusal and yet did not lose their

mediallions, which were worth over $15,000. The review of the history of taxi regulation in Section V makes it clear that the enforcement cost argument was not originally used to motivate entry restrictions.

40. Verkuil (1970, p. 693) reports that "rate regulation in New York is completely haphazard."

41. Palmer (1983, ch. 3, p. 11), reports that in 1977 in London, Ontario, the "City Council was initially hesitant about increasing fares until it was pointed out to them that a taxi fare increase would generate additional bus ridership, reducing the necessary subsidy to the bus system."

42. Paratransit Services (1983, pp. 6–7) reports: "In the 1970s, Atlanta emerged as a major commercial and convention center. These changes alerted the business community that Atlanta's taxicab industry was a key element in creating a progressive and attractive image for the city. These concerns were highlighted by frequent visitors' complaints about taxicab service. In fact, the concern among business leaders was so great that the Atlanta Chamber of Commerce donated staff resources to draft a new ordinance."

43. In each comparison, Eckert finds statistically significant differences between bureaucracies and commissions. However, Eckert's results are not particularly strong. Usable data exist on only six commissions in the set of 33 cities. Eckert (1970) uses this model to rationalize taxi regulation in Los Angeles in the 1920s and 1930s.

44. Gallick and Sisk (1984) suggest this justification for minimum fare regulations but not for entry barriers.

45. Regulations that held up air fares led to inefficiently high levels of service that people did not want to pay for; Douglas and Miller (1974a,b).

46. It is sometimes suggested that taxi licensing is motivated by government revenue considerations, but this is refuted by the low level of license fees (except at some airports) and the high level of medallion values. It is also suggested that taxi regulations reduce accident rates or costs. However, taxis do not have a higher accident rate per mile than do other automobiles (Kirby et al., 1974, p. 97). In any event, concern for the safety of third parties would jusify only regulations relating to driver qualifications, vehicle condition, and insurance coverage. Finally, it is suggested that taxi regulations reduce criminal activity on the part of drivers and associated law enforcement costs. While this might be true for regulations concerning driver qualifications, it does not provide a rationale for other taxi regulations.

47. Although a requirement to use meters can be rationalized as a measure to protect consumers from being overcharged, a major motivation for the requirement was to protect public transit by restricting ride sharing in taxis.

48. Eckert and Hilton (1972) provide a detailed discussion of the restrictions imposed on jitneys.

49. Gilbert and Samuels (1982, ch. 5). A 1925 entry restriction in Los Angeles is an exception.

50. For discussions of the beginnings of entry and fare regulation in the late 1920s and early 1930s in Los Angeles, Chicago, Boston, Seattle, and New York, see Eckert (1970), Kitch et al. (1971, 1972), Rosenbloom (1968, p. 413), Zerbe (1983a, p. 1), and Schreiber (1975). Efforts to impose entry restrictions and meters in Washington, D.C., were blocked by Congress (*Transit Journal*, 80, January 1936, p. 25, and Eckert, 1973).

51. A contemporary account dealing with 1932 describes in detail how taxi regulations proliferated during this period: "Briefly the developments of the year may be summarized as follows: Codes, setting forth in detail the regulations for every phase of taxicab operations, were prepared and adopted in three cities with a population of more than 100,000 during 1932. Ten cities enacted laws placing taxis under the jurisdiction of a Public Service Commission or a Taxicab Board, eight required a showing of convenience and necessity before issuing licenses, four required permits or licenses and fourteen adopted measures intended specifically to limit the number of cabs in operation. To drive out the cut-rate cabs and to end rate wars, three cities increased the minimum rate of charge, fifteen established a minimum rate, and two adopted a uniform rate. Seven cities specified a maximum fare, and most of these also set a minimum rate. Flat rate taxis were dealt several serious blows, for three cities eliminated the zone system and fourteen required the installation and use of taximeters. Eleven cities made it compulsory to carry liability insurance, one increased the amount of insur-

ance to be carried, two asked for posting of bonds, and three required a privilege tax or increased the license fee. Measures were passed in six cities to reduce cruising on the streets.'' *Transit Journal* 77, March 1933, p. 84.

52.   *Transit Journal* 77, March 1933, p. 84. The call to drive out cut-throat pricers and to end destructive competition was not unique to the taxicab industry. The formation of government approved codes of conduct under the National Industrial Recovery Act of 1933 for many industries was justified by the same fear of competition.

53.   For information on deregulated cities, we have used Gelb (1982, 1983a,b); Gilbert and Gelb (1980); Knight et al. (1983); Paratransit Services (1983); Rosenbloom (1983); Shaw et al. (1983); Teal et al. (1983); and Zerbe (1983a,b).

54.   In almost all cases, deregulation has been accompanied by an increase in nominal fares. However, fares generally had not been increased for some time prior to deregulation, and they would have increased eventually even if there had been no change in the taxicab ordinance. The important question is whether over a significant period of time following deregulation fares were above or below the level that would have been predicted in the absence of deregulation.

55.   Zerbe, letter to J. Philpott, May 10, 1984. See also Zerbe (1983b, p. 44).

56.   Since open entry leads to zero industry profits regardless of the chosen fare level, taxicab firms would have little incentive to request higher fares from regulators.

57.   In 1970 Honolulu had 4.3 cabs per thousand residents.

58.   Gelb (1983a, p. 133). Reason (August 1983), p. 16, reported that response time appeared to have declined dramatically as a result of regulatory reform.

59.   Zerbe (1983a, p. 3, and 1983b, p. 44). See also Gelb (1983b, p. xiv).

60.   Knight et al. (1983) concluded that open entry in Oakland and Berkeley led to a reduction in average vehicle age, and they found that new entrants devoted more resources to maintenance than did incumbents. There are reports that vehicle quality increased and/or average vehicle age declined following regulatory reform in Sacramento, Charlotte, and Jacksonville. There are reports of the opposite in Seattle, San Diego, Indianapolis, and Fresno.

61.   Kitch et al (1971, p. 291), and *Regulation* (1982), p. 13.

62.   Olson and Kuehl (1976, p. 67), McGrath (1976, p. 241), and Gelb (1983a, p. 133); (1983b), pp. 94-95).

63.   As we noted in Section V.B., entry regulation began about the same time as federal trucking and airline regulation. Perhaps the same general forces that lead to deregulation of these industries in the late 1970s and early 1980s led to local taxicab regulatory reform.

64.   Schroeter (1983, p. 92) suggests that a toll levied on cabs in the airport queue would be efficient, given the high fare. See also La Croix et al. (1984).

REFERENCES

Abe, M. A., and B. C. Brush. (Autumn 1976) ''On the Regulation of Price and Service Quality: The Taxicab Problem,'' *Quarterly Review of Economics and Business*, Vol. 16, pp. 105–111.

Allred, J., A. Saltzman, and S. Rosenbloom. (1978) ''Factors Affecting the Use of Taxicabs by Lower Income Groups,'' *Transportation Research Record*, Vol. 688, pp. 21–27.

American Public Transit Association. (1981) *Transit Fact Book*, Washington, D.C.

Beesley, M. E., and S. Glaister. (May 1979) ''Criteria for Regulation of Taxis,'' mimeo, London School of Economics.

————. (September 1983) ''Information for Regulation: The Case of Taxis,'' *Economic Journal*, Vol. 93, pp. 594–615.

Brown, T. A. (1973) *Economic Analysis of the Taxicab Industry in Pennsylvania*, U.S. Department of Transportation, Report No. DOT-TST-75-15.

Coe, G. A., and R. L. Jackson. (1983) ''Some New Evidence Relating to Quantity Control in the

Taxi Industry,'' Transport and Road Research Laboratory, Department of Transport, Crowthorne, Berkshire, England.

Coffman, R. B. (September 1977) ''The Economic Reasons for Price and Entry Regulation of Taxicabs: A Comment,'' *Journal of Transport Economics and Policy,* Vol. 11, No. 3, pp. 288–297.

De Vany, A. S. (February 1975a) ''Capacity Utilization under Alternative Regulatory Restraints: An Analysis of Taxi Markets,'' *Journal of Political Economy,* Vol. 83, No. 1, pp. 83–94.

_____ . (Spring 1975b) ''The Effect of Price and Entry Regulation on Airline Output, Capacity and Efficiency,'' *Bell Journal of Economics and Management Science,* Vol. 6, No. 1, pp. 327–345.

_____ . (June 1976) ''Uncertainty, Waiting Time, and Capacity Utilization: A Stochastic Theory of Product Quality,'' *Journal of Political Economy,* Vol. 84(3), pp. 523–541.

_____ . (June 1977) ''Alternative Ground Transportation Systems of Dallas/Fort Worth Airport,'' Texas A&M University, mimeo, prepared for the Federal Trade Commission's Dallas Regional Office, File No. 741—0015.

De Vany, A. S., and T. R. Saving. (September 1977) ''Product Quality, Uncertainty, and Regulation: The Trucking Industry,'' *American Economic Review,* Vol. 67, No. 4, pp. 583–594.

_____ . (December 1983) ''The Economics of Quality,'' *Journal of Political Economy,* Vol. 91, No. 6, pp. 979–1000.

Douglas, G. W. (May 1972) ''Price Regulation and Optimal Service Standards: The Taxicab Industry,'' *Journal of Transport Economics and Policy,* Vol. 6, No. 2, pp. 116–127.

Douglas, G. W. and J. C. Miller III. (Spring 1974a) ''The CAB's Domestic Passenger Fare Investigation,'' *Bell Journal of Economics and Management Science,* Vol. 5, pp. 205–222.

_____ . (September 1974b) ''Quality Competition, Industry Equilibrium, and Efficiency in the Price-Constrained Airline Market,'' *American Economic Review,* Vol. 64, pp. 657–669.

Eckert, R. D. (1970) ''The Los Angeles Taxi Monopoly: An Economic Inquiry,'' *Southern California Law Review,* Vol. 43, No. 2, pp. 407–453.

_____ . (Spring 1973) ''On the Incentives of Regulators: The Case of Taxicabs,'' *Public Choice,* Vol. 14, pp. 83–99.

Eckert, R. D., and G. Hilton. (October 1972) ''The Jitneys,'' *Journal of Law and Economics,* Vol. 15, No. 2, pp. 293–326.

Frankena, M. (1979) *Urban Transportation Economics,* Butterworths, Toronto.

_____ . (June 1981) ''The Effects of Alternative Urban Transit Subsidy Formulas,'' *Journal of Public Economics,* Vol. 15, pp. 337–348.

_____ . (1982) *Urban Transportation Financing: Theory and Policy in Ontario,* University of Toronto, Toronto.

_____ . (January 1983) ''The Efficiency of Public Transport Objectives and Subsidy Formulas,'' *Journal of Transport Economics and Policy,* Vol. 17, No. 1, pp. 67–76.

Frankena, M. W., and P. A. Pautler. (1984) *An Economic Analysis of Taxicab Regulation,* Federal Trade Commission, Washington, D. C.

Gallick, E. C., and D. E. Sisk. (1984) ''Specialized Assets and Taxi Regulation: An Inquiry into the Possible Efficiency Motivation of Regulation,'' draft mimeo, Federal Trade Commission, Washington, D. C.

Gelb, P. M. (September 1982) *Taxi Regulatory Revision in Portland, Oregon: A Case Study,* U.S. Department of Transportation, Report No. UMTA-MA-06-0049-82-7.

_____ . (May 1983a) *Effects of Taxi Regulatory Revision in San Diego, California,* U.S. Department of Transportation, Report No. UMTA-CA-06-0127-83-1.

_____ . (May 1983b) *Effects of Taxi Regulation Revision in Seattle, Washington,* U.S. Department of Transportation, Report No. UMTA-WA-06-0019-83-1.

Gilbert, G., R. J. Burby, and C. E. Feibel. (1982) ''Taxicab Operating Statistics,'' Center for Urban and Regional Studies, University of North Carolina at Chapel Hill.

Gilbert, G., and P M. Gelb. (September 1980) *The Indianapolis Experience with Open Entry in the Taxi Industry,* U.S. Department of Transportation, Report No. UMTA-MA-06-0049-80-17.

Gilbert, G., and R. E. Samuels. (1982) *The Taxicab: An Urban Transportation Survivor*, University of North Carolina Press, Chapel Hill.

Glaister, S. (1981) *Fundamentals of Transport Economics*, Oxford, Blackwell.

Kirby, R. F., K. U. Bhatt, M. A. Kemp, R. G. McGillivray, and M. Wohl. (1974) *Para-Transit: Neglected Options for Urban Mobility*, Urban Institute, Washington, D. C.

Kitch, E. W. (October 1972) "The Yellow Cab Antitrust Case," *Journal of Law and Economics*, Vol. 15, No. 2, pp. 327–336.

Kitch, E. W., M. Isaacson, and D. Kasper (October 1971) "The Regulation of Taxicabs in Chicago," *Journal of Law and Economics*, Vol. 14, No. 2, pp. 285–350.

Knight, R. L., D. F. May, and D. Koffman. (June 1983) *Taxi Regulatory Revision in Oakland and Berkeley, California: Two Case Studies*, U.S. Department of Transportation, Report No. UMTA-CA-06-0127-83-2.

La Croix, S. J., J. Mak, and W. Miklius. (February 1984) "Airport Taxi Service Regulation: An Analysis of the Merits of an Exclusive Contract," Department of Economics, University of Hawaii.

Langenfeld, J. (1983) "The Costs and Benefits of Automobile Emissions Controls and Safety Regulations," Center for the Study of American Business, Washington University, St. Louis.

Manski, C. F., and J. D. Wright. (1976) "Nature of Equilibrium in the Market for Taxi Services," *Transportation Research Record*, Vol. 619, pp. 11–15.

McGrath, J. P. (April 12, 1976) "Regulation of the Taxicab Industry in Washington, D.C.," in U.S. House of Representatives, Committee on the District of Columbia, *Taxicab Regulation*, 94th Cong., 2d. sess., Serial No. S-9.

Meyer, J. R., J. F. Kain, and W. Wohl. (1965) *The Urban Transportation Problem*, Cambridge, Harvard University Press.

Mohring, H. (September 1972) "Optimization and Scale Economies in Urban Bus Transportation," *American Economic Review*, Vol. 62, No. 4, pp. 591–604.

Olson, C. E., and P. G. Kuehl. (April 12, 1976) "The Taxicab Industry of Washington, D.C.: Regulatory Prespectives," in U.S. House of Representatives, Committee on the District of Columbia, *Taxicab Regulation*, 94th Cong. 2d. sess., Serial No. S-9.

Orr, D. (January 1969) "The Taxicab Problem: A Proposed Solution," *Journal of Political Economy*, Vol. 77, No. 1, pp. 141–147.

Palmer, J. P. (1983) *Municipal Transportation Regulation: Cartage and Taxicabs*, mimeo, Ontario Economic Council, Toronto.

Paratransit Services. (1983) "The Experiences of U.S. Cities with Taxicab Open Entry," International Taxicab Association, Rockville, Maryland.

Pickrel, L. J., and W. C. Rogers, eds. (1978) *Paratransit: The Idea May Be Nifty, But . . . .*, Agricultural Extension Service, University of Minnesota, Special Report 68.

Reason. (August 1983) The Reason Foundation, Washington, D.C.

Regulation. (March/April 1982) American Enterprise Institute for Public Policy Research, Washington, D.C.

Rosenbloom, S. (1968) "Characteristics of Taxicab Supply and Demand in Selected Metropolitan Areas," pp. 393–441 in *Systems Analysis of Urban Transportation*, Vol. 4, General Research Corporation, Santa Barbara.

—————. (1985) "The Taxi in the Urban Transport System," in C. Lave, ed., *Urban Transit: The Private Challenge to Public Transportation*, Pacific Institute for Public Policy Research, San Francisco.

Schreiber, C. (September 1975) "The Economic Reasons for Price and Entry Regulation of Taxicabs," *Journal of Transport Economics and Policy*, Vol. 9, No. 3, pp. 268–293.

Schroeter, J. R. (Spring 1983) "A Model of Taxi Service under Fare Structure and Fleet Size Regulation," *Bell Journal of Economics*, Vol. 14, No. 1, pp. 81–96.

Shaw, L. C., G. Gilbert, C. Bishop, and E. Pruitt. (October 1983) *Taxicab Regulation in U.S. Cities*, Vols. 1 and 2, U.S. Department of Transportation, Report No. UMTA-NC-11-0011.

Sheshinski, E. (1976) "Price, Quality and Quantity Regulation in Monopoly Situations," *Economica*, Vol. 43, pp. 127–137.

Stelzer, I. M. (c. 1980) "Deregulation of New York's Taxicabs: An Idea Whose Time Has Come," *NERA Topics*, National Economic Research Associates, New York.

Teal, R., M. Berglund, and T. Nemer. (December 1983) "Urban Transportation Deregulation in Arizona," Institute of Transportation Studies, University of California, Irvine.

Tolley, G. S., R. D. Eckert, S. J. Bruce, and R. D. Ranson. (March 1984) *Regulatory Impediments to Private Sector Urban Transit*, Vol. II, U.S. Department of Transportation, Report No. UMTA-MA-06-0146-82-3.

Transportation Center. (1958) *The Operation and Regulation of Taxicabs in the City of Chicago*, Northwestern University.

Tullock, G. (Autumn 1975) "The Transitional Gains Trap," *Bell Journal of Economics*, Vol. 6, No. 2, pp. 67–78.

Turvey, R. (March 1960) "Some Economic Features of the London Cab Trade," *Economic Journal*, Vol. 71, pp. 79–92.

Verkuil, P. RR. (Summer 1970) "The Economic Regulation of Taxicabs," *Rutgers Law Review*, Vol. 24, No. 4, pp. 672–711.

Wainwright, H. C., and Co. (March 1984) *Regulatory Impediments to Private Sector Urban Transit*, U.S. Department of Transportation, Report No. UMTA-MA-06-0146-82-3.

Williams, D. J. (January 1980a) "The Economic Reasons for Price and Entry Regulation of Taxicabs: A Comment," *Journal of Transport Economics and Policy*, Vol. 14, No. 1, pp. 105–112.

_____ . (Winter 1980b) "Information and Price Determination in Taxi Markets," *Quarterly Review of Economics and Business*, Vol. 20, No. 4, pp. 36–43.

Zerbe, Jr., R. O. (Summer 1983a) "New Trip for Taxicabs: Deregulation in Seattle," *Washington Public Policy Notes*, Vol. 2, Institute for Public Policy and Management, University of Washington.

_____ . (November/December 1983b) "Seattle Taxis: Deregulation Hits a Pothole," *Regulation*, pp. 43–48.

Zerbe, Jr., R. O., and K. Croke. (1975) *Urban Transportation for the Environment*, Cambridge, Mass., Ballinger.

FREQUENCY COORDINATION AND SPECTRUM ECONOMICS

Carson E. Agnew and Richard G. Gould

ABSTRACT

Radio engineers use formal procedures called "frequency coordination" to ensure that users of the same radio frequencies do not cause harmful interference. However, such procedures, particularly those used by the Fixed and Fixed-satellite services in several microwave frequency bands, have important economic aspects. As explained in this paper, the rules of frequency coordination institutionalize an implicit market in property rights to interference-free reception. As a consequence, the frequency coordination process is seen to allocate the radio spectrum in an economically efficient manner, without using a formal market arrangement such as an auction.

I. INTRODUCTION

It is striking how often professionals from different disciplines, while considering the same problem, emphasize different aspects of its solution. Such is the case, we believe, with formal frequency coordination procedures, particularly

Research in Law and Economics, volume 9, pages 167–183.
ISBN: 0-89232-657-3

those used by the Fixed and Fixed-satellite services in several frequency bands in the microwave region. Most engineers see frequency coordination rules as a practical way of ensuring that new entrants in a particular geographic region do not cause harmful interference to existing users operating on the same frequencies. In short, the rules are seen as a technical response to a technical problem.

The authors, however, see frequency coordination as an economic activity with some technical aspects. As we explain below, the rules of frequency coordination institutionalize an implicit "property rights" market. The cumulative effect of the frequency coordination process is to transfer these rights to the users who value them the most. This is an economically efficient outcome even though it is not achieved using a formal market arrangement, such as an auction. In short, although technical and economic efficiency are different concepts,[1] we believe frequency coordination promotes both. Indeed, as far as we know, it provides one of the few successful working examples of an economically efficient technique for spectrum management. As such, it deserves consideration when procedures must be devised for ensuring electromagnetic compatibility in new services or modifying them in existing services.

Economic techniques for spectrum management are often thought to involve formally organized markets. In recent years, auctions (Robinson, 1978), "shadow prices" (Levin, 1971; Russell and Lusignan, 1977; Webbink, 1971), markets of "output rights" (DeVany *et al.*, 1969), geostationary "orbital slots" (Jackson, 1976), and other formal markets have been proposed. However, use of these organized markets is not the only possible, useful spectrum management technique. Economically efficient use has much more to do with *use* than with *markets*. Loosely, economic efficiency requires that a good or service be provided to its users in a least-cost manner.[2] While formal markets can be shown to promote such use, less highly structured arrangements can serve this purpose just as well. In fact, the earliest proposals for economically efficient spectrum use (Coase, 1959; Minasian, 1975) envisioned markets operating more along the lines of frequency coordination than did later proposals.

From an economic standpoint, frequency coordination (a requirement for the issuance of a construction permit and license) works because it provides everyone using it with incentives to use spectrum efficiently. Coordination's rules are based on the principle that existing users should be protected from harmful interference caused by later users. This principle gives limited property rights in a portion of the spectrum to whoever uses it first in a given geographic area. These rights include permission to transmit a signal with specific technical characteristics from a particular point in a specified direction. Subsequent applicants for that portion of the spectrum must first determine a "coordination area" within which interference *might* be caused to existing users. The newcomer must then demonstrate to existing users that they will not cause interference above a specified level to any of those existing users. The method of calculation and the characteristics of the most sensitive system to be protected are set forth in the rules. Thus, coordination assigns the liability for harmful interference to new users, while simultaneously giving those users a mechanism for "coordinating" (i.e., informing, discussing, and amending as necessary) their plans with existing users. This combination of (1) well-defined liability rules with (2) simple procedures for identifying and resolving conflicts makes frequency coordination effective from an economic standpoint.

The principles just summarized need not be restricted to the 4 and 6 GHz frequency bands shared by the Fixed and Fixed-satellite services[3] on a "Primary" (or coequal) basis and heavily used by both. Indeed, coordination is also required in other bands shared by these two services, and is used by the Fixed service in bands allocated only to it. The principles used in coordination are transferable to other bands and services, and, in fact, recent proposals have been made to use these ideas in Multipoint Distribution Service (MDS) (FCC, 1980) and in FM broadcasting (Agnew *et al.,* 1979, ch. 6).

II. BACKGROUND

When communication satellites first became feasible, desirable frequencies for such systems were already allocated to point-to-point microwave relay systems operating in the Fixed service. These allocations were heavily used in many urban areas, and it was thought that little additional use could be made of them. However, it soon was discovered that the technical characteristics of the satellite and terrestrial services were sufficiently different to permit earth stations to be installed not only in parts of the country where there was little Fixed service operation, but even in congested areas where another radio-relay system could not be accommodated. Coordination procedures to facilitate the sharing of bands used by these services were first developed by the International Radio Consultative Committee (CCIR) of the International Telecommunications Union (ITU). These procedures were subsequently adopted internationally and are currently embodied in Appendix 28 of the Radio Regulations. These procedures have also been incorporated into the FCC *Rules and Regulations (Rules)* with only a few changes in interference criteria and assumed system characteristics.

The Fixed-satellite service (FSS) shares the 500 MHz wide 4 and 6 GHz bands (among others) with the Fixed (terrestrial microwave) service. To make such sharing possible, interference must be prevented between the two services. Among the possible interference situations are signals from the Fixed service (terrestrial station transmitters) to the Fixed-satellite service (earth station receivers) and from earth station transmitters to terrestrial microwave station receivers.[4] These two interference cases, which are subject to the rules for coordination provide a clear and interesting illustration of the economic aspects of this technique and will be discussed in the balance of this paper.

A. International and Domestic Coordination Rules

As noted, interference between the earth stations of satellite systems and fixed stations, and the associated requirement to coordinate the establishment of a new earth station or radio-relay station with other users, is covered by Appendix 28 to the Radio Regulations. Appendix 28 gives a "worst-case" method for calculating the so-called coordination area within which harmful interference *may* occur. These calculations are based on assumed characteristics for existing systems and the actual characteristics of the proposed system. The Radio Regulations, which have treaty status, then call for coordination (that is, discussion) between the administration (government) of an operator of the proposed new space or terrestrial station and administration of the operator(s) of existing station(s) within the coordination area around the new station. However, this requirement does *not* set a specific limit on how much interference a new station can cause—that is subject to a negotiation between the new station operator and each of the existing users in the coordination area.[5] Of course, the interfering signal level used in the calculation of the coordination area can, in some cases, cause interference. This level becomes the starting point in the subsequent negotiations during which the newcomer tries to demonstrate that the proposed operation will not cause unacceptable interference in this specific situation with its particular characteristics and complement of equipment.

The FCC *Rules* (specifically, 47 CFR 25.203) contain the requirement for coordination. The procedures set forth in Appendix 28 are incorporated in Sections 25.251–254. The *Rules* also require coordination with the fixed (terrestrial) service (47 CFR 25.203(c)–(d)). The requirements for the Fixed service [47 CFR 21.100(d)] are typical:

> All applicants . . . shall, before filing an application or major amendment, . . . coordinate proposed frequency usage with existing users in the area and other applicants with previously filed applications, whose facilities could affect or be affected by the new proposal in terms of frequency interference or restricted ultimate system capacity.

Thus, in the United States an applicant for a construction permit must (a) determine if harmful interference may be caused to existing users, (b) inform those users potentially affected of his plans, and, if possible (c) take whatever steps are needed to obtain these users' agreement to the proposed operation. Under point (b), every applicant must communicate the technical details of his proposed station to every existing user within the coordination area who, calculations show, may suffer harmful interference, and obtain the concurrence of *all* such users in his plan. Following the successful coordination, and the grant of a construction permit by the FCC, the station is protected in turn.[6] In practice, the FCC will not issue a construction permit for any station unless all existing users within the coordination area assent.

B. Effect of Coordination Calculations

Coordination distance calculations are, as noted, based on a number of worst case assumptions, which depend on the frequencies involved and the state of the art in the service, as well as an allowable incursion into the "noise budget" of a particular type of system. Given a particular level of "permissible noise," specified propagation models are used to estimate the distance at which this interference could be caused. These distances define the boundary of the coordination area. For example, Appendix 28 and the associated Recommendations of the CCIR contain methods for calculating areas where harmful interference may occur by either great-circle propagation or by scattering from precipitation. The boundary of the coordination area is the union of the areas found by applying each of the two methods separately.

Because operators of systems outside the coordination area need not be consulted by a newcomer, the selection of a permissible noise level and of particular interference models determine both the level of protection afforded to existing systems and the number of systems with which a newcomer must deal before being licensed. The current rules are conservative in this respect; the worst case assumptions embodied in them mean that many or even most systems identified by coordination calculations will *not*, in fact, suffer harmful interference from the newcomer's operation. The actual coordination between service operators is intended to identify *probable* as opposed to *possible interference*. In the United States this is done through data bases of licenses, construction permits, and pending applications which are maintained by independent companies and by certain of the common carriers who use the microwave bands extensively. These data bases serve the same role that a data base of land titles serves in real estate—they economize on the cost of obtaining a clear "title" to the spectrum.

If a detailed examination shows that harmful interference may be caused, the newcomer has several alternatives.[7] Of course, the applicant could abandon the proposed site and seek another further away from conflicting stations, or where the antenna pointing directions would be more favorable. Furthermore, our investigation has found other alternatives which are employed including:[8]

- Restricting the direction in which the earth station antenna might point (thereby limiting the orbital locations of satellites with which the station could communicate);
- Restricting the frequencies on which the station would operate (i.e., coordinate less than the full 500 MHz band, thereby limiting the total number of channels that could be carried by the station, and therefore both the maximum communication capacity of the station and the flexibility in assigning channels to and from the station and within the system it serves);
- Constructing artificial barriers to transmitted and/or received interference (e.g., pits, earthen embankments, and metallic shielding fences);

- Replacement of conventional IF strip filters in radio relay receiver with ones having better performance;
- Retuning of entire radio relay systems to convert from a so-called split frequency plan to a "standard T" plan to reduce the interference protection requirements;
- Installation of "blinders" (also termed "eyebrows") on horn antennas to improve their interference-rejection capability;
- Reduction of power of an existing, potentially interfering station or reducing the "deviation" of one or more FM carriers;
- In certain cases, installing a more directional or better shielded antenna at the proposed and/or one or more *existing* stations.

In fact, the last remedy is embodied in the FCC *Rules* (47 CFR 25.251(d)), which states that although a less discriminating,[9] so-called Standard B antenna may be used in areas of low traffic density, an existing operator must install a better Standard A antenna if this would eliminate the harmful interference. However, antennas even more discriminating than Standard A are available from several manufacturers at somewhat higher prices.[10]

In many cases, use of such ultra-high performance antennas by a Fixed station would eliminate the possibility of interference between a new station (either a fixed terrestrial or a satellite earth station) and an existing one, but the installation of such antennas are *not* required under current FCC *Rules*. However, these superdirective antennas are sometimes installed with the newcomer voluntarily paying some or all of the cost of purchase (and sometimes even of installation) even if the antenna is installed on an existing system. As we demonstrate below, such economically efficient and technically desirable solutions to an interference situation are to be expected in a market system.

III. PROPERTY RIGHTS AND COORDINATION

Having reviewed the operation of coordination, we now can refer to the economic theory of property rights to analyze coordination's effects.[11] The basic idea is simply stated: achieving economically efficient use involves finding an allocation of goods or services to users in which no further gains from trade are possible. However, before such an allocation can be found there must be well-defined goods or services, and it has to be possible to trade them. The rules of frequency coordination *define* a tradable service, that is, the right to operate a system with known characteristics, free from harmful interference.

Although we refer in this paper to "spectrum," the property rights involved in coordination do not involve some abstract "invisible resource" (Levin, 1971) "ether" (suggested in Coase, 1959), or a right to use some "time-area-frequency" combination (as in DeVany et al., 1969). The rights provided under coordination guarantee the reception at one or more receivers of the signal from a particular transmitter which is free from harmful interference. Harmful interference can be prevented by any technically feasible means, including separation of systems in space, time, or frequency, but the means used are not a part of the right. In short, an existing user has a right to a "clear" communications channel.[12] This right must be respected by newcomers, although the existing user is free to surrender all or part of it if this is in his best interest. The trading of rights occurs when the characteristics of one or both systems are modified. Since such trades are voluntary, only those that leave at least one trader better off than he would be without the trade will be made. Moreover, each completed coordination moves the situation one step toward more efficient use of the spectrum.

C. An Example of the Economics of Frequency Coordination

To demonstrate how coordination promotes efficient use, consider the following example. Suppose the coordination calculations determine that if an operator A builds a new earth station at some location, harmful interference will be caused to an existing Fixed system operated by B. Installing a superdirective antenna on B's system to protect it from the interference has a net cost of $15,000. However, if the interference is not reduced by the antenna, A's earth station must be located at another site further from its intended service area. The additional cost of using this location could be many times $15,000, perhaps because an additional relay station, or more power transmitters are required at the new location.[13] Let us assume these costs are $40,000.

First, what is the economically efficient outcome? We assume, in doing this, that costs to either A or B represent costs to society, that is, the value of resources diverted from some other use is $15,000 in one case and $40,000 in the other. If the antenna is installed, society is better off the difference between the $40,000 cost avoided for the earth station and the $15,000 cost of the antenna, that is, $25,000. Installing the antenna and allowing the new earth station to operate is therefore the economically efficient solution to this spectrum management problem. This solution also makes more intensive use of the spectrum in this area, so installing the station would probably be judged technically "efficient" as well.[14]

Under the coordination rules, A is liable for harmful interference caused to B's system. When notified by A of the potential interference, it is in B's interest to refuse to allow A to operate unless compensated in some way by at least enough to pay for the installation of the antenna. That is, the compensation must be worth at least $15,000. Since this amount costs A less than the $40,000 required to relocate the earth station, it is in A's interest to make such compensation. The value of the compensation offered will be somewhere between $15,000 and $40,000—the exact amount depends on the bargaining power of A and B. In any case, compensation is often "in kind." For instance, A may offer to install the antenna at no cost to B.

The key point is that if both users act according to their self-interest the negotiations arising from coordination can lead both to the installation of the antenna and the establishment of the new earth station. The economically (and technically) efficient solution is thus achieved without regulatory intervention.

The efficient solution also will be chosen if A is the existing user of the spectrum and B the newcomer. In this case, however, B will choose to build his system from the first with the superdirective antenna, since paying the extra cost of $15,000 is less expensive than paying A at least the $40,000 assumed in this example to relocate his earth station.[15]

D. Coordination When Spectrum Use Is Growing

Coordination also can achieve efficient use where business growth or new technology lead to growing spectrum use. Assume that initially the frequency allocation in a particular area is unused. Coordination is trivial for whoever first establishes a station. Indeed, it will probably be easy to accommodate many early users in this relatively uncongested environment. Transactions such as the antenna upgrading discussed above will rarely be needed, because each newcomer will probably be able to locate his facilities so as to avoid interference with any existing user.

However, as the available frequencies and sites are filled with users, coordination will require adjustments to someone's system more and more often. These adjustments will be of the kind reviewed above—antenna upgrades, changes in transmitter or receiver design, and so forth. In each case, users who follow their self-interest will adopt economically efficient solutions to their electromagnetic compatibility problems. The cumulative effect of the individual decisions will be to substitute technological sophistication for spectrum use in a least cost manner.

If growth continues long enough, the intensity of spectrum use will be as great as can be accommodated by the state of the art. Specifically, no technical alternatives will exist that are worth installing. New systems can operate in a particular area only if existing systems cease to operate.

As far as we know, this state of affairs has not been reached. Although many urban areas are highly congested, the steady advance of communications technology has kept spectrum use from being completely constrained.[16] But even if saturation occurs, coordination would still promote efficiency. In this case, the new system's operator would have to be willing to pay enough to persuade the operator of some existing system to cease operation. This might be feasible, for example, if an alternative to radio transmission such as coaxial cables or optical fibers were available to some users at a cost below what the new operator was willing to pay. Thus, coordination encourages economic substitution between technologies that use spectrum and other information transmission media.

Finally, there may come a time, in a given area for a given technological state of the art, where no amount of ingenuity will permit the addition of another microwave radio relay station or a new satellite earth station. However, some time after such saturation has occurred, newly discovered practices or equipment of higher performance will become practicable. At such time, astute prospective operators may be able to "squeeze in" another station or system following a coordination process based on this new technology. In this sense, coordination promotes innovation in the long run.

E. Effect of the First-Come, First-Served Principle

This discussion shows that the use of spectrum will be economically efficient, provided negotiations are possible at relatively low cost. However, the final distribution of wealth between the operators of the different systems is different depending on who is the existing user and who is the newcomer. In the example, B's fixed station is the earlier user, and A must pay B at least $15,000 to effect a coordination. If A's earth station is earlier, B would pay $15,000. In short, the first-come first-served principle transfers wealth from newcomers to established spectrum users.

The fact that the first-come first-served principle imposes the cost of any adjustments on newcomers is a central issue in the ongoing international debate over rigid, a priori "planning" of orbit-spectrum use in the Broadcasting Satellite service in ITU Region 2, which includes the United States. The above argument suggests that frequency coordination (an alternative to a priori planning) would lead to more efficient use of the available orbit-spectrum. However, the developing countries argue that the coordination principle may impose an unfair hardship on them, since they will almost certainly wish to use the resource later than the developed countries. While this paper is not the place for a discussion of the debate over planning international orbit-spectrum, it seems to us that efficient use and wealth-transfer ought to be regarded as separate issues, amenable to separate solutions. In particular, coordination could be used to promote efficient use, and some arrangement that reallocates some of the costs from newcomers to earlier users might be required in order to achieve equity.

F. Are There Incentives To Abuse the First-Come First-Served Principle?

It might be thought that the requirement for coordination, that is, for getting the acquiescence of existing users, coupled with the FCC's invariable policy of not granting a construction permit if even one such user objects (and of not intervening to make a technical decision of whether interference is likely), would be open to abuse. This abuse could be in the form of "warehousing" frequencies against a possible future requirement; holding them for "trafficking" (i.e., for sale or release to another carrier); or to block a competitor from access to a par-

ticular market. It is the widespread opinion of coordinators for the major carriers
and for the coordination services, that instances of abuse probably are rare. The
major carriers probably refrain from such practices because they know that they
can become victims of it on a subsequent occasion. Coordination for small users
is usually performed by a commercial service, and that company has the same
self-interest objective of maintaining good will in the industry. (Often the same
commercial coordination company will represent *both* the newcomer and many
of the existing users in different licensing proceedings.)

We can also investigate the economics of "warehousing" spectrum under the
first-come, first-served rule. Obviously, an early entrant is entitled to be compensated by latecomers, and avoids the need to make such compensation. This might
be sufficient reason to build and coordinate a system before its use is otherwise
justifiable. However, the size of the incentive to premature use depends on the
present value of the cost of expected future modifications (and associated
compensation) to the early entrant system, since these costs are avoided by
early entry.

The argument is as follows. A potential early entrant has two choices. Early
entry means that at some future time engineering changes in his system may be
required. However, the costs of these changes will be borne by latecomers. On
the other hand, if construction of the system is delayed these changes may have
to be incorporated from the start, but the operator will have saved any capital and
operating costs associated with the system during the time prior to its eventual
use. The difference between the cost of these two alternatives measures the
strength of the incentive to be an early entrant.

This cost difference will only be significant if (1) upgrades to an existing system are substantially less costly than changes to a proposed system, but (2) they
are nevertheless very costly in comparison to the system's other costs. Our investigation (Agnew *et al.*, ch. 5) indicates that neither condition holds very often.
Upgrades are seldom substantially cheaper than design changes because
continuing technological advances reduce costs. And, most cases of coordination
involve incremental, relatively inexpensive changes such as antenna improvements. Therefore, it seems to us that the incentive to prematurely claim spectrum
through coordination, although a theoretical possibility, is not practically important in systems built to date.

IV. SOME PROBLEMS WITH COORDINATION

This is not to say, however, that coordination is without problems. It has them,
although some can be ameliorated by changes in the existing rules.

A. Coordination Over Time

One issue that needs to be addressed is the extent to which coordination leads to optimal decisions over time when there are so-called irreversible investments. We illustrate this problem using the example introduced above, involving users A and B. Suppose that the first system introduced is B's fixed system. Since it is the only system, it suffers from no interference. If B designs the system to be more resistant to interference than is initially required (e.g., using a superdirective antenna, installing it in a manmade pit, or erecting a fence around it), the additional cost of this *ab initio* protection might be, say, $10,000. However, retrofitting the system at a later date to give equivalent protection is more expensive because unanticipated changes must be made. Suppose this alternative costs $50,000. Now, let A's earth station be the newcomer, with a $40,000 cost saving if it uses its most preferred site, which will cause harmful interference to B's system unless it is protected. If no preplanning is undertaken, the same reasoning used above shows that A will not be able to obtain B's agreement, because the locational advantage is worth only $40,000, but the cost of modifying the fixed system is $50,000. Is this the economically efficient outcome?

As discussed in Agnew et al. (1979), the answer to this question depends on:

1. The comparative costs of retrofitting versus *ab initio* protection.
2. The time lag between the start of B's operation and the entry of A.
3. The interest rate applicable to B's investment.

For example, suppose that the time lag between the start of B's operation and the start of A's operation is T years, and the real rate of interest applicable to both investments is r. To determine the efficient alternative, we compare the present value of three alternatives:

1. Build the protection into B's system *ab initio*: $10,000.
2. Retrofit A's system when B is ready to share the spectrum: $50,000 $(1+r)^{-T}$.
3. Deny A's system access to the spectrum at its most preferred location: $40,000 $(1+r)^{-T}$.

As noted, coordination will avoid choosing alternative (2), the worst of the three. But, notice that the first alternative (build protection in *ab initio*) may be less costly to society than the third alternative (deny access). Alternative one, for example, is best if the rate of discount is 10 percent and the time lag is less than fifteen years. However, alternative (1) requires some mechanism that gives A an There incentive to spend the extra $10,000 at a time when his system needs no protection.[17]

There are several ways to provide this incentive. The FCC rule allowing fixed service operators to assert protection for systems up to five years in advance of their operation is one way to address this problem. For example, if A's earth station were allowed five-year advance protection (and if it were actually optimal to install it in less than five years), A would be willing to compensate B to build in protection *ab initio*. Alternatively, if A's earth station were granted protection before B's was, B would build in the extra protection in order to operate.

B. Limitations on Trading

Unfortunately, empirical evidence on the frequency or types of agreements made during coordination is lacking. So is evidence on how often transactions costs or other limitations cause potentially fruitful coordinations to fail. This is because nothing related to coordination is a matter of legal record. Once a newcomer and existing user have reached some kind of agreement, the existing user merely provides a letter asserting to the newcomer's application. All the letters obtained from existing users are filed by the newcomer with the Commission, but there is nothing to indicate what was required in order to obtain agreement.

One theoretical impediment to trading is that it may be difficult to transfer the implicit "rights" for reasons similar to those that arise in water rights law (Posner, 1972, ch. 2). The problem arises as follows.

Suppose an operator A has established rights through coordination. As noted above, these rights are to interference-free use of a particular communications channel. The problem is that A's ability to transfer this right to another party B depends on how B will use them. If A's and B's uses of spectrum were identical (and if B's use were in fact the more valued of the two), B could "buy" A's permission to operate, and A would cease operation. The problem arises when B's use is not identical to A's. Specifically, if B plans to cause less interference than A, he may want only a part of A's implicit rights. But A cannot necessarily retain whatever portion of his rights B doesn't acquire. For instance, A's rights lapse if he ceases operation at the old location—hence, he cannot be compensated for them. As a result, examples can be constructed where A and B are not able to reach an agreement (Agnew et al., 1979) even if agreement would promote efficiency.

Of course, other users in the area presumably suffer less interference when B replaces A. If transactions costs were truly zero, it would be possible for all the other users of spectrum to band together and buy those rights that B doesn't want. The coalition of other users benefits by the reduced interference, and A is compensated for his rights in this case. But transactions costs are not zero, and the formation of such coalitions may violate the antitrust laws. As a result, negotiation solely between A and B may fail to produce an efficient solution.

An attractive solution to this problem is similar to one proposed for water rights (Mishan, 1967, p. 35). Under it, A's rights could be transferred in their entirety to B, even though B didn't use all of them. B could coordinate his system in the future *as if* it were A's. This solution allows A and B to complete their transaction, and gives B an asset (the rights he isn't using) to dispose of during future coordinations. This possibility is not allowed by the existing rules.

C. How Much Protection Is Reasonable?

A third problem is a technical one: the fact that there have been few, if any, proven cases of interference between operating satellite earth stations and fixed terrestrial stations (Agnew *et al.*, 1979) suggests that the interference criteria and/or propaganda models used in coordination may be overprotective. The implication is that much greater use could be made of these frequencies with only a small increase in the likelihood of interference.

An analogy from another field may be helpful in illustrating this point: a criterion employed by bridge players is that "if you make every slam contract you bid, you're not bidding enough slams." If the interference criteria employed to date have resulted in essentially no interference they probably are too restrictive. The increased use which could be made of the spectrum through relaxed criteria could be so much more productive, and profitable, that it would outweigh the occasional instances of interference that might result. Unfortunately there is no easy way to determine empirically how much more interference should be tolerated. This is because interference that occurs sporadically in different systems at different times and places, as might be expected under relaxed coordination criteria, is hard to distinguish from interference from natural causes such as fading. Consequently it is difficult to assign liability for such sporadic interference.

V. CHANGES TO AND EXTENSIONS OF COORDINATION

We have already noted that coordination's costs are relatively small: for example, independent coordination companies charge as little as $1500 for coordinating a simple receive-only early station (Agnew *et al.*, 1979). But the proliferation of small earth stations and their attendant low cost has made coordination relatively expensive for some systems.

This problem is especially acute when we consider the possibility of systems costing less than $5,000 that transmit at very low powers (less than one watt) (Equatorial Communications Corp., 1983). These systems, with their low per-unit cost and large numbers of transmitters, would find traditional coordination procedures prohibitively expensive. Relaxed criteria in this case would reduce the cost of coordinating individual systems, allowing more of the newer systems to operate but possibly impairing quality of service provided by existing users.

The FCC has responded to the proliferation of receive-only stations by allowing such stations to operate without a license. However, unlicensed stations receive no protection against harmful interference by newcomers (or, obviously, from existing users). Receive-only stations that are coordinated and licensed can still claim protection from interference. However, if such a station employs an antenna poorer than specified in the *Rules* [§ 25.209(a),(b)], it can claim protection only to the degree that one meeting these requirements would get.

In both these cases, the problem is that the present rules make the costs of coordinating a terminal prohibitive. "Transactions costs" are thus nonnegligible, and it may be appropriate for regulators either to reduce these costs or to establish rules such that the economically efficient outcome is reached without in most cases incurring the costs of a full coordination (Posner, 1972). The FCC's action in the case of receive-only earth stations appears to be an example of the latter sort. Changes in the rules to accommodate very low power transmit-receive systems would be an example of the former type. We feel it is beyond the scope of this paper to recommend specific changes in the rules. However, we think that the technical changes continually occurring in the field will make them necessary before too long.

The incentives for efficient use provided by frequency coordination make it attractive in other services. For instance, there are a number of "one-to-many" services, such as the Multipoint Distribution Service (MDS), the Instructional Fixed Television Service (ITFS) and the FM and television broadcasting services, where one transmitter sends to a large number of receivers. What is needed here is some way to give the operator of a transmitter protection from harmful interference in some service area around each transmitter. Such areas are sometimes called "protected service areas" by spectrum managers (e.g., FCC, 1980). Methods of calculation exist (see, for example, Close, 1981) which allow realistic contours defining such areas to be drawn.

We believe that the rules for defining and using protected service areas should also do two things:

1. *Require* newcomers to demonstrate to existing users that their proposed operation will not generate interference that encroaches on the existing users' protection areas.
2. *Permit* existing users to allow a newcomer who may encroach on a protection area to operate, that is, permit voluntary modification of an existing user's protection area.

Such rules are a part of the FCC's technical proposals for MDS in Docket 80-113 (FCC, 1980). In Agnew et al. (1979) we discuss a similar set of rules for FM broadcasting and, as does Close (1981), present calculations showing that gains in the number of people served are possible if realistic protection areas are used and if technical trade-offs which alter these areas are made between existing users and newcomers.

There are also services to which we believe coordination could not be usefully extended. These are services where propagation calculations of the kind used in coordination are not straightforward. HF (high frequency) band radio operations are a case in point. Here signals may skip and fade in an unpredictable fashion, making it difficult to determine a well-defined group of existing users with whom a newcomer would have to deal.

VI. CONCLUSION

The preceding sections have pointed out how frequency coordination defines a system of property rights and also promotes spectrum efficiency. Despite the problems just discussed, coordination in practice works reasonably well. As noted above, there are no known instances of interference in coordination situations in the United States, and as far as we know there has never been a case where the FCC has had to decide on a license application in which all coordination conflicts had not been resolved. In our earlier study (1979) we summarized discussions with a number of members of the user community; none expressed a willingness to replace coordination with direct regulation by a government agency such as the FCC. *A fortiori* staff members at the FCC have stated in private communications that the Commission would be unable to cope with the current volume of applications for construction permits for new stations if it had to determine if unacceptable interference would be caused to existing users.

Coordination provides a lesson in how to promote efficient spectrum use that should be considered by other spectrum users. Basically, all that is required is a workable mechanism for determining which receivers and transmitters are likely to suffer from and cause unacceptable interference, combined with a clear statement as to which party is responsible for correcting any interference problem. Good information about the location and technical characteristics of stations also needs to be provided to users, but in most cases, such information is available from radio license applications, or from domestic or international records on radio assignments.

We feel that frequency coordination has a role to play in efficient spectrum management that is too little recognized. If its key features are adopted more widely, we believe that all users of spectrum can benefit from the flexibility and efficiency that coordination provides.

NOTES

1. A number of articles in a recent special issue of the *IEEE Transactions on Electromagnetic Compatibility* (1977) discuss this point.
2. For a discussion of technical vs. economic efficiency, see Agnew *et al.* (1979), ch. 2.
3. The Fixed-satellite service transmits signals to and from the earth's surface to satellites overhead, whereas the Fixed service is a terrestrial relay service which transmits signals from one micro-

wave antenna to another along the surface of the earth. Hence, the signals in the two services are often more or less perpendicular to each other, and not likely to interfere.

4. Typically a terrestrial station will operate in either the 4 *or* 6 GHz bands. On the other hand, a transmit/receive satellite earth station must use both bands and will therefore need to coordinate, and be licensed for, operation in both 4 *and* 6 GHz.

5. While CCIR Recommendations 356 and 357 recommend an *aggregate* limit for this interference, they provide no guidance as to the allowable contribution to this overall interference from a *single* system.

6. The FCC allows operators of receive-only earth stations in the Fixed-satellite service to elect to operate without coordination. However, stations operated in this way do not receive protection from interference.

7. No specific procedures are stipulated in the Radio Regulations (or the FCC *Rules* for that matter) and administrations (i.e., governments) are thus free to use any mutually agreed method for resolving the conflict.

8. In addition to the alternatives cited, electronic sidelobe interference cancellers may become practical in the future (Gould and Schmitt, 1977).

9. A less discriminating antenna permits more off-axis interfering signals to enter, when used as a receiving antenna, and emits more off-axis interference when used as a transmitting antenna.

10. As an indication of relative costs, a 10-foot diameter antenna for use in the 4 GHz band will cost about $5,000 if standard B; about $9,000 if standard A, and about $10,000 if of the "ultra high performance" type.

11. Interestingly, research on the economic theory of property rights has had a considerable rebirth in the last twenty years, due in no small part to Ronald Coase's study of spectrum management. His paper, "The Problem of Social Cost" (1960) appeared only a year after his study of the FCC (1959) which proposed a market in spectrum as an alternative to regulation. Coases's work on property rights stimulated others. In particular, there are Demsetz (1967), Mishan (1967), and Posner (1972), whose chapter on the property law provides probably the clearest summary of the economic issues.

12. Mueller (1982), pp. 6–11, discusses this kind of right in greater detail.

13. In one case we know of, a newcomer paid $250,000 to completely *relocate* an existing user.

14. Moreover, the performance of B's system will often be improved in other ways than merely interference rejection to A's signals: the new antenna typically increases the signal-to-noise ratio, and the margin against fading, and hence increases system quality and availability in the bargain.

15. It can also be shown that coordination achieves the economically efficient solution if the numbers are reversed (i.e., if the antenna cost is $40,000 and the cost saving associated with the earth station's location is only $15,000). In this case the economically efficient solution is for the earth station not to operate at its most preferred location. Under coordination, the earth station operator (A) is willing to pay only $15,000, but the fixed system's operator (B) demands at least $40,000 to modify his system. Clearly, no transaction will take place, and the earth station will be located elsewhere in order to minimize costs. If B is the newcomer, on the other hand, he will be willing to pay at least $15,000 to relocate A's earth station.

16. Recent proposals to build so-called teleports on the outskirts of major cities suggest another way that local saturation of the available spectrum can be overcome. In such cases technology is used to concentrate communications traffic in the city center, and transport it to an earth station in an outlying area where the spectrum is still available for use.

17. The general argument behind this example is as follows. Let the cost of alternative (1), *ab initio* protection, be normalized to unity; let $\phi = (1+r)^{-T}$, and let v and w be the costs of alternatives (2) and (3), retrofitting and denying access, respectively. The economically efficient decision minimizes over the triple $(1, v\phi, w\phi)$. Coordination results in choices that only minimize the pair (v,w). So an inefficient choice will be made if $\min(v\phi, w\phi) > 1$, that is, if the relative cost of the alternative chosen by coordination is greater than the cost of building protection into the initial system. A measure of the overall loss in efficiency would be the average value of the nonlinear function $\max(0, \min(v\phi, w\phi) - 1)$.

We do not have direct evidence about the magnitude of this measure. If incentives of the kind discussed in the text are considered, additional research should be done to validate this model of losses and determine the relevant values.

ACKNOWLEDGMENTS

This paper was written while Carson E. Agnew was an assistant professor of Engineering-Economic Systems at Stanford University. The research was supported by the Stanford Center for Economic Policy Research, the National Science Foundation's grant IST-8108350 and the National Telecommunications and Information Administration's contract NT79RAC96005. Don Ewing and Dale Hatfield, and Harvey Levin provided thoughtful comments on earlier drafts.

REFERENCES

Agnew, C. E., R. G. Gould, D. A. Dunn, and R. D. Stibolt. (December 1979) *Economic Techniques for Spectrum Management*, Princeton, N.J., Mathtech, Inc.

Close, J. S. (1981) "Spectrum Utilization in Broadcasting," in L. Lewin, ed., *Telecommunications in the United States: Trends and Policies*, Dedham, Mass., Artech House.

Coase, R. H. (October 1959) "The Federal Communications Commission," *Journal of Law and Economics*, Vol. 2, pp. 1–40.

——————. (October 1960) "The Problem of Social Cost," *Journal of Law and Economics*, Vol. 3, pp. 1–44.

Demsetz, H. (May 1967) "Toward a Theory of Property Rights," *American Economic Review Papers and Proceedings*, Vol. 57, No. 2, pp. 347–359.

DeVany, A. S. et al. (June 1969) "A Property System for Market Allocation of the Electromagnetic Spectrum: A Legal-Economic-Engineering Study," *Stanford Law Review*, Vol. 21, No. 6, pp. 1499–1561.

Equatorial Communiations Corp. (September 1983) *Prospectus*, Mountain View, Calif.

Federal Communications Commission. (1980) *Notice of Inquiry and Notice of Proposed Rulemaking*, Docket 80-113, adopted March 19 (FCC 80-137).

Gould, R. G., and K. Schmitt. (1977) "Interference Reduction Techniques for Satellite Earth Stations," *Second Symposium and Technical Exhibition on Electromagnetic Compatibility*, Montreaux, Switzerland, June 28–30.

IEEE Transactions on Electromagnetic Compatibility. (August 1977) Vol. EMC-19, No. 3.

Jackson, C. L. (November 1976) *Technology for Spectrum Markets*, Ph.D. dissertation, Massachusetts Institute of Technology.

Levin, H. J. (1971) *The Invisible Resource: Use and Regulation of the Radio Spectrum*, Baltimore, Johns Hopkins Press.

Minasian, J. P. (April 1975) "Property Rights in Radiation: An Alternative Approach to Radio Frequency Allocations," *Journal of Law and Economics*, Vol. 18, pp. 221–272.

Mishan, E. J. (1967) "Pareto Optimality and the Law" *Oxford Economic Papers*, New Series, No. 19, p. 255.

Mueller, M. (June 1982) "Property Rights in Radio Communication: The Key to the Reform of Telecommunications Regulation," Washington, D.C. Cato Institute.

Posner, R. A. (1972) *Economic Analysis of Law*, Boston, Little, Brown.

Robinson, J. O. (May 1978) "Assignment of Channels in the Multipoint Distribution Service by Auction," presented at the Sixth Telecommunications Policy Research Conference, Airlie, Va.

Russell, S. P., and B. Lusignan. (August 1977) "A Techno-Economic Approach to U.S. Domestic

Satellite Orbit Spectrum Regulation,'' *IEEE Trans. on* Electro-magnetic Compatibility, EMC-19, No. 3, pp. 351–357.

Webbink, D. W. (September 1977) ''Setting FCC License Fees according to Frequency Spectrum: A Suggestion,'' IEEE Trans. Broadcasting, BC-17, pp. 64–69.

MUNICIPAL EMPLOYEE RESIDENCY REQUIREMENT STATUTES:

AN ECONOMIC ANALYSIS

Kenneth V. Greene and George D. Moulton

ABSTRACT

Our purpose is to use economic analysis to develop reasons why important segments of a city's population would perceive the benefits from municipal employee residency requirements to be large or the costs low. Many of the hypotheses are consistent with judicial justifications for the legality of such statutes. But the economic analysis provides additional insights about their effects not considered by the law.

An empirical analysis of the use of such statutes by the 50 biggest cities in the United States reveals some empirical support for hypotheses about what encourages the usage of residency requirements, implying that economic analysis can be fruitful in informing rational discussion of such laws.

Research in Law and Economics, volume 9, pages 185–204.
Copyright © 1986 by JAI Press Inc.
All rights of reproduction in any form reserved.
ISBN: 0-89232-657-3

I. INTRODUCTION

The use of municipal residency requirements for public employees has generated much litigation and subsequently considerable comment in law journals. The substance of the scholarly literature has been concerned with the question of what criteria the courts have used and should use in deciding about the constitutionality of such laws. Contained within this literature are some of the reasons defendants have proferred in defending their use of residency requirements.

In contrast, the economics literature has devoted little space to any analysis of such laws. This is despite the use of the public choice mode of analysis which is intensely concerned with the economic analysis of the formation of government institutions and the fact that such laws might have consequences predictable by traditional economic analysis.

The purpose of this paper is to try to fill some of the gaps in the economic analysis of residency requirements and at the same time to bring some empirical data to bear on the rationales for residency requirements exposed in the legal literature and our own economic analysis. The paper is divided into four sections. The first reviews the essence of the questions considered by the legal literature. Section III provides an economic analysis of the use and possible effects of residency requirements. Section IV provides a statistical analysis of the tendency of cities to use residency requirements, focusing upon the 50 largest cities in the United States. The final section contains concluding remarks.

II. THE LEGAL LITERATURE

The usage of municipal residency requirements has often been challenged in court. The attacks have usually centered on the equal protection clause of the United States Constitution. The argument is that the law deprives an employee of the ability to live where he or she desires and of the ability to travel both across and within state borders. The laws are alleged to discriminate against nonresidents denying them their fundamental right to travel freely.

In adjudication of these cases, courts have proceeded along two lines. Finding that no "fundamental" right has been abridged, some courts apply the minimum scrutiny or rational basis test to see whether the discrimination created by the statute could be justified by a reasonably conceived state of facts. When such an approach is used, the courts find a violation of equal protection only if the distinction between resident and nonresident employees is entirely irrelevant to the state's purpose.

In other cases, the courts have reasoned that the residency requirements infringe upon fundamental constitutional rights and uphold the statute only if there is a compelling state interest in the distinction. Here the standard is strict scrutiny. There must be a strong argument that the means are necessary for the accomplishment of the end.

Generally when the courts use a rational basis test, they have declared the residency laws to be constitutional.[1] Some of the reasonable bases outlined have been the "public coffer" theory and the "stakes in the community" theory. The former concludes that the state may reasonably wish to give jobs to its own citizens rather than citizens of other communities because its own citizens presumably spend more of their monies within the municipality. The "stakes in the community" theory reasons that such laws give employees bigger interests in the welfare of the community and, therefore, encourage incentives for better performance.[2]

Furthermore, in *Ector v. City of Torrance,*[3] the California Supreme Court developed other rationales that would pass the minimum scrutiny test, including the promotion of ethnic balance, reduction of high city unemployment rates, improvement of employee performance because of either greater knowledge of local conditions or better relationships with local residents, reduced absenteeism and tardiness, and greater availability in emergency situations.

When the courts have found that the residency requirement chills the exercise of a fundamental right and can only be justified if there is a compelling state interest, some courts have found the requirements unconstitutional while others have upheld the laws. In *Donelly v. City of Manchester*[4] a fundamental right to travel was established and the courts could find no compelling interest to transcend it. In *Krzeninski v. Kusler*[5] the court recognized the infringement of a fundamental right, but felt that an "identity with the community" argument developed a compelling interest in light of contemporary urban fragmentation.

In the most recent employee residence requirements case to come before it,[6] the Supreme Court found no constitutionality protected right of interstate travel. This would imply that precedent will require only the application of a rational means test for the acceptability of a residency requirement which is nondurational in character.[7]

Considerable discussion in the law journal literature has arisen about whether this is the "right" test. Kramer (1977), for instance, argues that a compelling interest rule should have been created because employee residency requirements limit the fundamental right to interstate travel and that they are not different in this regard from durational residency requirements for welfare benefits that the Supreme Court has struck down. Hager (1980) argues that the dire financial, economic, and social straits of cities justify the existence of these laws even if a compelling interest is the correct test. Lamer (1975) reasons that there are always better means to the same ends of preserving municipal viability such as job retraining programs and municipal income taxes on resident employees. Richman (1974) concludes that different laws infringe on basic rights to different degrees and also create different sized benefits for the municipality. In each case the costs should be weighted against these benefits. Reiter (1975) agrees and suggest the use of a substantial relation test based on whether or not the laws accomplish their purposes.

A review of the legal literature's discussion of employee residency requirements displays a typical concern with whether residency requirements *should* be used. But it also leads us to two insights capable of generating some positive analysis. One is that there are some conditions that would encourage a city to attempt to use a residency requirement for the benefit of its general citizenry. The second is that there exists extremely little analysis of the effects of residency requirements. In the next section of this paper we will try to apply some economic analysis to derive some hypotheses about when such a requirement will be favored and by which city residents. In the course of doing so we will discuss some of the potential effects[8] (such as the possibility of raising employee wages and therefore possibly even encouraging suburban flight).

III. AN ECONOMIC ANALYSIS

If we turn to an economic analysis of the decision to use residency requirements, it is important to distinguish between different models of the public choice process. One familiar model is the median voter or representative voter model (Downs, 1957). Here the implicit assumption is that the collectivity is an institution designed to facilitate the choices of the majority of the people that it serves. Another model is that of Leviathan wherein the collectivity is conceived as a mechanism wherein certain groups—whether politicians, bureaucrats, or other special interest groups—maximize their own welfare at the expense of "the general public" or the majority (Brennan and Buchanan, 1977; Niskanen, 1972). We attempt an analysis of municipal residency requirements using a representative voter model, but supplement it by considering both the voting power of city employees and the interest of incumbent politicians.

In order to simplify our analysis we assume that all individuals in the collectivity that are consumer-taxpayers (CTS) are identical. In other words, all such individuals in the community have the same income and tastes, face the same tax price for purchasing a public service, and all desire the same quantity of the public service. There is, however, another possible type of consumer-taxpayer who may work for the community as a public employee. We call these individuals employee consumer-taxpayers (ECTS).

Now let us consider the cost of providing a single public service producible at constant per unit cost. Assume it is a private good in the Samuelsonian sense and that the collectivity chooses the desired amount by a majority voting process. If the ECTS are a null set it follows that the desired amount will be unanimously agreed upon. This will also be the case if employees are in perfectly elastic supply to the community. If they are not, the public employees may demand greater public services simply to acquire economic rents. Presuming they remain a minority, the identical CTS will obtain their own preferred service levels.[9]

Within this context, let us build a theory of the demand for the use of residency requirements. The individual consumer-taxpayer's utility is assumed to depend on two goods: the publicly provided, G, and the privately provided, Z.

$$U = U(G, Z). \tag{1}$$

This G is produced with three types of inputs: resident labor, L_R, nonresident labor, L_N, and a composite input, K.

$$G = G(L_R, L_{NR}, K). \tag{2}$$

The amount of the public service entering the utility function depends on the way it is produced. The resident and nonresident labor are presumed to be imperfect substitutes in the production process. Moreover, given a level of capital services and total labor services we assume that a unit of residential labor always produces more public service than a nonresidential unit. We are supposing, for instance, that an extra policeman residing in the suburbs, together with a fixed amount of other inputs into the police protection production process, might create the same additional safety as an incremental policeman residing in the city, but that the city consumer sees this police protection produced with the use of suburban resources yielding less "policing" and hence less utility. This may be due to the fact that the city resident is of the same racial character as the ultimate consumer of safety, because he is viewed to be more "accessible," or the like.

Our discussion may be summarized by noting that the CTS's problem is presumed to be the selection of G that maximizes his utility subject to a presumed fixed-income constraint. If P_z is the per unit price of the private good and P_G is the voter's share of the marginal cost of another unit of the public good, then Eq. (3) illustrates the constrained maximization problem:

$$U(Z, G) + [ZP_z + P_G G(L_R, L_{NR}, K) - Y], \tag{3}$$

and Eq. (4) contains the necessary first-order conditions for utility maximization,

$$\frac{\partial U}{\partial Z} \bigg/ \frac{\partial U}{\partial G} = \frac{P_z}{PG}. \tag{4}$$

Fulfillment of this condition presumes that the public service G is produced in a cost-minimizing way or if G* is the consumer-taxpayer voter's optimal public service level that its cost is minimized. Writing W_R, W_{NR}, and r as the per unit prices of residential labor, nonresidential labor, and capital, the cost minimization problem is illustrated in Eq. (5):

$$W_R L_R + W_{NR} L_{NR} + r K + \lambda [G(L_R, L_{NR}, K) - G*]. \tag{5}$$

Cost minimization requires that

$$\frac{W_R}{W_{NR}} = \frac{\partial G}{\partial L_R} \bigg/ \frac{\partial G}{\partial L_{NR}}. \tag{6}$$

Now if, as we presume, an incremental unit of residential labor is always perceived to produce more G than an incremental unit of nonresidential labor and if $W_R/W_{NR} = 1$, then a corner solution with only residential labor is called for. Whatever police protection is chosen will be produced using only city residents. If there are such benefits, however slight, from using domestic resources, the city would always use a residency requirement. To even conjecture about its nonuse is to admit of the possibility of cost considerations.

To analyze these cost considerations, let us turn to a model of the labor market wherein the amount of either domestic city or suburban labor supplied depends positively on the wage rates paid and where antidiscrimination laws prevent the payment of different wages to one type of this objectively identical[10] labor rather than another. Within this context, it follows that suburban labor could be used if the extra cost of restricting employment to domestic labor (precipitated by going further up the supply curve for domestic labor rather than only up along the aggregate supply curve) fell short of the benefits from using solely domestic labor. Thus suppose the city requires X policemen. The total cost would be OXAB if bought on a market without residency requirements or OXEF if bought on a market restricted to residents. The extra cost OXEF-OXAB would have to be less than the extra subjective benefits of services provided solely by domestic labor.

Among the conditions which increase the expected benefits or increase the relative marginal productivity of L_R in producing that which ultimately enters the utility function are many of the same things mentioned by the law literature. If there is a substantial difference between the racial composition of the city and suburban labor forces, the expected benefits might be high. If the city's unemployment rate is high and city residents are concerned only with the unemployment in the city, expected benefits will be higher than if the unemployment rate is lower. If the distance between the physical location of the average city resident and the average suburban resident is high, then the expected benefits in case of emergency need will be higher.

Anything which would lower the subjective cost of any extra tax burden would lower the expected costs of residency requirements and the usage of exclusively residential labor. Two factors immediately come to mind. One is the fraction of city revenues that are financed by other levels of government. Another might be income which could lower the subjective cost of sacrificing additional dollars. But since the private good also has a positive elasticity, it is clear that income need not have an unambiguous effect.

This line of reasoning alerts us to the possibility that a residency requirement could impose either net costs or benefits on the ordinary consumer-taxpayers.

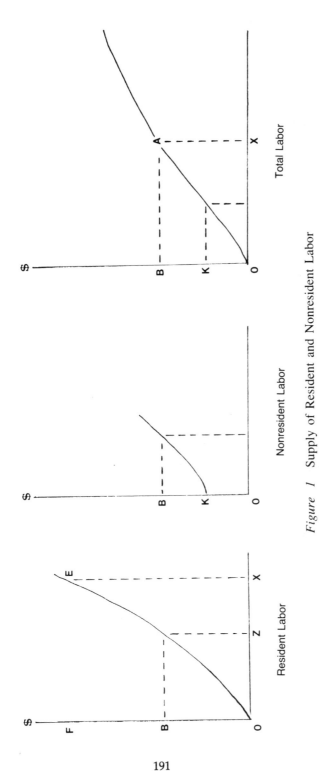

Figure 1 Supply of Resident and Nonresident Labor

191

However, there is another group of voters for whom it can apparently create only a boon. All those ECTS who would work in the public sector at a wage illustrated in the figure of B or below receive a bigger producer surplus if residency requirements are imposed and at least Z units of labor are still utilized. Naturally, it does not follow that all public sector employees would favor residency requirements. Consider the imposition of such a law *de novo*. The identical suburban and resident laborers are assumed to obtain the same wage in the absence of the law. Then some suburban laborers would oppose the move because it would eliminate their economic rent. Realistically, if conditions are changing, it does not follow that residency requirements would find unanimous support even from resident employees. The same phenomena which the rent gradient theories of urban economics employ to explain an increased desire for suburban residential location may precipitate employee opposition to residency requirements even if their effect would be increased wage levels. This type of reasoning leads to one important insight: if the process of "suburbanization" in a metropolitan area is especially strong there is likely to be less support for residency requirements among public employees.[11]

Our prior reasoning builds upon a model of informed rational behavior on the part of both public sector employees and ordinary consumer-taxpayers. In this framework it is possible for the members of either group to favor or oppose the use of residency requirements. There is an alternative framework that some might view as more descriptive of reality. In it individuals may see the direct and obvious consequences of a policy such as employee residency requirements but fail to perceive the indirect effects on resource and, ultimately, product prices. The taxpayer-consumers see an obvious benefit in services provided by people living within a city rather than elsewhere and no associated cost. Public employees see such residency laws restricting their mobility and not having any beneficial effect on their wages.[12] In general, public employees would oppose residency requirements, while the general public would approve of them in these circumstances. This is certainly consistent with the phenomena of substantial support for residency requirements found in public opinion polls and public employees instituting many of the suits challenging residency requirements. Of course, the model of rational, fully informed decision-making is also generally consistent with these phenomena.

Our analysis also reveals that it is conceivable that residency requirements will lead to bigger public sector wages, a possibility not considered by the legal process or literature. There is a general presumption that somehow residency requirements will maintain or improve the fiscal health of the city by maintaining a job base that will support middle-income residents and by assuring that city revenues would be bigger than otherwise would be the case. While this makes some sense, if such employees generate more extra revenues than extra costs from locations in the city rather than the suburbs,[13] this reasoning ignores the possibility that the increased cost of public services precipitated by the residency requirements could also create a fiscal incentive toward suburban location.

The rising public sector wage rates that could follow from the use of residency requirements might not be solely a source of opposition among those who would oppose residency requirements apart from their supposed benefits in terms of improved services. The higher the public sector wages, the more attractive public sector jobs and the more likely a consumer-taxpayer will favor the use of residency requirements as a possible means of reserving such plums for himself or other members of his family in the future. In other words, historical circumstances leading to high public sector wages can lead to increased demand for residency requirements.

Our analysis, of course, assumes that the labor market is competitive. But even if public employees are unionized, residency requirements could be analyzed in the same framework if such an institution led to increased bargaining power for public sector employees as a result of decreased supply alternatives on the municipal employer's part.

The previous analysis precludes the influence of employee-citizen voters on the public choices of a community. Even if they might prefer bigger public sectors because their economic rents would be boosted by the expansion, as long as they face a group of identical majority citizen-voters their desires will be thwarted. The mere lifting of the assumption of identical citizen votes and its replacement with a frequency distribution of desired public sector outcomes by citizen-voters leads to the employees having some influence. Moreover, the greater the number of these employee-consumer voters, ceteris paribus, the greater will be the desired public service level of the median voter and, in a purely democratic decision-making world, the greater the actual choice level.

This leads to a possibly favorable rationale for residency requirements as far as public employees are concerned. Residency requirements assure that a greater fraction of the voting populace will be public sector employees. They would therefore increase public service levels and possibly public sector wages and generate increased economic rents. The relationship between the residency requirements and increased political power may be more readily apparent to union leaders and unionization might work to increase their usage.

In the model developed by Fiorina and Noll (1978), bureaucrats (public sector employees) and incumbent politicians live in a somewhat symbiotic relationship. Any increase in the size of the public sector leads to an increased use of bureaucrats (which is assumed beneficial to the original bureaucrats by increasing their chances of promotion and the like) and this in turn increases the marginal productivity of facilitative services. These are the types of services political officeholders provide to their constituents by "cutting through bureaucratic red tape." Incumbents, having acquired a substantial human capital stock which increases their productivity as facilitators, have a comparative advantage in producing such services and hence an increased size of the public sector increases their chance of re-election. Where the city's main executive officer is a mayor elected via an explicit political process, it is possible that the benefits of municipal residency requirements may be larger for at least some important players in the political arena.

IV. AN EMPIRICAL ANALYSIS OF
MUNICIPAL USE OF RESIDENCY REQUIREMENTS

We wish to test some of the implications of the economic models developed in the previous section. Our models imply certain causative relationships between certain phenomena and the likelihood that any employee residency requirement will garner sufficient support to be politically viable. Thus if a city suffers a great deal of unemployment it is more likely to try to restrict its employment to its own residents. Moreover, we would reason that if there were considerable racial differences between the populations of a city and its surrounding suburbs, the more likely a residency requirement would be used as a tool to assure racial balance (or even racial superiority) for a group dominant in the city but a minority in the entire metropolitan area. The greater this difference the greater might also be the perceived advantage of having "interested" city residents serve their fellow citizens. One might also reason that the physical inaccessibility of suburban residents might affect the perceived benefits of residency requirements for public employees especially in emergency situations. At first glance, land area of a city might be an appropriate proxy for inaccessibility of suburban workers.[14] It is conceivable, however, that as the physical size of the city increases the marginal effect falls off. One might also predict that where the city's recent suburbanization process had been slow there would be a smaller resistance to the use of the requirements from public employees because of their costs in constraining residential location choices.

The analysis also reasons that a community might be more likely to adopt a residency requirement, if in fact they lead to higher costs of service provision, if a large fraction of those costs were paid for outside of the jurisdiction. Thus the local fiscal structure might be important and the residency requirements might be more frequently used where the fraction of revenues that are locally financed is low. Similarly, if income is high and the perceived benefits from provision by local residents as opposed to nonresidents possesses a high income elasticity, income might have a positive effect on the usage of residency requirements. Also we conjecture that where those responsible for the operation of a city are elected in a process where political affiliation and the direct voting process are important it is more likely that politicians and bureaucrats will support residency requirements as a means of boosting the fraction of all voters who support big public sectors. When the main administrative office of a city is a city manager or a group of commissioners and is less politically oriented, support for the residency requirements will be smaller.

Finally, we have reasoned that the higher the wages of city government employees compared to their wages in similar jobs the more likely will people support a residency requirement as a means of increasing the likelihood that they or their heirs will acquire a part of this surplus. The bigger are these relative wages also the more likely it is that some fiscal resources will be lost if city residents are employed in suburban jobs and suburban residents are employed in city jobs but individuals generate the majority of their tax payments in their domiciles.

We attempted to test these hypotheses by utilizing survey results on the usage of employee residency requirements by the 50 largest cities in the United States published by Reiter (1975) (see Table 1). A city was deemed to have a residency requirement if an ordinance existed which applied to all employees and required residency in the city and which was in place on January 1, 1972. Thirty percent of the cities had residency requirements according to this criterion.

Employing a linear probability model, we utilized independent variables, as defined in Table 2, to explain the usage of residency requirements. The reader

Table 1.   Cities in Sample

New York	Kansas City, Mo.
Chicago	Atlanta
Los Angeles	Buffalo
Philadelphia	Cincinnati
Detroit	Nashville
Houston	San Jose
Baltimore	Minneapolis
Dallas	Fort Worth
Washington, D.C.	Toledo
Cleveland	Newark
Indianapolis	Portland
Milwaukee	Oklahoma City
San Francisco	Louisville
San Diego	Oakland
San Antonio	Long Beach, Calif.
Boston	Omaha
Memphis	Miami
St. Louis	Tulsa
New Orleans	Honolulu
Phoenix	El Paso
Columbus	St. Paul
Seattle	Norfolk
Jacksonville, Fla.	Birmingham
Pittsburgh	Rochester
Denver	Tampa

Note: Listed in order of city population size.
Source: Reiter (1975).

Table 2. Definition, Means, and Standard Deviations of Independent Variables

	Variable Definition	Source	Mean	σ
Ū	Average unemployment rate of city 1960-1970	Manpower Report of President, 1972	7.16	2.06
NWD	1970. Difference in the percentage of the population which was nonwhite between city and the remainder of Standard Metropolitan Statistical Area .	1970 Census of Population	.166	.138
LOW SUB	Low degree of suburbanization: Growth rate in city population minus growth rate in suburban population between 1960 and 1970 using 1970 as base.	Ibid.	−.189	.465
POP	Total population in city	Ibid.	812.812	117.970
Y	Median income of city families	County and City Data Book, 1972	$9,262.00	$1,621.00
SURPLUS	Average October earnings of full-time city employees minus average October earnings of full-time county employees in rest of SMSA	1972 Census of Governments	$137.89	$93.81
LA	Land area of city in 1969 in square miles	County and City Data	166.9	162.3
MANG	A dummy variable equal to one if a city had a city manager or commission form of government in 1972	Municipal Yearbook, 1972	.340	.479
LFIN	Percentage of city revenues locally financed 1972; total local governmental revenues less intergovernmental transfers as a percentage of total local governmental revenues	City Government Finances, 1972	.677	.127

will note that these include a variable which measures the difference between a city's public sector wages and the same wages in its suburbs. Our theory reasons that such wage differences could in part be caused by the usage of residency requirements and thus a simultaneous equations problem could arise. In order to deal with this we attempted to utilize two-stage least squares by explaining this variable by all the other exogenous variables mentioned in Table 1 and some other exogenous determinants. This attempt was unsuccessful in that none of the hypothesized additional determinants of the variable we labeled Surplus were significantly related to its size.[15]

The empirical experiment as reported in OLS results in Table 3 may be marred, given our small sample size, by the heteroskedasticity arising from the use of a dichotomous dependent variable. This can bias the estimated variances, although it will leave the estimated coefficients unbiased. In trying to avoid the problem, we turned to probit and multinomial logit equations as well. They are reported in Tables 4 and 5 and generally corroborate the results arrived at through ordinary least squares. In each of the tables, equations (1) through (4) employ a squared land area term. Since it is not significant, equations (5) through (8) drop it. Equations (2) and (6) drop the insignificant income variable. Equations (3) and (7) also drop the local finance variable and equations (4) and (8) add the population term to the list of deleted explanatory variables.

Only one of the traditional rationales for the use of residency requirements which are found in legal defenses and which economic analysis would also predict to have explanatory power proves consistently statistically significant. The probability of using a residency requirement is enhanced and the effect is statistically significant if the rate of suburban population growth is relatively low compared to city population growth. This effect is always significant at the 1 percent level of confidence, indicating that less rapid suburbanization might reduce the subjective costs of city residency requirements.

The average unemployment rate in the decade of the 1960s possesses the expected positive sign but never achieves the ordinarily acceptable degree of significance. The difference in the percentage of nonwhite population between the city and the suburban ring proves somewhat more significant. While the OLS results display a positive coefficient with t-values ranging from 1.18 to 1.94, the probit and logit results generate asymptotic t-values ranging from 1.62 to 2.26. There is then at least some evidence that the racial imbalance between city and suburban populations leads to more frequent use of residency requirements.

The city's land area has a significant negative effect on the probability that a residency law will be utilized. If this variable is a proxy for the distance that a suburban resident may be from his municipal job, and the bigger this distance the less the accessibility of such employees and the greater the benefits from residency requirements, then a positive effect might be expected. But it is the relative advantage of city as opposed to suburban location for the productivity of the labor input in producing the public service which counts. In a world where ser-

Table 3. OLS Regression Results Explaining Residency Requirement Usage by Fifty Largest U.S. Cities in 1972

Coefficients of Independent Variables
(t values in parentheses)

Equation	C	$\bar{U}$	NWD	LOW SUB	LA	LA^2	SURP	POP	Y	LFIN	MANG	$\bar{R}^2$	Standard Error of Estimate
(1)	.219	.029	.611	.475	-.003	$.003 \times 10^{-3}$	.0019	$.002 \times 10^{-5}$	$.005 \times 10^{-2}$	.662	-.191	.310	.385
	(.33)	(.93)	(1.18)	(2.26)	(2.46)	(1.60)	(2.70)	(.41)	(.86)	(1.33)	(1.52)		
(2)	-.189	.022	.726	.475	-.003	$.004 \times 10^{-3}$	.0019	$.002 \times 10^{-5}$	—	.695	-.191	.314	.383
	(.41)	(.74)	(1.46)	(2.27)	(2.66)	(1.75)	(2.70)	(.34)		(1.41)	(1.53)		
(3)	-.330	.011	.627	.465	-.003	$.003 \times 10^{-3}$	.0021	$.001 \times 10^{-6}$	—	—	-.187	.298	.388
	(1.18)	(.37)	(1.26)	(2.19)	(2.45)	(1.62)	(3.05)	(.02)			(1.47)		
(4)	-.330	.011	.630	.466	-.003	$.003 \times 10^{-3}$	.0021	—	—	—	-.187	.315	.383
	(1.20)	(.37)	(1.33)	(2.39)	(2.79)	(1.83)	(3.15)				(1.51)		
(5)	.262	.031	.786	.663	-.001	—	.0020	$-.002 \times 10^{-5}$	$.005 \times 10^{-2}$	.586	-.191	.283	.392
	(.39)	(.96)	(1.53)	(3.72)	(2.80)		(2.74)	(.34)	(1.09)	(1.16)	(1.16)		
(6)	.266	.022	.954	.682	-.001	—	.0020	$-.003 \times 10^{-5}$	—	.621	-0.191	.280	.393
	(1.23)	(.71)	(1.94)	(3.84)	(2.92)		(2.73)	(.52)		(1.23)	(1.49)		
(7)	.206	.011	.851	.660	-.001	—	.0021	$-.004 \times 10^{-5}$	—	—	-.187	.271	.395
	(.76)	(.38)	(1.75)	(3.72)	(2.70)		(3.05)	(.80)			(1.45)		
(8)	.182	.013	.790	.639	-.001	—	.0200	—	—	—	-.171	.277	.394
	(.68)	(.44)	(1.65)	(3.65)	(2.82)		(2.96)				(1.35)		

Table 4. Probit Regression Results Explaining Residency Requirement Usage by Fifty Largest U.S. Cities in 1972

Coefficients of Independent Variables
(t values in parentheses)

Equation	C	$\bar{U}$	NWD	LOW SUB	LA	LA^2	SURP	POP	Y	LFIN	MANG	−2 Log of Likelihood Function
(9)	−4.12 (.99)	.192 (1.23)	5.77 (1.73)	4.62 (2.39)	−.021 (2.00)	$.001 \times 10^{-2}$ (.72)	.0122 (2.69)	$.020 \times 10^{-5}$ (.68)	$.008 \times 10^{-5}$ (.29)	5.03 (1.58)	−1.27 (1.84)	27.15
(10)	−5.01 (1.74)	.179 (1.23)	6.10 (1.95)	4.68 (2.42)	−.022 (2.19)	$.001 \times 10^{-2}$ (.80)	.0123 (2.72)	$.020 \times 10^{-5}$ (.72)	—	5.36 (1.79)	−1.26 (1.84)	27.23
(11)	−.56 (.48)	.087 (.69)	4.21 (1.72)	3.84 (2.60)	−.018 (2.10)	$.001 \times 10^{-2}$ (.80)	.0112 (2.82)	$.031 \times 10^{-6}$ (.13)	—	—	−1.26 (2.01)	31.00
(12)	−.58 (.49)	.085 (.68)	4.30 (1.83)	3.90 (2.76)	−.017 (2.42)	$.001 \times 10^{-2}$ (.84)	.0112 (2.88)	—	—	—	−1.27 (2.04)	30.32
(13)	−3.97 (.98)	.203 (1.31)	6.26 (1.87)	5.33 (3.03)	−.015 (2.65)	—	.0126 (2.75)	$.073 \times 10^{-6}$ (.33)	$.013 \times 10^{-2}$ (.49)	4.97 (1.55)	−1.38 (1.96)	27.73
(14)	−5.41 (1.87)	.181 (1.26)	6.93 (2.26)	5.55 (3.17)	−.015 (2.78)	—	.0128 (2.80)	$.069 \times 10^{-6}$ (.30)	—	5.44 (1.75)	−1.37 (1.96)	27.98
(15)	−.86 (.78)	.084 (.68)	4.84 (2.07)	4.46 (3.45)	−.012 (2.90)	—	.0115 (2.91)	$.086 \times 10^{-6}$ (.43)	—	—	−1.29 (2.03)	31.74
(16)	−.92 (.84)	.091 (.74)	4.70 (2.03)	4.43 (3.44)	−.012 (2.97)	—	.011 (2.87)	—	—	—	−1.26 (2.00)	31.94

Table 5. Logit Regression Results Explaining Residency Requirement Usage by Fifty Largest U.S. Cities in 1972

Coefficients of Independent Variables
(t values in parentheses)

Equation	C	$\bar{U}$	NWD	LOW SUB	LA	LA^2	SURP	POP	Y	LFIN	MANG	-2 Log of Likelihood Function
(17)	-7.28 (1.04)	.284 (1.03)	9.57 (1.62)	8.04 (2.35)	-.038 (1.91)	$.002 \times 10^{-2}$ (.73)	.0220 (2.54)	$.035 \times 10^{-5}$ (.71)	$.009 \times 10^{-2}$ (.19)	8.81 (1.60)	-2.13 (1.75)	27.39
(18)	-8.24 (1.67)	.269 (1.03)	9.98 (1.81)	8.12 (2.38)	-.039 (2.05)	$.002 \times 10^{-2}$ (.79)	.0221 (2.57)	$.036 \times 10^{-5}$ (.73)	—	9.15 (1.74)	-2.13 (1.75)	27.43
(19)	-1.22 (.54)	.167 (.72)	7.30 (1.63)	6.87 (2.47)	-.029 (1.92)	$.002 \times 10^{-2}$ (.64)	.0200 (2.63)	$.014 \times 10^{-6}$ (.04)	—	—	-2.36 (1.98)	30.98
(20)	-1.24 (.56)	.167 (.72)	7.35 (1.73)	6.91 (2.63)	-.029 (2.25)	$.002 \times 10^{-2}$ (.72)	.0200 (2.67)	—	—	—	-2.37 (2.02)	30.98
(21)	-7.09 (1.06)	.319 (1.19)	10.49 (1.78)	9.23 (2.91)	-.025 (2.56)	—	.0222 (2.59)	$.012 \times 10^{-5}$ (.33)	$.017 \times 10^{-2}$ (.37)	8.51 (1.54)	-2.38 (1.88)	28.03
(22)	-8.89 (1.82)	.292 (1.16)	11.47 (2.15)	9.52 (3.04)	-.023 (2.64)	—	.0225 (2.64)	$.011 \times 10^{-5}$ (.30)	—	8.93 (1.65)	-2.40 (1.90)	28.18
(23)	-1.88 (.91)	.190 (.83)	8.43 (1.98)	7.86 (3.14)	-.021 (2.72)	—	.0205 (2.70)	$.014 \times 10^{-5}$ (.45)	—	—	-2.54 (2.06)	31.44
(24)	-1.99 (.97)	.204 (.90)	8.17 (1.94)	7.78 (3.15)	-.021 (2.78)	—	.0200 (2.68)	—	—	—	-2.47 (2.03)	31.66

vice delivery points are distributed evenly throughout (or alternatively are concentrated at the center of) the city and where residencies are evenly distributed elsewhere in the SMSA, then if the size of the SMSA is fixed, a big city land area means a big relative distance of city residencies from city delivery points compared to suburban residencies. If big and small cities are connected with suburbs of equal size, the same argument holds and large land areas would lead to less advantage for residency requirements. Only if big city land areas are connected with big suburban land areas would it be even possible for the relative advantage of city residency to increase with city land size.[16] Generally then a more thorough examination of this variable leads to an expected negative sign.

The likely negative sign of land area would also be predicted if large city land areas are connected with small suburban land areas and this leads to superfluity of residency requirements because the city labor market dominates the SMSA labor market. Another explanation of a negative effect could be a connection between large land areas and a philosophy of "wide open space" that is antipathetic toward imposing restraints on employee locations. Finally, if big land areas mean low density and residency requirements are policies advocated by minorities, the greater organizational difficulties confronting minority groups in areas of low density may be the explanation of a negative causal relationship. It should be noted that dropping land area as an explanatory variable leaves the values and significance of the rest of the coefficients virtually unaffected and adding its square leaves the coefficient on land areas significantly negative, exhibits a positive but insignificant coefficient for the squared term but leaves the substance of our results basically unaltered.

While we fail to find a significant effect of income and population size, our admittedly crude measure of the difference between the earnings of civil servants in the city and its suburbs has a significant positive effect in all specifications. This is in accord with the predictions of either the public coffer theory or our own hypotheses that if such surpluses exist, a city resident will be more likely to favor a residency requirement to enhance his own family's chances of benefiting from the surplus. It also may be due to the presence of a simultaneity problem with which we cannot cope.

Interestingly, the dummy variable which measures the existence of a city manager or commissioner form of government is always negative, and often significant at the 5 percent level of confidence. This is in accord with the hypothesis that there could be more support for residency requirements when political institutions enhance the advantage for bureaucrats of large numbers of voters who are civil servants and in favor of large public sectors. Political institutions may be determinants of the acceptability of residency requirements.

The fraction of the revenues that are locally financed was hypothesized possibly to have a negative effect on the use of residency requirements. The argument was that *if* residency requirements led to more expensive public services, the opposition to them would be larger if the city itself picked up a larger share of the financial burden. While not generally significant, at the 5 percent confidence level, the coefficient of this variable is positive.

It should be pointed out that if we drop all of the insignificant variables in the equations reported in Tables 2 through 4, there are no substantive changes in the coefficients of the other variables. Moreover, earlier we referred to the possibility that labor union strength could conceivably lead to increased support for residency requirement. While we only possessed qualitative information in the form of the presence of police and/or firefighters' union within the city, the incorporation of these variables and their interaction into our explanatory equations yielded insignificant signs for the union variables while the significance levels of those variables passing significance tests in Tables 2 through 4 remained robust. This was true even when we confined our analysis to only 47 cities, excluding from our observations those that did not possess general residency requirements but which did place some sort of restriction on the residency of either their police or firemen.

V. CONCLUSION

Construed within the context of a model of demand for services produced by residential inputs and for enhanced earnings prospects, many of the rationales for the use of residency requirements alluded to in legal proceedings make economic sense. Economic theory itself would suggest some other possible explanations of the use of residency requirements. This paper tests whether these hypotheses can help explain the tendency to use residency requirements. Focusing on the 50 largest U.S cities, empirical corroboration is found for the idea that phenomena that increase perceived benefits from or reduce the costs of using resident requirements increase the likelihood of its use. Since it is less than definitive, the paper points toward the possible need for further theoretical and empirical work on the effect of residency requirements on public sector wages, the perceived quality of delivered services, and the political effects of the imposition of such laws. It does imply, however, that economic analysis can be fruitful in informing rational discussion about such laws.

ACKNOWLEDGMENTS

The authors thank Hadi Salavitabar and Elias Links for capable assistance and Phillip Nelson and Stanley Masters for useful comments.

NOTES

1. Examples are *Williamson v. Lee Optical*, 348 U.S. 634 (1973) and *F. S. Royster Guano Co. v. Virginia*, 253 U.S. 412 (1920).
2. Both theories are elucidated in *Kennedy v. City of Newark*, 148 A2d 473 (1959).

3. *Ector v. City of Torrance*, 314 P2d 433 (1973).
4. *Donnelly v. City of Manchester*, 274 A2d 789 (1971).
5. *Krzeninski v. Kusler*, 338 F. Supp. 492 (D.N.J. 1972).
6. *McCarthy v. Philadelphia Civil Service Commission*, 424 U.S. 645 (1976) (per curiam).
7. The same does not hold true for durational residency requirements. The U.S. Supreme Court has found against such laws; the cases involve welfare benefits: *Shapiro v. Thompson*, 394 U.S. 618 (1969); voter registration, *Dunn v. Blumstein*, 405 U.S. 331 (1972); and hospital care, *Memorial Hospital v. Maricopa County*, 415 U.S. 250 (1974). Employee residency requirement laws which specify previous residence have been struck down by both federal and state courts: *Mary L. Justice et al. v. Jerry Manzagol*, N.M. State Personnel Director, USCD for the District of New Mexico. Case No. 74-64 (Jan. 29, 1970) and *Fraternal Order of Policy etc. v. Huter*, 303 NE2d 103 (1973).
8. We have nothing at all to say about some of the purported effects such as actually increasing the fiscal resources of the community or fostering racial integration of the city and its work force.
9. For a model which incorporates a distribution of preferred outcomes among civil servants and among the rest of the population, see Courant et al. (1979).
10. These types of labor are perfectly substitutable as far as the production of safety, but not necessarily "policing," is concerned.
11. By suburbanization we mean the tendency of residential location to become increasingly concentrated outside of the city boundaries.
12. The assumed ignorance on the part of public sector employees is less believable to the extent that knowledge capable of changing wages would be more valuable per public employee than per general taxpayer.
13. It is by no means clear that suburban residents do not generate revenues more than the costs of the services they consumer in the city. See Greene et al. (1974).
14. If we hold population constant, land area is an inverse measure of density. Density might have its own effect in promoting the use of residency requirements if such serve the interests of minority groups and these groups find political organization less costly when density is high. On this point see Phillip Nelson (1982). Thus the hypothesized effect of land area would be ambiguous.
15. We tried to explain the size of the surplus by all the other exogenous variables mentioned in Table 1: dummy variables for the existence of a police union, a firefighters' union and location in the northeast, the difference between civilian wages in the city and the remainder of the SMSA, and the differences in the percentages of public employees in high wage categories such as education, police, and fire. Only the slow suburbanization and local finance variables were significant (negatively and positively, respectively), but the coefficient of determination in this first stage was .36.
16. All our arguments assume that distance from the service delivery point is proportional to the amount of service a unit of labor delivers.

REFERENCES

Brennan, Geoffrey, and James M. Buchanan. (1977) "Towards a Tax Constitution for Leviathan," *Journal of Public Economics*, Vol. 8, pp. 255–273.
Courant, P. N., E. M. Gramlich, and D. Rubinfeld. (1979) "Public Employee Market Power and the Level of Government Spending," *American Economic Review*, Vol. 69, pp. 806–817.
Downs, Anthony. (1957) *An Economic Theory of Democracy*, New York, Harper.
Fiorina, M. P., and Roger Noll. (1978) "Voters, Bureaucrats and Legislators," *Journal of Public Economics*, Vol. 9, pp. 239–254.
Greene, Kenneth V., W. B. Neenan, and C. D. Scott. (1974) *Fiscal Interactions in a Metropolitan Area*, Lexington, Mass., D.C. Heath.
Hager, Connie M. (1980) "Residency Requirements for City Employees: Important Incentives in Today's Urban Crisis," *Urban Law Annual*, Vol. 18, pp. 197–222.
Kramer, Daniel C. (1977) "The Constitutionality of Post-Employment Residency Requirements," *Urban Lawyer*, Vol. 9, pp. 157–182.

Lamer, Dana (1975) "The Constitutionality of Residence Requirements for Municipal Employees,"
    Emory Law Journal, Vol. 24, pp. 447–470.
Nelson, Phillip. (1982) "Information and Political Behavior," Unpublished manuscript, Economics
    Department, SUNY-Binghamton.
Niskanen, William. (1972) *Bureaucracy and Representative Government,* Chicago: Aldine.
Reiter, G. M. (1975) "Municipal Employee Residence Requirements and Equal Protection," *Yale
    Law Journal,* Vol. 84, pp. 1684–1704.
Richman, James D. (1974) "Residency Requirements for Municipal Employees," *California Law
    Review,* Vol. 62, pp. 434–447.

INDEX

Research Annuals and Monographs in Series in
BUSINESS, ECONOMICS AND MANAGEMENT

Research Annuals

Advances in Accounting
General Editor: Bill N. Schwartz, *School of Business Administration, Temple University*

Advances in Accounting Information Systems
Edited by Gary Grudnitski, *Graduate School of Business, The University of Texas at Austin*

Advances in Applied Business Strategy
Edited by Robert B. Lamb, *Graduate School of Business Administration, New York University*

Advances in Applied Micro-Economics
Edited by V. Kerry Smith, *Department of Economics and Business Administration, Vanderbilt University*

Advances in Artificial Intelligence
Edited by David Hertz, *Institute for Artifical Intelligence, University of Miami*

Advances in Business Marketing
Edited by Arch G. Woodside, *College of Business Administration, University of South Carolina*

Advances in Econometrics
Edited by Robert L. Basmann, *Ecometric Statisician, Alto, New Mexico* and George Rhodes, *Department of Economics, Colorado State University*

Advances in Financial Planning and Forecasting
Edited by Cheng F. Lee, *Department of Finance, University of Illinois*

Advances in Group Processes
Edited by Edward J. Lawler, *Department of Sociology, University of Iowa*

Advances in Health Economics and Health Services Research
Edited by Richard M. Scheffler, *School of Public Health, University of California, Berkeley.* Associate Editor: Louis F. Rossiter, *Department of Health Administration, Medical College of Virginia, Virginia Commonwealth University*

Advances in Industrial and Labor Relations
Edited by David B. Lipsky, *New York State School of Industrial and Labor Relations, Cornell University*

Advances in Information Processing in Organizations
Edited by Lee S. Sproull and Patrick D. Larkey, *Department of Social Science, Carnegie-Mellon University*

Advances in International Comparative Management
Edited by Richard N. Farmer, *Graduate School of Business, Indiana University*

Advances in Investment Analysis and Portfolio Management
Edited by Frank K. Reilly, *College of Business Administration, University of Notre Dame*

Advances in Marketing and Public Policy
Edited by Paul N. Bloom, *Department of Marketing, University of Maryland*

Advances in Mathematical Programming and Financial Planning
Edited by Kenneth D. Lawrence, *North Brunswick, N.J.,* Gary R. Reeves, *University of South Carolina* and John Guerard, *Department of Finance, Lehigh University*

Advances in Nonprofit Marketing
Edited by Russell W. Belk, *Department of Marketing, University of Utah*

Advances in Public Interest Accounting
Edited by Marilyn Neimark, *Baruch College, The City University of New York.* Associate Editors: Barbara D. Merino, *College of Business Administration, North Texas State University* and Tony Tinker, *Baruch College, The City University of New York*

Advances in Statistical Analysis and Statistical Computing
Edited by Roberto S. Marino, *Department of Economics, University of Pennsylvania*

Advances in Strategic Management
Edited by Robert B. Lamb, *Graduate School of Business Administration, New York University*

Advances in the Economic Analysis of Participatory and Labor Managed Firms
Edited by Derek C. Jones, *Department of Economics, Hamilton College* and Jan Svejnar, *Department of Economics and Program on Labor Managed Systems, Cornell University*

Advances in the Economics of Energy and Resources
Edited by John R. Moroney, *Department of Economics, Texas A & M University*

Applications of Management Science
Edited by Randall L. Schultz, *School of Management, The University of Texas at Dallas*

Perspectives on Local Public Finance and Public Policy
Edited by John M. Quigley, *Graduate School of Public Policy, University of California, Berkeley*

Public Policy and Government Organizations
Edited by John P. Crecine, *College of Humanities and Social Sciences, Carnegie-Mellon University*

Research in Consumer Behavior
Edited by Jagdish N. Sheth, *School of Business, University of Southern California*

Research in Corporate Social Performance and Policy
Edited by Lee E. Preston, *Center for Business and Public Policy, University of Maryland*

Research in Domestic and International Agribusiness Management
Edited by Ray A. Goldberg, *Graduate School of Business Administration, Harvard University*

Research in Economic History
Edited by Paul Uselding, *Department of Economics, University of Illinois*

Research in Experimental Economics
Edited by Vernon L. Smith, *Department of Economics, University of Arizona*

Research in Finance
Edited by Haim Levy, *School of Business, The Hebrew University and The Wharton School, University of Pennsylvania*

Research in Governmental and Non-Profit Accounting
Edited by James L. Chan, *Department of Accounting, University of Illinois*

Research in Human Captial and Development
Edited by Ismail Sirageldin, *Departments of Population Dynamics and Policital Economy, The Johns Hopkins University*

Research in International Business and Finance
Edited by H. Peter Grey, *Department of Economics, Rutgers University*

Research in International Business and International Relations
Edited by Anant R. Negandhi, *Department of Business Administration, University of Illinois*

Research in Labor Economics
Edited by Ronald G. Ehrenberg, *School of Industrial and Labor Relations, Cornell University*

Research in Law and Economics
Edited by Richard O. Zerbe, Jr., *School of Public Affairs, University of Washington*

Research in Marketing
Edited by Jagdish N. Sheth, *School of Business, University of Southern California*

Research in Organizational Behavior
Edited by Barry M. Staw, *School of Business Administration, University of California, Berkeley* and L.L. Cummings, *J.L. Kellogg Graduate School of Management, Northwestern University*

Research in Personnel and Human Resources Management
Edited by Kendrith M. Rowland, *Department of Business Administration, University of Illinois* and Gerald R. Ferris, *Department of Management, Texas A & M University*

Research in Philosophy and Technology
Edited by Paul T. Durbin, *Philosophy Department and Center for Science and Culture, University at Delaware.* Review and Bibliography Editor: Carl Mitcham, *New York Polytechnic Institute*

Research in Political Economy
Edited by Paul Zarembka, *Department of Economics, State University of New York at Buffalo*

Research in Population Economics
Edited by T. Paul Schultz, *Department of Economics, Yale University* and Kenneth I. Wolpin, *Department of Economics, Ohio State University*

Research in Public Sector Economics
Edited by P.M. Jackson, *Department of Economics, Leicester University*

Research in Real Estate
Edited by C.F. Sirmans, *Department of Finance, Louisiana State University*

Research in the History of Economic Thought and Methodology
Edited by Warren J. Samuels, *Department of Economics, Michigan State University*

Research in the Sociology of Organizations
Edited by Samuel B. Bacharach, *Department of Organizational Behavior, New York State School of Industrial and Labor Relations, Cornell University*

Research in Transportation Economics
Edited by Theordore E. Keeler, *Department of Economics, University of California, Berkeley*

Research in Urban Economics
Edited by J. Vernon Henderson, *Department of Economics, Brown University*

Research on Technological Innovation, Management and Policy
Edited by Richard S. Rosenbloom, *Graduate School of Business Administration, Harvard University*

Monographs in Series

Contemporary Studies in Applied Behavioral Science
Series Editor: Louis A. Zurcher, *School of Social Work, University of Texas at Austin*

Contemporary Studies in Economics and Financial Analysis
Series Editors: Edward I. Altman and Ingo Walter, *Graduate School of Business Administration, New York University*

Contemporary Studies in Energy Analysis and Policy
Series Editor: Noel D. Uri, *Bureau of Economics; Federal Trade Commission*

Decision Research - A Series of Monographs
Edited by Howard Thomas, *Department of Business Administration, University of Illinois*

Handbook in Behavioral Economics
Edited by Stanley Kaish and Benny Gilad, *Department of Economics, Rutgers University*

Industrial Development and the Social Fabric
Edited by John P. McKay, *Department of History, University of Illinois*

Monographs in Organizational Behavior and Industrial Relations
Edited by Samuel B. Bacharach, *Department of Organizational Behavior, New York State School of Industrial and Labor Relations, Cornell University*

Political Economy and Public Policy
Edited by William Breit, *Department of Economics, Trinity University* and Kenneth G. Elzinga, *Department of Economics, University of Virginia*

Please inquire for detailed brochure on each series

 JAI PRESS INC., 36 Sherwood Place, P.O. Box 1678
Greenwich, Connecticut 06836

Telephone: 203-661-7602   Cable Address: JAIPUBL